Archaeo-Volunteers

The World Guide to Archaeological and Heritage Volunteering

Charles Seale-Hayne Library
University of Plymouth
(01752) 588 588
LibraryandITenquiries@plymouth.ac.uk

Green Volunteers
Publications

Archaeo-Volunteers

The World Guide to Archaeological and Heritage Volunteering

Editor:	Erin McCloskey
Project Editors:	Fabio Ausenda, Erin McCloskey
Concept:	Fabio Ausenda
Cover design:	Studio Cappellato e Laurent srl, Milano
Cover photo:	Gaelle Le Calve volunteering at the Canterbury Whitefriars Site, a Canterbury Archaeological Trust Excavation. Photo Andrew Savage/Canterbury Archaeological Trust, Ltd.
Acknowledgements:	Special thanks to Gaelle Le Calve and Marion Green, and to the Canterbury Archaeological Trust, Ltd.

This Guide is not an annual publication: the useful websites section, the suggestions for contacting the organisations in the introductory pages, and the link page of our website (see bottom of next page) allow the reader to find continuous new opportunities and to keep the information in this Guide always up to date.

Published by: Green Volunteers di Fabio Ausenda
Via Canonica 72 - 20154 Milano, Italy
www.greenvol.com
e-mail: greenvol@iol.it

US & Canada distribution:	Universe Publishing A division of Rizzoli International Publications, Inc. 300 Park Avenue South, New York, NY 10010
UK distribution:	Vacation Work Publications 9 Park End Street, Oxford OX1 1HJ, England
Printed in Mar. 2003 by:	Consorzio Artigiano L.V.G. srl, Azzate (VA), Italy

ISBN: 88-900167-7-9
Library of Congress Control Number: 2002116393

The Editor wishes to thank, for the academic support, Giorgio and Julie; for the field support, Tamara and Robin; and for the unconditional support in every other department, Connie, Vince, and Sebastian.

The Editors highly recommend the following introductory pages are read. These pages explain what humanitarian and development volunteering involves and will increase the volunteer's chances of being accepted by an organisation.

HOW TO FIND MANY MORE ORGANISATIONS TO VOLUNTEER FOR:

The "useful websites" section (see page 20) and our website—www.archaevolunteers.org/links.html—list many links to other websites useful for finding hundreds of organisations in the UK, US, Canada, Australia, Europe, and in other countries offering various volunteering opportunities worlwide. Our links webpage is frequently updated, allowing the reader to constantly find new opportunities.

TABLE OF CONTENTS

INTRODUCTION

Although the title is *Archaeo-Volunteers*, the scope of the Guide include organisations and projects involved in archaeology, anthropology, cultural heritage and awareness, historical restoration and maintenance, and palaeontology. Archaeology, and its related fields, provide a fascinating and lifelong pastime for anyone with an interest and is not an exclusively professional arena. Amateurs and enthusiasts have important roles to play and can do valuable work. Most projects are led by experienced archaeologists, palaeontologists, or other scientists and specialists to teach volunteers and students new skills and information. The following definitions provide a general description and overview of the major fields of discipline and the sectors occupied by this guide.

Archaeology is a subfield of anthropology. It is the study of the material remains and environmental effects of past human activities. These investigations can be of the recent past to millions of years ago. The study involves that of cultural processes through looking at the remains of past human behaviour including old farm field systems and housing. They can reveal insights about the migrations of human habitation, to the early adoption of agriculture, to the development of industries, to the origin and possible demise of ancient civilisations, etc., through the discovery of entire lost cities down to the discovery of microscopic remains of flora or fauna associated with human activities. Archaeology forms interdisciplinary approaches to research by collaborating with many other disciplines, including geography, history, social sciences, maths, physics, biology, chemistry, art, religion, and technology.

Anthropology can be considered a four-field discipline that studies human culture. Archaeology, as defined above, is one of these subfields. However, beyond archaeology is physical/biological anthropology, which focuses on primates and human biology; social/cultural anthropology, which studies present or the recent past human societies; and linguistic or socio-linguistic anthropology, which is the study of human language. It could be argued that medical anthropology and applied anthropology are two additional an emerging subfields.

Palaeontology is the branch of archaeology that studies fossil organisms and related remains of life of past geological ages. It is the study of plant and animal life forms that provide evolutionary clues to understand the relationship between present species and their ancient ancestors, how their development led to their present forms, and which factors, such as behaviour and environment, were catalysts to their evolution and survival or, contrarily, their extinction.

Cultural Heritage and Historical Restoration is not a defined science but a categorisation established for the purpose of defining this sector with the Guide. The recognition of sites of cultural significance such as buildings, structures, or gardens allow for the preservation of heritage to be appreciated by visitors as well as the local community and its future generations. These areas are often within or of themselves World Heritage sites as they have been defined by UNESCO – United Nations Educational, Scientific and Cultural Organisation, or government protected historical sites.

ARCHAEOLOGICAL FIELDWORK

Archaeology is a fascinating and even romantic field of discovery for a traveller. However, do not be disillusioned by its Hollywood glamour; it is hard work! Do not expect to be unearthing vast chambers of forgotten treasures. Your entire dig experience may be within a single square meter of substrate that you excavate with a tiny pick and a brush. It may involve only uncovering small broken fragments of pottery or the remains of a small wall. There is always the possibility though of discovering the unexpected, and the tangible connection to history by discovering an artefact that is thousands of years old is a privileged and thrilling experience. Ultimately, you are given the opportunity to contribute personally to the recovery and preservation of the past.

Excavation opportunities tend to fall under one of three categories: training courses, amateur digs, or day digs. The training courses are offered through universities and colleges with well-established archaeology, palaeontology, or anthropology departments. The field school is typically one or two months in the summer doing field survey or excavation with PhD students conducting research. These projects may not be open to non-students if competition for positions is high. Amateur digs are conducted by a research institution independently or in conjunction with an expedition company. The Earthwatch Institute is an example of a project where the volunteer requires no skills or experience and works alongside professional scientists in the field. This organisation is very reputable and the experience is bound to be rewarding but the cost to join is on the high end of the scale. Smaller projects offer similar programmes but undoubtedly have fewer resources and volunteers may have a 'rougher' experience. However, every project differs in accommodation and style; even with Earthwatch you may find yourself in a remote area, sleeping in a tent, and eating limited cuisine. Volunteering with a smaller organisation is more economically affordable and may be more rewarding in the sense that your volunteer contribution may be the lifeblood of the project's revenue. Without volunteer support in developing countries, valuable research would possibly not occur. However, always research the organisation well before joining and ensure that the programme is professional, trustworthy, and safe. Projects that are organised in conjunction with an expedition company will have several tourist and educative excursions built into the programme in order for the volunteers to discover the local area and culture. The third type of excavation category is the day dig. This type of programme is open to the public and often all ages are accommodated. Day digs are typically set at a museum site with staff supervision and instruction and are aimed at tourists, with individual, family, or school rates to participate in the programme. Alternatively the excavation may be organised through a small community organisation where local enthusiasts volunteer on a weekend or evening basis. These digs are free but offer no accommodation, meals, or transportation, and the volunteers may have to join the society in order to be covered by the project's insurance.

Archaeological excavation is often labour intensive and prospective volunteers should understand their physical ability and stamina before joining. Excavation is often considered the most exciting aspect of the work, but it is also the most physically demanding. Hours are spent kneeling or stooping, lifting and carrying, or digging with picks and shovels. Excavated soil is carried in buckets or bags to a sorting area that may be in close proximity to the dig or a fair distance walk off site. Work may be performed in heat or rain, in cold wind, or at high elevations. Higher elevations may make physical work seem more strenuous. Remote sites and survey work involves hiking, possibly up and down steep inclines or across difficult terrain. Fully understand what physical work is expected from the volunteers and whether you are able to meet this demand. Notify the project in advance of health concerns such as asthma or allergies. Reconstruction and excavation sites can be very dusty or in grassy fields.

Health and safety is the concern of the volunteer as well as the project or organisation. Even if insurance is provided it is always wise to have your own personal coverage against accident or illness, trip cancellation or early return, etc. Anti-tetanus vaccination is recommended and may be mandatory on some sites. Hygiene conditions are often very basic in the field. Organics or ground-water seepage in the soil dictates washing your hands after digging and before eating. It has been suggested that cattle bones found in the soil can still carry viable germs such as anthrax, hoof and mouth disease, etc., although this has never been proven. If the field setting offers no clean water with which to wash, dry soap or disinfectant may be a good idea to carry along with you. Archaeological fieldwork has risks owing to the physical demands and the work setting. Deep stratification, unstable masonry, shoring and scaffolding, unstable deposits, and ground-water seepage all pose hazards. The project should supply safety equipment and take all precautions to ensure a safe worksite. However, use your own common sense and best judgement and do not put yourself in an uncomfortable or dangerous situation.

Beyond Excavation

There is more to archaeology than excavation. There is considerable work that is undertaken in the laboratory processing and archiving finds. Volunteers can also become involved in setting up museum displays and public outreach programmes. Cultural programmes that focus more on anthropological study of culture involves participants more in community projects, festivals, and cultural exchanges, and there are also the historical restoration projects where volunteers help restore architecture or other significant structures requiring preservation. Some cultural programmes referenced in this guide tour cities and villages and museums offering an educational tour rather than a work situation.

WHY VOLUNTEER?

The philosophy behind voluntary work as an alternative vacation is one of reciprocal favour. Travel and tourism can be very beneficial for the economy of a country, especially a developing country, but is can also be damaging culturally and ecologically. However, the ability to 'give back' through voluntary service while travelling helps the host country in many ways. An international demand for cultural programmes incites employment and volunteer/participant fees provide funding for the project infrastructure. Volunteers provide labour that may not otherwise be affordable as well as additional funding for research, reconstruction, and community development projects, etc., but they also bring a message of international goodwill and heighten cultural awareness, especially among the youth. Cultural programmes that teach volunteers indigenous languages, arts, folklore, dance, music, etc., are invaluable in preserving cultural heritage, not only for foreign study but especially for local pride and enthusiasm to continue passing along these cultural keystones to future generations.

Locally, in their own countries or communities, volunteers can also provide a public demand and the necessary physical or monetary resources for important research to be undertaken. Enthusiasts can get involved with local or national societies that hold lectures, publish newsletters and journals, organise excursions, and launch archaeological fieldwork investigations. Many projects provide students with an opportunity to gain field experience or thesis material while becoming involved in important scientific research efforts. And non-students may be interested in educational or alternative travel and contributing their energies to a worthy cause.

VOLUNTEER PROJECTS AND ORGANISATIONS

Until recently, volunteer opportunities were mainly offered by large organisations but the costs/fees charged limited the number of people who could afford them and participate. However, there are many smaller projects with a constant shortage of funding that greatly need volunteers. Often the contributions made by volunteers can maintain projects for years. This guide aims to introduce prospective volunteers to the many valuable projects throughout the world in need of volunteer assistance.

Voluntary organisations are often directed at people interested in alternative vacation. Many of the projects are aimed at youth but there are a considerable number who accept all ages, including retired people, with or without skills or a background in archaeology.

Museum associations take volunteers for administrative, public outreach work and sometimes take volunteers to assist in the laboratory and with associated fieldwork. There are regional and national museum associations throughout the world. A simple internet search will provide an extensive list (see Useful Websites)

Universities with well-established departments of anthropology or archaeology offer training courses or coordinate PhD projects requiring field staff. Participants pay tuition for credit and often must pay auditing fees for non-credit participation. The tuition is paid to the facilitating university but credit must be approved through the home institution of the student.

Independent research projects with established or inter-government organisations offer outreach programmes. Funding or (non-monetary) assistance may be provided by municipal or regional governments or on a national level.

Non-Government Organisations (NGOs) are typically non-profit and self-sufficient in the sense that they receive no funding from government agencies. They are strongly dependant upon public contributions and volunteer support.

Workcamps (International workcamp associations) organise voluntary projects for young participants, from all over the world, and in collaboration with local authorities. They are the ideal setting for young people or volunteers with no previous experience not wanting to commit too much time. They are therefore particularly suitable for students and young people as a meaningful way to spend a summer vacation or visit a new country or take part in a cultural exchange. Workcamp experience could be considered more of an alternative vacation than a true volunteering commitment. Nevertheless workcamps offer a good introduction to volunteering, and they are an enriching life experience for the work accomplished and for meeting people from many different countries and cultures who share the same interests and lifestyle.

Often no previous experience is required for workcamps; the structure is organised to lodge and cater to a certain number of volunteers, the tasks to be accomplished are simple, and the work is never in extreme situations. Often the only requirement is to know the language of the workcamp (most often English). For these reasons the workcamps are preferred by young people and students. Older volunteers may also be accepted but they should first verify that the type of work involved is of interest and within physical capabilities and know the average age of the other volunteers, in order not to feel too isolated from the rest of the group. More experienced volunteers can always apply for a coordinating position.

Workcamps and unpaid volunteer positions obviously have less competition but they may not be able to take volunteers with little notice because if the camp is popular the few available positions may already be filled. They may also require specific qualifications to meet the needs of the association or project at that particular time. And even though volunteers may be financially self-supporting and willing to work, they still require considerable engagement on the part of the organisation. Organisations often take only a limited number of volunteers since they require space, attention, coordination, assistance, transportation, and they must be provided with higher standards of hygiene and safety than what may be normally found in that country. It is advisable to make as large a search spectrum as possible to increase the chance of finding an organisation that is not only interested but also ready to accept a prospective volunteer to their project.

The following is a list of some of the organisations that coordinate international workcamps. Several already listed in the Guide are: Alliance of European Voluntary Service Organisations, CCIVS, Chantiers Jeunesse, Compagnons Batisseurs, Concordia, Conservation Volunteers Greece, Cooperation for Voluntary Service Bulgaria, Cotravaux, GMS, Horizon Cosmopolite, FIYE, NICE, Jeunesse et Réconstruction, Pro International, SCI, UNESCO, Volunteers for Peace, Workcamps for Young People in Brittany, and YAP.

AFSAI started as one of the Italian partners of EVS and regularly organises workcamps in the sectors of community development, culture, education, etc. See: www.afsai.it

AJED organises different activities for young people in Senegal such as workcamps, stays with guest families, and education programmes. The workcamps promote cultural exchanges. See: www.go.to/ajed

AJUDE was born during the post.civil-war period in Mozambique when the region faced deep transformations. Workcamps involve community development, constructions, education, human rights, and women's issues. See: www.ajude.org

AVSO (Association of Voluntary Service Overseas) organises international workcamps in culture, education, community development, etc., for European Union residents. See: www.avso.org

BWCA (Bangladesh Work Camps Association) organises national and international workcamps, study tours, international youth exchange, and leadership training on issues proclaimed by UNESCO towards establishing world peace. See www.mybwca.org

Council Exchanges USA runs international volunteer projects for Amercans to work overseas on projects on cultural, construction, community development, etc. See www.councilexchanges.org

Eurocultura organises cultural exchanges and youth workcamps throughout Europe. See: http://www.eurocultura.it

EVS (European Voluntary Service) offers a contact point between other workcamp or volunteer associations and volunteers and is a reference for National agencies working in close collaboration with the European Commission. See: http://wwwyouth.cec.eu.int

Inventaire des monuments et chantiers is a French workcamp organisation; they also have a Guide Book for work camps. See: http://cvmclubduvieuxmanoir.free.fr/club/inventaire_chantiers.php

Jeunesse et Réconstruction (see listing) is an organisation for volunteer camps and activities abroad and in France in reconstruction, renovation, and conservation. See: http://www.volontariat.org

Solidarités Jeunesses is related to the Minister of Youth and Sport in France and is the French branch of YAP. It organises international camps in the world for long- and short-term voluntary service. See: http://www.solidaritesjeunesses.org/solidarites_jeunesses/index.php3

Voluntary Service International (VSI)) Africa/Asia/Latin America Exchange programme enables Irish people and people from other European countries to gain an insight and understanding of developing countries by participating in voluntary workcamps organised by local voluntary/community organisations working as part of a group of international volunteers alongside local volunteers and villagers on projects of a practical nature, such as building a school or health clinic, planting trees, or repairing village roads. See http://www.iol.ie/~vsi/AALA.htm

Volunteer Africa lets volunteers work with villagers on projects and get involved in village life.See: www.volunteerafrica.org

HOW TO START

Tips for Contacting an Organisation

Having a copy of *Archaeo-Volunteers* has been the first step. Below are some suggestions to help you find the organisation most suited to your interests and be accepted on their project.

Have clear in mind what you want to do, the subject you prefer, the geographical location, the duration of your volunteering period, and the costs you can afford. This will help you select and reduce the number of organisations you need to apply to. If you are professionally qualified in a specific field, and you think that your skills may be useful, look specifically for organisations in your sector where you would best be able to use your qualifications. Conversely, do not consider organisations that do not need your skills. Select a list of organisations and divide them into priorities and start contacting both groups systematically.

Use the fastest possible method to contact an organisation. Remember that interesting projects or organisations also have many applicants, and they usually fill their available positions on a first come, first serve basis. Therefore, you want to be as fast as possible in letting them know that you are interested in taking a position with them. Do not lose time by sending a letter by regular mail, unless you are required to do so, but immediately start sending e-mails, even if only as preliminary enquiries. E-mail is usually a good way to make a first contact with an organisation and get to know who they are without being too committed. It is also a good idea to verify before applying whether or not you have a good chance to be accepted. If not, do not waste time, go on to the next organisation on your list. Should you not receive a reply within 3–5 days, be prepared to send reminders or telephone to confirm their e-mail address or verify whether or not it is worth continuing your application process with them, particularly if it requires filling out lengthy forms.

If an organisation is in a developing country, make it easy for them to respond to you. Remember that organisations in poorer countries often are short of funds. Therefore, help them by enclosing self-addressed stamped envelopes should you exchange regular mail (for example you may need an original letter in their stationary paper to obtain the Visa). Always enclose one or more international postal reply coupon as a form of courtesy, even if you are not required to do so. You may also offer an organisation to fax you collect (give them an appointment, because in order to receive a fax collect you should first be able to answer vocally, accept the call, then switch on the fax mode). Better still, since a fax goes both ways regardless of who calls, you can offer to call the organisation on their fax line and have them fax back the information. Remember that you should arrange this over the phone. If you interact with a large organisation, well-equipped for recruiting volunteers, they will have all the means to contact you.

Contact many organisations to select an organisation, or a specific project, well in advance. Properly planning your vacation or time in advance will allow you to find the best airfares and select the best period suitable to you. Get detailed information on what to expect: the type of work, accommodation, food, climate, clothing, equipment necessary, etc. Owing to a lack of space this information cannot be included in the projects' description in this guide.

Research the history and culture of the subject of the project as well as the culture, customs, and climate of the host country. A basic understanding of archaeological techniques is a good idea for personal preparation but if no experience is required by the project, they will likely provide all the necessary training to give you the skills to work effectively and enjoyably. They should also confirm the project details, such as the living, working and safety conditions, prior to departure. Request contact information of previous volunteers and correspond with them to further verify the conditions of the projects.

This guide aims to give a general overview of a given organisation and give you tools to find many others. Never show up at a project location without having first applied and having been accepted and confirmed. Most projects have limited positions, lodging and personnel. Very rarely are they equipped to take on an unexpected volunteer. Unless very clearly stated by the project or organisation, never arrive at a project unannounced. It is disruptive, unprofessional, and awkward for the project leader. If you choose to inquire while already travelling in a certain area, do not be disappointed if you are rejected.

Application Advise

Do exactly what is required by an organisation for being accepted. If they require you to complete their application form, whether it is sent to you or whether you download it from their website, do fill it out, even if you have already submitted your detailed CV. If you apply with an organisation where the official language is not English but another major international language that you will be expected to use if accepted by them, send at least the cover letter in this language and be prepared to translate your CV if necessary. The competition to participate in some projects may be high. Treat your applications as you would a job application. In the application or on your CV state your skills: language, computer or web design, or artistic (e.g., for illustrating and photography) that may be useful to archaeological projects. State your educational background, elaborate if you have a relevant specialisation in the arts and sciences, and reference any previous volunteer experience you may have. Research projects associated with Universities may require only experienced volunteers or research assistants. Field positions such as these offer opportunities for graduate students to gain thesis material or practical field experience to advance them in their careers. Letters of recommendation or presentation from professors or recognised academics may be required.

Many organisations with workcamp programmes often request an advanced deposit or membership to their organisation. If accepted, do not be late in paying. Inquire about the fastest method to transfer funds: by international telegraph money order, credit card, and money wire from bank to bank, etc.

Preliminary meetings or training courses – attendance may not be feasible for international participants, but be sure to have this requirement waived if it is not possible to attend.

Prospective volunteers should exchange frequent e-mails, or even fax or phone calls, with project leaders and ensure that communication is always prompt and clear. Follow up upon the status of your application to make sure that it has been received and at what point in time you should expect to receive a response by.

WHAT TO BRING

Documentation to Bring

Necessary documentation includes passports, visas, permission clearance for some countries, and insurance (personal, medical, and travel may or may not be included in the project fees – see below for further details on insurance). Make photocopies of all important documentation and leave one set with an emergency contact at home and carry another set with you, separate from the originals, as a back-ups in case you lose the originals. Carry on you, and provide to the organisation you are joining, the name of a person to contact in case of emergency. Be sure that your family or your friends know exactly where you are going and for how long. Give them the information for where you can be contacted or found in case of emergency.

If you intend to travel abroad to a country requiring extensive visas and permissions, begin all the documentation acquisitions at least six months prior to your departure. When in transit or in non-secure areas keep your money, passport and important documents in a purse or small sack under your clothing, even when sleeping, or at arm's reach and eye's view when bathing. Do not put all your resources in one place. Divide your money and other resources and stash them in different bags.

Passport: Up to date and valid for at least six months beyond your intended stay abroad. Carry the original in a secure place. Keep one copy separate from the original as a back-up while travelling and another left at home with an emergency contact.

Visas: It is often necessary to have either a tourist or student visa to enter a foreign country or to participate in a study or research project. It may take several months to apply for the visa, in which case make sure that you have initiated the bureaucratic process enough in advance, or the visa may be purchased in the airport upon arrival, like a form of tax – in this case ensure you have the money on you to pay for it and local currency may be the only option. Information concerning visa requirements is usually provided from the project or organisation you will be joining, but you should also consult the embassy or consulate of the country of destination in your home country.

Currency: Bring small amounts of local currency (enough to cover you for a couple of days of room, board, and local travel upon arrival) and the remainder of your resources in the form of traveller's cheques. The exchange rate may not be as favourable in this method, but the security against loss or theft is worth the cost. Keep sound records of the traveller's checks that you have already used. Bring a bank card that works internationally and possibly a credit card (carry the international emergency phone number with you to cancel the card in case of loss or theft).

Insurances: Travel, medical, and personal/life insurances are highly recommended and may be necessary. There may be special rates available to students and seniors. Even if the organisation you are joining has insurance, it is better to have your own personal policy as well in case of any litigation. Have insurance that covers theft, lost of luggage, flight delay or cancellation, emergency evacuation, change of return flight, and emergency health coverage for ambulance, hospital, and medication. If you are a citizen of a European Union (EU) country and you will be attending a project in another EU country, request an E111 form from your National Health Service, which will qualify you for coverage by the health system of the host country. If you have an insurance against theft, have receipts at home of any valuable you are taking with you and if this is not possible take photographs of the items. Keep receipts of things that you purchase while travelling.

Vaccination card: Carry a vaccination card (stating current vaccinations stamped from the medical board where the vaccinations were taken) and health card stating your blood type and any allergies you may have. Inquire at the relevant embassy for vaccination requirements. Realise that certain vaccinations or preventative medications, such as antimalarial drugs, must be started at least a couple of weeks before entering the country that hosts the risk. Obviously, most precautions only apply to visiting developing or tropical countries, but almost all projects that involve excavation work require an anti-tetanus and possibly a hepatitis vaccination.

Clothing and Equipment to Bring

Always request a detailed list of clothing and equipment that is required to bring to the project. Most projects will supply the heavy and technical equipment and safety gear such as hard hats. Volunteers may need to purchase a personal trowel in advance (not riveted and no greater than 4 inches/10cm long) to bring for their own use. Bring a measuring tape, water bottle, alarm clock, flashlight, batteries, and sunglasses. Various types footwear may be required: steel-toed boots for certain work settings or soft flat-soled shoes for delicate areas with artefacts being photographed *in-situ*. Kneeling pads and gardening gloves are recommended.

Clothing must be climate appropriate and protective against sun, wind, or rain. Comfort is very important. Tight or restrictive clothing will make excavation work difficult. Bring sufficient clothing to last with limited laundry possibilities but do not over pack as you may be responsible to carry your supplies between various locations and space may be limited. Bring a hat suitable for the climate in which you will be working (sun, rain, cold, etc.). Raingear should include jacket and pants, hat, and perhaps even rubber boots.

Bring all necessary medical and personal hygiene supplies. A personal first aid kit is advisable and include within it sunscreen, insect repellent, and other items to deal with skin concerns: cuts, scrapes, rashes, bug bites, burns, slivers, blisters, etc., especially if you will be joining a workcamp or an excavation project. If travelling overseas, it may be a good idea to take a medical and dental examination prior to your trip to help ensure against any medical problems while away.

If the project is a camp setting, you may be required to bring your own tent, sleeping bag and mat, cutlery, etc.

Some final suggestions on what to bring include a regional travel guide and a personal journal describing the work you are doing, camp life, your impressions of the local culture, etc., by which to remember you experience by years later.

USEFUL WEBSITES

The World Wide Web is the most comprehensive source of information on voluntary work worldwide. Most of the websites of the organisations listed in this guide provide good links, however, the following pages highlight the most useful websites to help the prospective volunteer find opportunities in archaeology, anthropology, palaeontology, etc. Recommended books include *The International Directory of Voluntary Work* by Vacation Works Publications (Oxford UK) listing thousands of voluntary placements worldwide in different sectors including archaeology and related fields; and directly in the field of archaeology the Archaeological *Fieldwork Opportunities Bulletin* is one of the best guides and is published by the Archaeological Institute of America (see website next page).

The following list offers a variety of useful websites and is a sampling from the links page of the *Archaeo-Volunteers* website, accessible only to those who have purchased this Guide, which is updated periodically. The address of the link web page is:

http://www.archaeovolunteers.org/archaeo/links.htm

The Internet allows rapid access to information from almost anywhere in the world on practically every subject. The organisations involved with volunteers are certainly a primary use of the Internet. Non-profit organisations in developing countries have little funding and considerable demand for communicating their calls for assistance, fundraising, public awareness campaigns, volunteers, and other needs. After choosing a sector of interest, the type of work, the country of destination, etc., the Internet becomes a great tool for prospective volunteers to find the most suitable project. Search-engines, links to other sites, and organisation newsletters are valuable tools for researching volunteer opportunities and finding associations either close to home or in a specific country. Use a good search engine and look for "association + volunteering + the city/country name" to find nearby associations. To find workcamps type in the key word "workcamp" and the country name. The volunteer positions are typically listed in the menu under "Get involved!" or "Join us". Most often, after a section dedicated to fundraising, there is a section concerning volunteering.

About.com: Archaeology
Articles and directory of Internet sites, including a world atlas of archaeology on the web, and excellent links.
http://archaeology.about.com

Amazing Worlds of Archaeology, Anthropology, and Ancient Civilizations
Resource for students and others interested in the fields of archaeology, anthropology, and ancient civilisations divided by topic.
http://www.archaeolink.com/index.html

Ancient World Web
Links to several sectors and categories of antiquity, archaeology, literature, etc.
http://www.julen.net/aw/

Anthropology Resources on the Internet
Anthropology directory of academic to amateur level. Projects, associations, and relevant resources with focus on academic objectivity.
http://www.archeodroit.net/anthro/Contents/contents.html

Archaeologic.com
Directory of fieldwork opportunities and other relevant resources.
http://archaeologic.com/fieldwork_directory.htm

Archaeological Adventure
Think Quest project explaining what archaeology is and its methods and techniques. Examples of significant discoveries including Troy, Shiqmim, the Egyptian Pyramids. http://library.thinkquest.org/3011

Archaeological Fieldwork Service
International volunteer and fieldschool opportunities.
http://www.cincpac.com/afos/testpit.html

Archaeological Institute of America (AIA)
North America's oldest and largest organisation devoted to the world of archaeology. Members include professional archaeologists, students, and enthusiasts from the US, Canada, and overseas. They publish annually the *Archaeological Fieldwork Opportunities Bulletin* listing fieldwork opportunities also with a searchable on-line database.
http://www.archaeological.org

Archaeological Research Resources
Internet directory maintained by Historic Archaeological Research of history and archaeology websites, including organisations, directories, technical references, and on-line publications.
http://www.har-indy.com/Links.html

Archaeological Resource Guide for Europe
The ARGE database contains links to evaluated Internet resources (mainly webpages, but also other resources such as discussion lists) concerning European archaeology.
http://odur.let.rug.nl/arge/

Archaeological Resource
French-English and German-English dictionaries, a dictionary of Art and Archaeology plus resources on archaeology, Egyptology, art history, and antiquity.
http://www.archaeologicalresource.com

Archaeology
Illustrated introduction to archaeology from Panorama Productions.
http://www.panoramaproductions.net/arch.htm

Archaeology Abroad
Information about archaeological fieldwork opportunities outside the UK through the University College London's Institute of Archaeology's publication *Archaeology Abroad*. Around 1000 placements advertised annually for volunteers, professional staff, and specialists on a wide variety of projects of all periods.
http://www.britarch.ac.uk/archabroad/

Archaeology Adventures
Site for archaeology enthusiasts. Focused primarily on history, archaeology, and numismatics of ancient cultures, as well as travelogues from historical destinations.
http://www.archad.org/

Archaeology: An Introduction
Links to web resources, archives, and documents about archaeology for students and enthusiasts.
http://www.staff.ncl.ac.uk/kevin.greene/wintro/

Archaeology Channel
Archaeology and related subjects presented through streaming media by the Oregon-based Archaeological Legacy Institute. Videos can be viewed on-line and purchased.
http://www.archaeologychannel.org

Archaeology Info
Significant archaeological discoveries on human origins. Illustrated and referenced descriptions of hominids. Articles, images, bookstore, and links.
http://www.archaeologyinfo.com

Archaeology on the Net
Directory of annotated, categorized links and fieldwork opportunities around the world.
http://www.serve.com/archaeology/fwork.html

Archaeology Pages
Archaeology related articles covering archaeo-geology, prehistory, palaeo-anthropology, the Andes, Meso-America, American Southwest and rock art.
http://www.jqjacobs.net/anthro/

Archeologia Italiana
Archaeology in Italy with links, a discussion forum (in Italian), information on excavations, etc.
http://www.archeologia.com/links/

Archeology
An introduction to archaeology by Ragz-International: the subject matter, history, specialisations, methods and techniques of the discipline.
http://ragz-international.com/archeology.htm

Archeopress
Archaeological news in the Internet.
http://www.archeopress.com/

ArchNet
Archaeology section of the World Wide Web Virtual Library.
http://archnet.asu.edu

Archonnet Discussion Group
For announcements and reviews of on-line archaeology resources.
http://www.serve.com/archaeology/archonnet

Athena Review Guide to Archaeology on the Internet
Primary information on archaeology and history. Combination of graphic images and on-line sources and databases.
http://www.athenapub.com/inet/guide2.htm

Bosco's Rockpile
Recreational site of interest in archaeology, geology, and palaeontology. Links to related sites, photos, information, and digs in the USA.
http://www.boscarelli.com/where2dig.htm

BuildingConservation.Com
On-line information centre for the conservation and restoration of historic buildings, churches, and garden landscapes.
http://www.buildingconservation.com/

CEAA Architecture et Archeologie
School with compulsory stage *in loco* about archaeology and architecture; collaboration with institutions in Greece and Egypt.
http://perso.wanadoo.fr/didier.laroche/CEAA_Archi_Archeo.html

Centro di Conservazione Archeologica
Various projects, research, and training courses have led to travel throughout the world and collaboration with many professionals and colleagues. Information on the field of archaeological conservation with the objective to facilitate and develop a network for professional exchange at the service of the conservation of archaeological heritage.
http://www.cca-roma.org/01en.html

Ciudad Virtual de Antropología y Arqueología
A portal of archaeology in Spanish.
http://www.arqueologia.com.ar – http://www.antropologia.com.ar
http://www.naya.org.ar

COIC Publications:
Working in History booklet with information about various careers including archaeology and related disciplines.
http://www.dfee.gov.uk/careerpubs/coic/welcome.cfm

Council for British Archaeology
Principal UK-wide NGO promoting knowledge, appreciation, and care of the historic environment. *British Archaeology*, published six times a year, contains the *CBA Briefing* produced by the British Archaeological Information Service with information on excavations and fieldwork, conferences, lectures, events, book reviews, and announcements.
http://www.britarch.ac.uk

Cultural Heritage Search Engine
Search engine about the conservation of cultural heritage, restoration, and maintenance of architecture and preservation of urban landscapes.
http://www.culturalheritage.net/

Current Archaeology
British archaeological bimonthly magazine referencing archaeological resources, digs, discoveries, events, and camps throughout the UK.
http://www.archaeology.co.uk/

DinoDon.com
Dinosaur art, dictionary, contests, news, digs, scientists, books, links, etc.
http://la.lti.cs.cmu.edu/callan/k12/ScavHunt2/hippos/WW6893.htm
http://www.dinosaurdon.com/dinosaurs/digs.html

EARP – European Archaeological Research Project
Database for excavation opportunities on the Internet.
http://archweb.LeidenUniv.nl/archeonet/fieldwork_oppor.html

European Association of Archaeologists
Membership-based association open to all archaeologists and other related or interested individuals or organisations worldwide working in prehistory, classical, medieval, and later archaeology: academics, environmental and field archaeologists, heritage managers, historians, museum curators, conservators, underwater archaeologists, etc.
http://www.e-a-a.org/

European Forum for Professional Associations in Archaeology
Institute of Field Archaeologists undertakes facilitating the standards setting work of the European Association of Archaeologists' Committee on Professional Associations in Archaeology.
http://www.archaeologists.net/europe.html

Institute of Cultural Affairs Worldwide
Non-profit organisation working on cultural programmes worldwide for individual, community, and organisational development. Highly participatory programmes in collaboration with other public, private, voluntary, or local community organizations.
http://www.icaworld.org

Institute of Field Archaeologists
Professional organisation for archaeologists in the UK promoting professional standards and ethics for conserving, managing, understanding, and promoting enjoyment of the heritage. Information for archaeologists, students, and purchasers of archaeological services.
http://www.archaeologists.net

Institute of Nautical Archaeology
Non-profit scientific and educational organisation looking for and excavate archaeologically important maritime sites in the world and disseminating this knowledge through scholarly and popular publications, seminars, and lectures as well as assisting the professional training and education of future nautical archaeologists through their participation in Institute projects.
http://ina.tamu.edu/

Into Archaeology
Resources for professionals and enthusiasts including software, articles, book reviews, news, multimedia, and specialised editor reviewed channels.
http://www.intoarch.com

LINK
Many links about archaeology, texts and inscriptions, sites and camps, museums, etc.
http://www.officenet.co.jp/~yoji/linke.html

Maritime Archaeology
Links page to international organisations, associations, resources, and projects.
http://www.vasamuseet.se/lankar/Eng_links/
links_maritime_archaeology.html

Maritime Underwater Nautical Archaeology
Private Institutes, centres, research groups, and private/non-profit
societies, associations, and organisations.
http://www.munarchaeology.com/munarchaeology/programs/private.htm

Marshalltown Trowel Company
Large manufacturer of masonry and related hand tools.
http://www.marshalltown.com

Prehistory.org
Large website is a collection of links in various sectors with strong
emphasis on archaeology and its related disciplines.
www.prehistory.org/links.htm

Public Archaeology
Information and advice about public archaeology for students,
professionals, and educators featuring a discussion forum on
contemporary issues in archaeology and public communication.
http://www.publicarchaeology.com

Smithsonian Institution's Anthropology Outreach Office
National Museum of Natural History listing of fieldwork opportunities
across the country.
http://www:nmnh.si.edu/departments/anthro.html/outreach/outreach1.html

Society for American Archaeology
International organisation dedicated to research, interpretation, and
protection of archaeological heritage of the Americas. Members include
professionals, students, and vocational archaeologists working in
government agencies, universities, museums, and the private sector.
http://www.saa.org/

UK Archaeology Opportunities
List of links to excavations by period in the UK.
http://www.ukarchaeology.org.uk

Underwater Archaeology Discussion List
Link list of the archives of sub-archaeology of the University of Arizona.
http://lists.asu.edu/archives/sub-arch.html

Underwater Archaeology In The World
Directory of underwater archaeology sites. Linked to the Humboldt State University.
http://sorrel.humboldt.edu/~archlab/under.html

Underwater Archaeology
Museums, shipwrecks, and projects.
http://www.pophaus.com/underwater/museums.html

World Archaeological Congress
Seeks to promote interest in the past of all countries and encourage the development of regionally based histories and international academic interaction.
http://www.wac.uct.ac.za/

Links to Museum Associations:

American Association of Museums
Focal point for professionals in museum and museum-related fields.
http://www.aam-us.org

Australian Archaeological Association
Largest archaeological organisation in Australia with excellent links.
http://www.australianarchaeologicalassociation.com.au/index.html

Canadian Museums Association
Non-profit museums, art galleries, science centres, aquaria, archives, sports halls of fame, artist-run centres, zoos, and historic sites.
http://www.museums.ca

Museums Association of Great Britain
Official Museums Body in the UK, with information, up to date news, events and a monthly debate topic.
http://www.museumsassociation.org

Museum Security Network
Internet service and mailing list for museum security professionals, curators, librarians, registrars, specialised police, journalists, collectors, galleries, national parks, archaeologists, universities, and students.
http://www.museum-security.org/indexb.html

RESPONSIBLE TOURISM

Responsible tourism deserves a separate mention. Indeed, it is not volunteering, but as the term suggests, "tourism made on tiptoe". The tourist tries to understand the local culture, to live with the locals, and to visit their villages, schools, farms, and cooperatives using the services offered by the local communities as much as possible so that they may increase their revenues. Responsible tourism is for those who want to travel, understand, and to be as little trouble to their host as possible. Several NGOs, in fact, are beginning to organise trips to the locations where their projects are carried out, so that the travellers may visit the volunteers and the communities being helped. Responsible tourism, in the context of this Guide, may be considered a gradual approach or introduction to volunteering.

HOW TO READ THE GUIDE

Archaeo-Volunteers is a directory. It lists organisations of many different sectors offering volunteer opportunities. The guide gives examples of the different kinds of opportunities but it cannot be considered comprehensive. If an organisation of interest cannot be found among the organisations listed, the section dedicated to resources on the Internet gives the reader the possibility of finding hundreds or thousands of additional organisations or projects. Organisations and projects are listed in alphabetical order. At the end of the Guide, there is an index with an Analytical Table listing the entries by the geographical area and period.

Meaning of Abbreviations

Where available, each entry in the Guide has listed:

The **address** and the **telephone** and **fax** numbers with the international codes. The local area code changes according to the country's telephone system. For example, to call the UK prefixed with the country and area code ++44 (20), calling from the UK do not dial ++44 (the international code) but add 0 (zero) before 20 (the local area code). Calling from Europe add 00 before 44 to call the UK, whereas from the US only dial 011 (the international code from the US to Europe) followed by 44.

E-mail and World Wide Web (**www**) addresses. Some organisations do not have a website: it can be useful to ask via e-mail or telephone if they have implemented one since the printing of this guide. If not, a prospective volunteer with good computer skills can help this organisation to make one; it is a good way to begin volunteering and an excellent introduction to the organisation. Organisations who do not have a website, and therefore do not have their e-mail address linked to a domain name, tend to change their e-mail address quite often. If, after a reasonable number of solicitations, an organisation does not answer to the e-mail messages, or a message bounces back, search for the project on the Internet to see if a new website has been established with new contact information. It is also possible to send an e-mail message to an organisation from the same country or of the same sector, which probably knows the organisation in question.

The reader should realise that projects are dynamic and details such as costs, accommodations, project duration, season dates, or countries in which the organisations operate may vary from year to year. New projects arise and old projects may end. Periodic verification of the websites of interest is highly recommended.

Desc.: The description outlines the activities and objectives of the organisation or the project details including information about the site, the history, the research ambitions, or other details.

Per.: The historical period to which the remnants that are excavated, studied, or restored belong to are defined. As much as possible, these definitions have been left as defined by the projects and organisations themselves and therefore do not fall into a rigid categorisation set by this guide. For organisations with cultural projects not involved with excavation or restoration 'modern' or 'contemporary' has been written. Considering that the Period is an important component in selecting a project to participate in, an Analytical Table of Geographic Areas and Periods has been provided (see page 242) to easily find the projects or organisations working on a particular subject or in a particular area. Period definitions are found on page 34.

Country: The country or countries the project or organisation works in is stated. Larger organisations may run several projects in more than one country or worldwide. In these cases their projects and locations may change year to year and prospective volunteers should always confirm that the project they are interested in is still running in any particular country. The head office may be in a different country from that of the project.

Loc.: The project location is a smaller, more specific reference than country. The city or village may be named or if the project is rural, a general geographic region may be explained.

Travel: Logistics for a meeting point for an international group is often difficult to assign and quite often the details of the travel arrangements are provided to the volunteers after their application has been approved. Often the volunteers will be picked up at a specified airport or bus or train station or are given instructions on how to arrive at the project site from these points. Always confirm prior to departure to a project whether there will be a pick-up arranged. If there is no pick-up, confirm the travel instructions and when you are to arrive at the project site.

Dur.: The duration of the volunteer or study period is the minimum length of stay and the months or the season in which the project is running. Longer periods of stay beyond what is specified may be possible if the project is ongoing upon approval from the project or organisation or if space permits. Typically the minimum stay is two weeks to have the time to efficiently apply new skills from training; single day digs are also common for all ages; six weeks are standard for University credited courses. Field projects are usually in the summer months.

Age: The minimum age accepted is stated. Typically this is 18 years of age. Younger volunteers may be accepted with permission but often must be accompanied by a guardian. Several projects have projects for families, school groups, and teenagers and are usually day or weekend events. There are usually no upper age restrictions stated but older volunteers must be comfortable with the physical demands of the project as all volunteers must be aware of their personal stamina and capabilities regardless of age.

Qualif.:   Any necessary qualifications or experience required by the volunteer is stated. Usually no experience is necessary however some professional digs may only accept students seeking course credit or field experience or professionals as experienced crewmembers or research collaborators.

Work: The type of work, such as excavation, survey, or laboratory work, is described as well as the work hours and days per week.

Lang.:   Typically the language of the projects are in English or the language of the host country. It is important that the volunteer has the necessary language skill requirements to successfully participate in the project.

Accom.:   The style and availability of accommodation varies greatly from project to project. Often excavation projects are in a camp setting. Volunteers may or may not have to provide their own camping gear (tent, sleeping bag, mat, etc.), and the availability of running and hot water, electricity, flush toilets may not exist. In camp settings understand prior to your arrival what the accommodation and field standards are and if you are comfortable with them. It is not unlikely to be in a field situation where there is no running or hot water and only outhouses or squat toilets. There is a wide range of hygiene facilities available from project to project. In some instances, showers (or makeshift saunas) are arranged but they may be as rare as once per week. Bathing may only be possible in a lake or a river. However, some projects house the participants in hotels or homes with all the modern comforts available and the worksite may also have a high infrastructure annex of buildings fully equipped with heating, plumbing, and electricity. The excavation site may even be situated in the middle of a large, modern city. Volunteers may be housed in dormitories, schoolhouses or other such buildings, hostels, hotels, motels, or bed and breakfasts, or be billeted by local families. Accommodation may not be provided but may provide suggestions for conveniently located and affordable options.

Cost: Project fees range from a small membership fee or project contribution to full room and board charges to complete travel package costs. If there is no fee, there are likely no benefits and the volunteer must be totally self-sufficient. Often the total cost stated is what covers the minimum or complete volunteer period. Some projects have introduced a very useful 'progressively decreasing cost' policy, depending on the length of stay. The rationale is that the longer a volunteer stays with a project, the more useful he or she becomes because of the experience gained. Always bring a reasonable amount of spending or emergency money in more than one form (local and home currency, a credit card, traveller's checks, or other).

Applic.: The first step in applying to a project or organisation should be to consult the website if one exists. Many websites for volunteer projects have an on-line form with which to apply. If application instructions are not provided, e-mail or telephone for a fast understanding of volunteer opportunities and then request further application instruction.

Notes: Additional information is provided when necessary, such as availability of academic credit, additional contacts, pertinent project details, what to bring, warnings or advice, etc.

See also:Related projects or organisations in the Guide are cross-referenced. If an organisation has project featured elsewhere in the guide, the names of these projects will be cited. These projects in turn will then reference the organisation. If two or more projects are related but there is no listing of their common organisation, the projects will cross-reference each other.

Analytical Table by Geographic Areas and Periods Definitions

The Classification of projects by cultural/historical periods is difficult and often debatable between historians and archaeologists. Moreover, every civilisation (in different geographical areas) has its own historic period definitions. Therefore, in order to help the reader easily find projects or organisations in their preferred subject and area, the Guide provides an **Analytical Table of Geographical Areas and Periods** (see page 242) where the periods are subdivided for the purposes of the index. These definitions are not to be regarded as an academic resource but simply as a tool in reading the guide. Please excuse any errors, inaccuracies, misinterpretations, or lack of information within the Table or the referenced projects. The geographical area, is obviously more comprehensible and more detailed information may be found on the possible website of any given project to help better historically locate a project of interest.

The categories are defined as follows:

Europe – Prehistory: encompasses from about the Palaeolithic (c. 100,000 years BP) to the Neolithic (c. 8,000 eBC) to the Bronze Age c. 800 years BC.

Europe – Classic/Iron Age: from c. 800 BC to the birth of Christ. It includes the Greek Classic period, early Italian civilisations, such as the Etruscan, and the early expansion of the Roman Republic in the Mediterranean. In Northern Europe this period can be generally defined as the Iron Age.

Europe – Roman: starts approximately at the birth of Christ, when the Roman Empire started its expansion in Europe (for example with the invasion of Britain in 43). The Roman period ends approximately in the years between 450 and 550 with barbarian invasions.

Europe – Early Medieval: from approximately the end of the Roman Empire in the year 500 in Western Europe, a period of crisis without a dominant culture follows and lasts approximately to the year 1000.

Europe – Medieval: by the year 1000 in Europe a clear subdivision starts between centres of power – France, England, and Germany. During this period, the Crusades take place. Art and literature begin to flourish and reach their highest peak at the Renaissance after the year 1400.

Europe – Renaissance/Post Medieval: is between 1400 and 1500. In Italy the Renaissance flourishes. The discovery and colonisation of the New World by other European countries begins.

Europe – Early Modern: from 1600 to 1800; from the Baroque Age to about the time of the French Revolution.

Europe – Modern: from 1800 to World War II, this period sees the growth of industrial societies, the beginning and end of large colonial empires and two World Wars.

Europe – Contemporary: this period considers the Art and Architecture after WWII.

Europe – Multiperiod: this definition includes organisations with different projects that encounter different layers in the excavation relating to successive periods.

Middle East – Prehistory: corresponds approximately to European Prehistory, from the Palaeolithic, c. 100,000 years BC, to the Iron Age, 500 years BC.

Middle East – Greek-Roman: the eastern shores of the Mediterranean were under the influence of what was happening on the Western shores between 300 BC and 500 AD; for simplicity this period has been classified in the Analytical Table as 'Greek-Roman'.

Middle East – Islamic/Medieval: in the year 700 the Islamic period starts and continues all the way to the Modern era. Christian architecture flourishes in the Medieval period in some countries, such as Armenia.

Asia – Prehistory: Far Eastern civilisations flourished from about 1000 BC. Prehistory can be considered to be belonging to the preceding periods.

Asia – Far East Civilisations: in China, Mongolia, Korea, and Japan history begins prior to 1000 BC. Although many periods (dynasties) can be identified among these important civilisations (just to name a few: the Qin, Han, Tang, and Song dynasties), for simplicity they have been grouped together.

Asia – Modern/Contemporary: grouped in this period are both the 19th and 20th centuries.

Africa – Prehistory/Palaeonthology: Africa saw the beginning of human evolution. Prehistory can be traced from about 3 million years BP to c. 2000 BC. For lack of space palaeonthological projects have been grouped in this category.

Africa – Modern/Contemporary: grouped mainly to consider cultural projects (such as projects on preserving traditional music or dances).

North America – Prehistory/Palaeonthology: from the early colonisation of the American continent by Asian populations, starting from about 20,000 years BP. For lack of space palaeonthological projects have been included in this group.

North America – Early Cultures: native American cultures were living undisturbed before the arrival of European colonists in 1600 on the East Coast and up to the early 1800s in the West. These cultures were well established from a few thousand years BC.

North America – Modern: this era corresponds approximately to the same period in Europe. The American Revolution in 1776 is animated by principles of freedom and democracy similar to those of the French Revolution in 1789.

Latin America – Maya/Precolombian: the Mayan civilisation flourished in central America from c. 500 BC to the arrival of the Spanish Conquistadores in 1500. The Maya period has been subdivided in pre-classic, classic and late classic; for simplicity, the Analytical Table does not refer to these periods.

Latin America – Pre-Inca/Inca: in South America the Inca empire flourished in the 15th century. Within this category projects related to earlier periods have been included for simplicity.

Latin America – Colonial/Modern: in Central America from 1500 to 1700 the Spaniards left beautiful examples of baroque religious architecture. Contemporary architecture has been included for simplicity.

Caribbean: referring to periods from 1492 to contemporary, including early colonialism, piracy, the slave trade, etc., up to the modern era.

Worldwide: organisations that have projects concentrating on various periods in several countries around the world are found in this category.

Before joining projects and organisations; prospective volunteers should carefully read the following considerations and warnings:

1)   **Because of obvious cost reasons**, which would then reflect on the cover price, **the Editor and Publisher cannot personally visit every project** listed in this guide but have to trust what projects and organisations (or the websites or previous volunteers) declare.

2)   **Small projects and organisations**, particularly in developing countries, mainly because of shortage of funding or qualified personnel or because of conflicts with local populations and/or local authorities, **often change their programmes or even interrupt their activities without informing the Editor and Publisher of** *Archaeo-Volunteers*.

3)   **Before joining a project volunteers should verify the validity of what is declared** on the project website (if one exists) or in this guide.

4)   **Prospective volunteers should exchange frequent e-mails**, or even fax or phone calls, **with project leaders** and ensure that communication is always prompt and clear. They should also confirm the project details, such as the living, working and safety conditions, prior to departure.

5)   **Prospective volunteers to any project should ask names** and addresses **of previous volunteers and correspond with them** to further verify the conditions of the projects.

6)   **Volunteers should never join a project by going directly to the location** without previous correspondence and verification of existing conditions.

7)   **Prospective volunteers should read carefully the WARNING on the third page of this book.**

Good luck with your "archaeo-volunteering"!

ORGANISATIONS AND PROJECTS LIST

Aang Serian Peace Village

PO Box 2113 Arusha Tanzania
Tel.: ++255 (744) 318 548 or 312 202
      ++44 (1865) 454 242 (in the UK)
E-mail: aang_serian@hotmail.com – businesslink1@compuserve.com
www.aangserian.org.uk

Desc.:   Aang Serian (meaning 'House of Peace' in Maasai language) is an independent, non-profit organisation. It is officially registered with the National Arts Council of Tanzania as an organisation for the promotion of arts and culture. Aang Serian is now establishing itself as a global NGO dedicated to preserving indigenous traditions and knowledge, and promoting intercultural dialogue around the world.

Per.:   Modern/contemporary.

Country: Tanzania

Loc.:   Arusha.

Travel: Details provided upon application.

Dur.:   3 months to 1 year, depending on project.

Age: Minimum 18.

Qualif.:   Non-professional volunteers with relevant skills to the project.

Work: Help to develop cultural programmes among local communities.

Lang.:   English.

Accom.:   Basic lodging.

Cost: Volunteers make a financial contribution to the projects of around GB£800 (US$1,200) for 3 months.

Applic.:   References will be required once the details of the project are confirmed.

Notes: Contact Antony Lunch.

Achill Island Field School

Folklife Centre
Dooagh, Achill, County Mayo Ireland
Tel.: ++353 (098) 43564
Fax: ++353 (098) 43564
E-mail: achill-fieldschool@iol.ie
www.archaeology.co.uk – www.achill-fieldschool.com

Desc.: Slievemore Archaeological Field School is involved in a research excavation at the Post Medieval Deserted Village at Slievemore on Achill Island, County Mayo. The school is an accredited field school of the National University of Ireland at Galway. Credits to students will be transferred through the University.

Per.: Post Medieval, 1600–1900 AD.

Country: United Kingdom.

Loc.: Dooagh Village, Achill Island in County Mayo off the west coast of Ireland.

Travel: Train from Dublin Heuston Station to Westport, then bus to Achill Island.

Dur.: 4–12 weeks; June to August.

Age: Minimum 18.

Qualif.: Students of archaeology, anthropology, and related disciplines.

Work: Excavation and survey of a post-medieval village.

Lang.: English.

Accom.: Self-catered.

Cost: EUR2,200–3,950 (approximately US$2,350–4,250).

Applic.: Contact field school directly.

AIEP – Association for Educational, Cultural and Work International Exchange Programs

42 Yeznik Coghbatsi Street, Room.22, Yerevan 375002 Armenia
Tel.: ++374 (1) 584 733
Fax: ++374 (1) 529 232
E-mail: aiep@arminco.com
www. aiep.am

Desc.:	AIEP sponsors historical restoration workcamps, technical internship and training programmes, and educational exchange programmes to students and youth as part of its goal to establish economic, cultural, and educational connections between Armenia and other countries. This sample project is at Dilijan, one of the largest health spa resorts in Armenia, within a national forest preserve with numerous historical monuments in the vicinity, the most interesting being the group of buildings of the Haghartsin Monastery.
Per.:	Medieval; 8th–13th centuries.
Country:	Armenia.
Loc.:	Dilijan is about 60 miles (100km) from Yerevan, the capital city of Armenia.
Travel:	Pick-up at Zvarnots airport and bus to workcamp.
Dur.:	15 days; July or August.
Age:	Minimum 18.
Qualif.:	No experience necessary.
Work:	Reconstruction of historic buildings and general cleaning. Monday to Friday; 4–5 hours per day.
Lang.:	English, Russian, Armenian.
Accom.:	The Holiday Hotels, near Dilijan and Ijevan. Some meals provided, others self-catered. Bring kitchen utensils and towels.
Cost:	US$100 registration fee plus US$10 per diem. Food, accommodation, and transfers included. Personal expenses, travel, and airport tax not included.
Applic.:	On-line form followed by printed formal application. Deadline 5 weeks before project start date. E-mail for further application information or consult the website of the Europe Cultural Cube Ltd. at www.culturalcube.co.uk.

Alchester Roman Fortress

Eberhard Sauer
Keble College, Oxford OX1 3PG   UK
Tel.: ++44 (1865) 272 720
Fax: ++44 (1865) 272 705
E-mail: eberhard.sauer@keble.oxford.ac.uk

Desc.: The annex of the fortress was founded as early as AD 44, less than 1 1/2 years after the original invasion. This is known because the high water table has preserved the bottom of the gateposts whose tree-rings allowed precise dating. The excavations have explored a large timber building with a courtyard in the annex, a granary in the main fortress, and the west gate of the annex. Future investigations aim to clarify whether the main fortress was constructed as early as the year of the invasion, 43 AD, and explore more of the military timber buildings and of a nearby Iron Age settlement.

Per: Excavation of invasion-period Roman fortress (1st century AD).

Country: United Kingdom.

Loc.: Near Wendlebury (Oxfordshire).

Travel: Transport between Oxford and the site on arrival and return.

Dur.: August to September.

Age: Minimum 16, preferably 18.

Qualif.: No experience necessary but of advantage.

Work: Excavation. Working hours 9:30–18:30 with a morning, lunch, and afternoon break. Participants work 5–6 days per week.

Lang.: English.

Accom.: Tent camping with basic sanitary, shower, and cooking facilities. Participant must bring their own tent. The site is self-catering (there is a pub in walking distance from the site that some participants use for evening meals). A supermarket is 5 minutes by car from the site.

Cost: None.

Applic.: Contact the project by early spring.

Alexandria Archaeology Museum

105 North Union Street, #327, Alexandria, Virginia 22314 USA
Tel.: ++1 (703) 838 4399
http://oha.ci.alexandria.va.us/archaeology/ar-support-become-volunteer.html
http://oha.ci.alexandria.va.us/archaeology/ar-programs-summercamp-appl.html

Desc.:   Alexandria was established on a crescent bay of the Potomac River by Scottish traders in the 1730s. It grew in the 18th century into one of the most important ports of the region. The city reflects many of the changes in economic focus, ethnic diversity, patterns of land use, and social stratification that characterise urban environments. Participants discover fragments and artefacts buried on Shuter's Hill, the site of 18th- and 19th-century mansions, a Civil War fort and barracks, and the George Washington Masonic National Memorial.

Per.:   18th–19th centuries.

Country: United States.

Loc.:   Old Town Alexandria, Virginia. Shuter's Hill is an historic period site close to the King Street Metro.

Travel: No travel provided. Contact the organisation for instructions.

Dur.:   10-day field and laboratory course in May; 1–2 weeks, 9:00–15:00 daily for Summer Camp in July; 1.5 hours (13:30–15:00 Saturdays) for Family/Public Dig Days.

Age: Minimum 18 for field school; 12–15 for Summer Camp; a participating adult must accompany children under the age of 16 for day digs.

Qualif.:   No experience necessary.

Work: Survey, excavation, artefact identification and recording, and laboratory processing. Public interpretation and lectures involved in field school; field trips and walking tours for Summer Camp.

Lang.:   English.

Accom.:   Tent camping for field school. No accommodation for Summer Camp and Day Digs as participants arrive at specific hours per day and do not stay overnight.

Cost: US$300 per week for Summer Camp; US$5 per person for Family/Public Dig Days.

Applic.: To register and for inquiries about tuition, course credit, etc., contact the George Washington University, Office of Summer, Special, and International Programs at sumprogs@gwu.edu or call (202) 994 9193. Before registering for the course, students should contact Alexandria Archaeology at (703) 838 4399 or e-mail via the on-line form at http://ci.alexandria.va.us/contactus/view_contactus.pxe. Print and fill out the Summer Camp Application and send it to Alexandria Archaeology. Enclose a check for the non-refundable US$50 deposit, made payable to the City of Alexandria. Family/Public Dig Days telephone reservations are required and accepted beginning at 10:00 on Tuesday for the next Saturday's sessions.

Alliance of European Voluntary Service Organisations

Secretariat c/o MS
Studsgade 20, DK-8000 Aarhus C. Denmark
Tel.: ++45 (8619) 7766
Fax: ++45 (8619) 7061
E-mail: alliance@alliance-network.org
www.alliance-network.org/

Desc.: This International Non-Governmental Youth Organisation (INGYO) represents national organisations running international voluntary service projects. Each organisation promotes community development, intercultural education, understanding, and peace through voluntary service. The Alliance consists of 28 member organisations from 20 countries. A workcamp involves 10–20 volunteers from 5–10 different countries. Projects take place in communities and provide volunteers the possibility to meet people from other countries and be hosted by the local community, thus gaining an intercultural experience while being a useful and active world citizen.

Per.: Modern, contemporary.

Country: Worldwide.

Loc.: Various.

Travel: Details provided upon application to specific project.

Dur.: They participate in short-term projects, lasting 2–3 weeks, or, in some cases, long-term projects of up to 12 months. Alliance members organise international workcamps throughout the year, mostly during the summer months.

Age: Minimum 18.

Qualif.: No experience necessary.

Work: Volunteers can engage in a wide variety of community development tasks, including environmental, construction, renovation, social, cultural and archaeological work.

Lang.: English or language of host country.

Accom.: Variable. May be group camping, dorms or hostels, or billeting with host families.

Cost: Typically a membership or administration fee plus travel and personal expenses.

Applic.: International Volunteer Projects are organised in each country by a national Alliance member, which also recruits volunteers within that country. All Alliance members place only individuals residing in their own country on projects. Interested volunteers should therefore only contact their national Alliance member! The members also work closely with similar national and international organisations in Europe and worldwide. Individuals or organisations in other countries who would like to get involved should contact the Coordinating Committee for International Voluntary Service (see listing) at UNESCO in Paris to find out the name of the voluntary service organisation in their own country.

See also:
CCIVS – Coordinating Committee for International Voluntary Service
UNESCO

Alutiiq Museum and Archaeological Repository

Community Archaeology
215 Mission Road, Suite 101, Kodiak, Alaska 99615 USA
Tel.: ++1 (907) 486 7004
Fax: ++1 (907) 486 7004
E-mail: alutiiq2@ptialaska.net
www.alutiiqmuseum.com/education.htm

Desc.: Every summer the Alutiiq Museum hosts an excavation at an archaeological site near the town of Kodiak. Museum archaeologists choose a deposit that will help to answer a significant question in Alutiiq prehistory while focusing on sites that are threatened by erosion, vandalism, or modern development. Participants are invited to join in the hands-on exploration of Alutiiq heritage and historic preservation. In 2000, this programme received the National Award for Museum Service.

Per.: Ocean Bay cultural tradition, 7500–4000 years before present.

Country: United States.

Loc.: Kodiak is an Island in the Gulf of Alaska. The site is Zaimka Mound, a prehistoric settlement on the eastern shore of Womens Bay, directly opposite the Kodiak Airport, a 30-minute drive from downtown Kodiak.

Travel: Access to the island is by plane or boat. The ferry docks downtown. Taxi from airport to town. Daily transportation between the museum and the site provided. Participants meet at the museum at 8:30 and are returned at 17:30.

Dur.: 1 day (8 hours) to 6 weeks; July to August.

Age: Minimum 14.

Qualif.: No experience necessary.

Work: Excavation, carrying and washing sediment, mapping, and site cleaning. In the laboratory, participants assist with washing, sorting, and labeling artefacts, drying and organising samples, entering information into a computer database, and cleaning field gear. 4 weeks of fieldwork followed by 2 weeks of laboratory work; Monday to Friday, 8 hours per day.

Lang.: English.

Accom.: No accommodation or meals provided. Motels, B&Bs, and camping available in Kodiak.

Cost: No fees are charged except tuition for those interested in obtaining academic credit. Participants are responsible for their room and board costs and personal expenses.

Applic.: Contact museum archaeologist Patrick Saltonstall for project dates, to schedule participation, and for academic registration procedures.

Notes: Bring rubber boots, raingear (Kodiak's summer weather can be cold and rainy), gloves, kneeling pads, and bug nets. Digging equipment is provided by the museum. Photography is permitted. Academic credit available through the University of Alaska's Kodiak College. Tuition fees apply.

Ancient Metal Production in Southern Jordan

University of California, San Deigo Archaeological Field School
Department of Anthropology
9500 Gilman Drive, La Jolla, California 92093-0532 USA
Tel.: ++1 (858) 534 4145 Fax: ++1 (858) 534 5946
E-mail: tlevy@weber.ucsd.edu
http://weber.ucsd.edu/Depts/Anthro/classes/tlevy/Fidan/

Desc.: The full name of this project is: Ancient Metal Production, Heterogeneity, and Social Change – Social Consolidation and Fragmentation During the Iron Age in Southern Jordan. The area this project occupies is considered the gateway to one of the Levant's largest copper ore deposits. The project provides an ideal open-air laboratory for studying the role of early copper ore extraction and metallurgy on the evolution of Levantine societies and involves archaeological survey along the Wadi al-Ghuwayb and excavation at the site of Khirbet en-Nahas, which has been known since early in the last century as one of the largest Iron Age metal production sites in the southern Levant.

Per.: Neolithic period to Iron Age; 11th–4th centuries BC.

Country: Jordan.

Loc.: Jabal Hamrat Fidan Region of southern Jordan. The base camp is located at the eastern end of the Wadi Fidan, on the edge of the local village of Qurayqira.

Travel: Fly to Amman aiport. Group pick-up or travel instructions for travel to Fidan provided. The campsite lies at the end of a paved road that runs from the village of Qurayqira to the main Aqaba-Dead Sea Road. The road to Ain el-Fidan is well sign posted. Initial transportation into the site and a pick-up of the group flight will be provided.

Dur.: 10 weeks; late September to December.

Age: Minimum 18.

Qualif.: No experience necessary.

Work: Fidan Orientation; Dana Reserve Ecology Program; Field Survey of Wadi al-Ghuwayb; Excavation at Khirbet en-Nahas; Post-excavation.

Lang.:   English, Arabic.

Accom.: Tent at the base camp or a tent camp near to the site. Permanent structures provide a kitchen, toilets, showers, and potable water. Camp beds with sleeping pads are provided but bring a personal sleeping bag or sleep sheets. A mosquito net is recommended. The tent camp has supplies transported in daily.

Cost: US$1,451 for 10 weeks plus US$150 registration fee. Tuition, room and board, and local project related travel expenses included. Airfare and personal expenses not included. US$275 for the ecology field school (see Notes); tuition fees not included.

Applic.: On-line form. Submit the non-refundable registration deposit and application and fulfill the subsequent payment deadlines. Passport, visa, and security forms also to be completed on-line. UCSD students must register through regular registration channels for the field school and the ecology course. Upon registration, an information packet will be sent. Limited to 40 students. Contact Dr. Thomas Levy for further details and instructions.

Notes: The Ecology Program is held a week prior to the archaeology field school providing a background understanding of the desert ecology and environment of the region.

Ancient Nomads of Mongolia

Earthwatch International
3 Clock Tower Place, Suite 100
Box 75, Maynard, Massachusetts 01754 USA
Tel.: ++1 (978) 461 0081 or toll free in NA 1 (800) 776 0188
Fax: ++1 (978) 461 2332
E-mail: info@earthwatch.org – www.earthwatch.org

Desc.:   Systematic survey of habitation, burial, and ritual sites answer some of the questions surrounding the pastoral lifestyle of nomadic herders of thousands of years ago in Mongolia. Hundreds of ancient stone structures, burial mounds, stone boundary lines, and large carved stone stelae or 'deer stones' have been discovered and researched in the Khanuy Valley.

Per.:.   Prehistoric.

Country: Mongolia.

Loc.:   Khanuy River Valley at 5000 feet (1500m), central Mongolia.

Travel: Details provided after application.

Dur.:   2 weeks; May to July.

Age: Inquire with organisation for minimum age restrictions.

Qualif.:   No experience necessary.

Work: Survey, GPS, excavation, archiving, and documenting finds.

Lang.:   English or local language.

Accom.:   Tent camping. No electricity or running water; pit toilets; bathing in nearby stream; food transported into the site and cooks prepare meals.

Cost: US$1,995 (approximately GB£1,350). Room and board included.

Applic.:   On-line form to e-mail, fax, or post. Select project and dates of preference. Reserve placement by submitting completed form with deposit of US$250. Full payment required 90 days in advance of project start date.

See also:
Earthwatch Institute

Anglo-American Project in Pompei

Department of Archaeological Sciences, University of Bradford
Bradford, West Yorkshire BD 7 1 DP UK
Tel.: ++44 (1274) 233 536
Fax: ++44 (1274) 235 190
E-mail: archsci-pompeii@bradford.ac.uk
www.brad.ac.uk/acad/archsci/field_proj/anampomp/

Desc.: The House of the Surgeon, the 2nd large residence in the *insula*, the bars and workshops, plus a complete block of the ancient city, the *insula*, are investigated to understand the social range of the ancient urban community and reveal how the urban fabric was created over 5 centuries.

Per.: Roman; 79 AD.

Country: Italy.

Loc.: Southern Italy on the Bay of Naples, south of Naples.

Travel: Arrive to Naples. Meeting point confirmed after application.

Dur.: 6 weeks; June to August.

Age: Minimum 16.

Qualif.: No experience necessary. Particularly suitable for students at all levels in archaeology, classics, and anthropology.

Work: Excavation, sediment, artefact, and ecofact processing, ceramics and glass, wall painting and architectural analysis, archaeozoology, botany, metallurgy, and illustration.

Lang.: English is the working language, but the team is international.

Accom.: Camping Spartacus, a modern camping facility 300m from the site entrance. The campsite has toilets, shower facilities, and washing machines. Bring all personal gear, a tent and bedding, and a trowel. There is an on-site restaurant, café/bar, small store, and Internet point. Other amenities are nearby.

Cost: US$3,000. Includes tuition, equipment, project handbook, campground fees, meals, visits, and project insurance. Travel and health and travel insurance not included.

Applic.: On-line form to returned via e-mail. Deadline March 7. Academic credit available from the University of Bradford.

Notes: Up-to-date tetanus vaccination required.

ArchaeoExpeditions

Cultural Expeditions MEC Canada, Inc.
Westgate PO Box 35012, Ottawa, Ontario K1Z 1A2 Canada
Tel.: ++1 (613) 264 0377 or toll free in NA 1 (866) 682 0562
Fax: ++1 (613) 264 0388
E-mail: info@archaeoexpeditions.com
www.archaeoexpeditions.com

Desc.: Volunteers are able to participate in real archaeological excavations or travel to important sites and museums while helping professional archaeologists undertake or continue important research.

Per.: Various.

Country: Various.

Loc.: Various.

Travel: Details provided with specific project.

Dur.: 16 weeks.

Age: Minimum 18.

Qualif.: No experience necessary but of advantage. The archaeologist will assign responsibilities at the site. Field training provided.

Work: Excavation involves kneeling and bending for long periods of time and lifting buckets full of dirt. Each project requires different levels of physical work.

Lang.: English or local language.

Accom.: Typically camping or modest hotel. Varies with projects.

Cost: Depending upon project. Details are identified in the expedition descriptions. All costs incurred while travelling to and from the project site are not included.

Applic.: Select a project and apply to ArchaeoExpeditions

Notes: No formal accreditation is offered. Volunteers should research the project, host country conditions and culture, tourist visas, insurances, currency matters, etc.

See also:
ArchaeoExpeditions – Belize
ArchaeoExpeditions – Canada
ArchaeoExpeditions – Spain

ArchaeoExpeditions – Belize

Cultural Expeditions MEC Canada, Inc.
Westgate PO Box 35012, Ottawa, Ontario K1Z 1A2 Canada
Tel.: ++1 (613) 624 0377 or toll free in NA 1 (866) 682 0562
Fax: ++1 (613) 264 0388
E-mail: info@archaeoexpeditions.com
www.archaeoexpeditions.com

Desc.: This long-term archaeological research and Maya studies programme in the Rio Bravo Biosphere Reserve is dedicated to the protection and management of a rich and sensitive ecological zone that includes many important cultural sites. The University of Texas in Austin and the local non-profit organisation, Program For Belize, have started an intensive survey and site inventory project with some 50 archaeological sites already identified. The Late Classic Centre of Dos Hombres (among others) is included as well as smaller site localities throughout the territory.

Per.: Pre-Classic through Late Classic Maya.

Country: Belize.

Loc.: Northwest Belize.

Travel: Belize City airport for pick up.

Dur.: 4 weeks; April to May.

Age: Minimum 18.

Qualif.: No experience necessary.

Work: Survey, excavation, and inventory. Participants will be assigned to 1 or more sites as the work is carried out.

Lang.: English with Spanish helpful.

Accom.: Field camp in rainforest environment.

Cost: US$620 for 1 week; US$1,140 for 2 weeks; US$1,560 for 3 weeks; US$1,880 for 4 weeks. Room and board included. Airfare not included.

Applic.: Maximum 10 volunteers per week.

See also:

ArchaeoExpeditions

ArchaeoExpeditions – Canada

Cultural Expeditions MEC Canada, Inc.
Westgate PO Box 35012, Ottawa, Ontario K1Z 1A2 Canada
Tel.: ++1 (613) 264 0377 or toll free in NA 1 (866) 682 0562
Fax: ++1 (613) 264 0388
E-mail: info@archaeoexpeditions.com
www.archaeoexpeditions.com

Desc: Explore the life of Iroquoian peoples in Canada 550 years ago at the Metate Site. This historic Neutral Indian village is the northern most settlement on top of the Niagara Escarpment in the Crawford Lake area. Between AD 1560 and 1580 it was home to at least 1,000 people. Excavation of the area is to define a long-house structure and its associated functions.

Per.: 1500s.

Country: Canada.

Loc.: Situated near Acton, Ontario with easy access from Toronto and highway 401.

Travel: Meeting point to be advised.

Dur.: 5–7 days; June to October intermittently.

Age: Students under18 must be accompanied by an adult.

Qualif.: No experience necessary.

Work: Survey, excavation, inventory, and laboratory work including washing, sorting, and cataloguing of artefacts. An introduction to the history of occupation of southern Ontario is given by native peoples, tours, and lectures.

Lang.: English.

Accom: Hotel.

Cost: CAD$1,225 per week plus CAD$400 deposit with registration; accommodation Sunday through Thursday night, meals, and transportation to and from the site included. CAD$500 per weekend; 2 nights hotel, meals, and programme included. CAD$250 for the project only with lunch Saturday and Sunday.

Applic.: Deadline is 45 days prior to start date of session. Groups of 4 or more should reserve early in the season with specific dates.

See also:
ArchaeoExpeditions

ArchaeoExpeditions – Spain

Cultural Expeditions MEC Canada, Inc.
Westgate PO Box 35012, Ottawa, Ontario K1Z 1A2 Canada
Tel.: ++1 (613) 624 0377 or toll free in NA 1 (866) 682 0562
Fax: ++1 (613) 264 0388
E-mail: info@archaeoexpeditions.com
www.archaeoexpeditions.com

Desc.: Since the 1980s directors of La Roca dels Bous archaeological project have been uncovering Neanderthal layers with hearths and associated faunal and lithic artefacts. Participants will collaborate with professors of Torre of the Universitat Autonoma de Barcelona. This research will help to understand the behaviour of the last Neanderthals. The access to the archaeological site is easy but the landscape is quite rugged and wild, with deep ravines and sheer cliffs.

Per.: Neanderthal, Palaeolithic.

Country: Spain.

Loc.: Northern Spain. La Roca dels Bous is located in the pre-Pyrénées mountain ranges, near to the town of Balaguer.

Travel: Participants make their own way to Balaguer.

Dur.: 4–2-week sessions; June to August.

Age: Minimum 18.

Qualif.: No experience necessary.

Work: Survey, excavation, and laboratory inventory. Everyone is expected to help in miscellaneous tasks needed for the normal development of the project. The nature of the site does not require strenuous digging, however participants should be moderately fit and able to hike on rugged terrain.

Lang.: English; Spanish helpful.

Accom.: Pension or camping.

Cost: US$1,300 per 2-week session. Meals and accommodation included.

Applic.: Maximum 10 volunteers per week.

See also:
ArchaeoExpeditions

Archaeolink Prehistory Park

Oyne, Insch, Aberdeenshire AB52 6QP UK
Tel.: ++44 (1464) 851 500
Fax: ++44 (1464) 851 544
Email: info@archaeolink.co.uk
www.archaeolink.co.uk

Desc.: Archaeolink opened in 1997 to act as a link between the public and Aberdeenshire's rich archaeological heritage. A series of reconstructions – all based on archaeological evidence from northeast Scotland – form a Path through Prehistory. There are reconstructions from stone age camps through to a Roman Marching camp and an Iron Age farm.

Per.: Prehistory to Roman.

Country: United Kingdom.

Loc.: Insch, near Aberdeen.

Travel: Volunteers are responsible for their travel to the sight.

Dur.: 1 day to full season; March to November.

Age: Minimum 14 with guardian.

Qualif.: No experience necessary.

Work: Reconstruction.

Lang.: English.

Accom.: Local B&B.

Cost: Volunteers must pay for their travel, food and accommodation, but no contribution is required from the Park.

Applic.: Contact the park for further info.

Archaeological and Architectural Field Work in Turkey
City Gate Restorations

Kivanc Tourism, Fabrika Caddesi, No. 23 Yalvac 32400 Turkey
Tel.: ++90 (246) 441 43 48 Fax: ++90 (246) 441 63 43
E-mail: info@pisidian.com
www.pisidian.com – www.anitsal.com
www.interimpact.com/expeditions/turkey.html

Desc.: The City Gate was built to welcome the Emperor Hadrian to Antioch on his visit to the Province of Asia in 129AD. Over the years the gate collapsed and many of the stones from the supporting pillars were removed and used for other purposes. However much of the superstructure survives including stones that bore a bronze letter dedication to Hadrian. The gate is now to be rebuilt under the supervision of the Turkish architects the Yalvac Museum.

Per.: Roman; 129 AD.

Country: Turkey.

Loc.: Pisidian Antioch, Yalvac.

Travel: Details provided upon application.

Dur.: 2–6 weeks; May to September.

Age: Minimum 18.

Qualif.: No experience necessary.

Work: Restoration work from 7:00–12:30 and 13:30–16:00, 4 days a week.

Lang.: English.

Accom.: Pension-style appartment in Yalvac, 2–4 people per room, computer, internet, TV, bar facilities and home-style meals.

Cost: US$1,300 for 2 weeks; US$2,000 for 4 weeks; US$2,500 for 6 weeks. US$300 deposit.

Applic.: On-line form.

Notes: On weekends participants may relax, travel, or join a tour to Lake Catalhuyuk.

Archaeological Excavations in Northern Spain

CA Cantabrian Quaternary – Institute of Human Origins
Anthropolgy Department, PO Box 872402 Arizona State University
Tempe, Arizona 85287-2402 USA
Tel.: ++1 (480) 727 6580 Fax: ++01 (480) 727 2402
E-mail: ana.pinto@asu.edu – cuaternario2@conectia.net
http://accuca.conectia.es

Desc.: Excavation of a Palaeolithic site in the mountains of northern Spain.

Per.: Palaeolithic.

Country: Spain.

Loc.: Asturias County, Northern Spain. The site is remote and volunteers will be taken in a 4x4 vehicle to a drop-off point after which they will hike 30 min. in the mountains to the site and return again for pick-up at day's end.

Travel: Arrive to Madrid or Bilbao airports, then get a ALSA or EASA coach to the city of Oviedo. Volunteers are collected in Oviedo following confirmation of dates.

Dur.: Minimum 6 weeks, maximum 8 weeks; July to August.

Age: Minimum 20.

Qualif.: The project favours archaeology or anthropology advanced students or professionals with prior experience in excavations and laboratory work, however will consider also other committed applicants.

Work: Excavation, collecting, and processing sediment. Monday to Saturday, 10 hours per day. Mountain hiking, wet weather, and carrying sacks of sediment requiring physical stamina.

Lang.: Spanish and English

Accom: Lodgings are provided in bunk beds in rooms holding up to 6 people. Volunteers must bring sleeping bags.

Cost: No charge. Room and board included. Travel expenses not included. Cooking or other home chores may be expected.

Applic.: Submit CV via e-mail stating studies and prior experience and a cover letter stating disposition to work for 6–8 weeks.

Notes: Bring mountain boots and raincoats or waterproofs.

Archaeology and Art

Perpetuum Mobile International (PMI)
c/o Grenzenlos, Liechtensteinstr. 20, A-1090 Vienna Austria
E-mail: sending@pm-int.org
Tel.: ++43 (1) 315 76 36
Fax: ++43 (1) 315 76 37
www.pm-int.org/en/workcamps.html

Desc.: This international workcamp organisation has an archaeology project aimed at physically and mentally disabled individuals and local youth. The site has not been previously excavated; the project will focus initially on an area near a church. The finds from the dig will be used to decorate a big music festival to take place at the end of the workcamp.

Per.: Pre-modern.

Country: Austria and worldwide.

Loc.: Styria near Straden, which is 40 miles (60km) south of Graz.

Travel: Airports are in Graz and Vienna. Train to Feldbach and then bus to Straden for pick-up.

Dur.: 3 weeks; August to September.

Age: Minimum 18.

Qualif.: No experience necessary. Up to 15 international and 5–10 local volunteers; 6–8 physically and mentally disabled people and 1–2 archaeology students.

Work: Exploratory dig. Monday to Friday; 8:00–14:00.

Lang.: English, French, German.

Accom.: Community centre with sleeping room with 15 places, bathroom, kitchen, and toilets. Bring a sleeping bag.

Cost: Fees paid to sending organisation in partnership with PMI. Room and board included. Additional workcamp fees may apply. Travel not included.

Applic.: Apply through PMI or local workcamp organisation. Archaeology students can contact Dr. Diether Kramer at the archaeology office at the University of Styria for the opportunity to join his students in leading this project.

Notes: Bring work shoes and clothes, raingear, swimming suit and cap, personal items, and travel insurance.

ArchaeoSpain

135 Pope Street
Fairfield, Connecticut 06825 USA
Tel./Fax: ++1 (203) 384 9700
E-mail: info@archaeospain.com
www.archaeospain.com

Desc.: ArchaeoSpain is a group of cultural resource specialists with a commitment to public education, providing opportunities for people to engage in scientific research. The International Archaeology Program allows participants to do archaeology with trained investigators and contribute to ongoing research efforts in several important sites in Spain and Italy.

Per.: Roman, Celtiberian, Visigothic, Medieval, and other.

Country: Spain and Italy.

Loc.: Various locations in Spain and Italy, depending on project.

Travel: Details provided upon application.

Dur.: 2–6 weeks; summer.

Age: Minimum 18.

Qualif.: No experience necessary.

Work: Excavation, land survey, mapping, photography, and conservation and exhibition of artefacts. Work is demanding owing to the heat and the physical demands. Participants should be in reasonable physical condition and in good health.

Lang.: English; Spanish helpful. While Spanish speaking ability is not a prerequisite or the goal of this project, participants will be immersed in the language daily, therefore it is hoped that they will take advantage and improve their spoken Spanish.

Accom.: Hostel, group house, etc., depending on project.

Cost: US$1,275 for 2-weeks; US$2,075 for 1 month. Meals, lodging, transportation, site and museum admissions, and administrative costs included. Airfare not included.

Applic.: On-line form.

Notes: Academic credit available with approval from home institution.

ArcheoClub D'Italia

Via Nomentana 263, 00161 Rome Italy
Tel.: ++39 (06) 44 20 22 50 or 44 20 22 39
Fax: ++39 (06) 44 20 24 93
E-mail sede-nazionale@archeoclubitalia.it
www.archeoclubitalia.it

Desc.: ArcheoClub d'Italia promotes the knowledge, protection, and care of the Italian archaeological and cultural heritage. The Association works throughout Italy and has more than 300 local chapters. Archeoclub organises many workcamps for the protection of the national heritage, such as the ones in Agrigento, in the archaeological area of Paestum, Campi Flegrei, for the restoration of castles, forts, and caves that were modified and used as churches in southern Italy. Volunteers are very important for the Association's activities.

Per.: Greek Classical, Roman, Early Christian.

Country: Italy.

Loc: Various.

Travel: Each camp is easily reachable with public transportation. Details provided upon application.

Dur.: Typically 2 weeks.

Age: Minimum 18.

Qualif: No experience necessary.

Work: Excavation, documentation, survey, etc.

Lang.: Italian, English.

Accom.: Generally in dormitory structures.

Cost: Approximately EUR300 (approx. US$320) per 2-week session plus EUR30 (US$32) membership fee. Food and accommodation included.

Applic.: On-line form.

Notes: Bring work boots, gloves, and clothes, a water bottle, hat, and sleeping bag.

See also:
ArcheoVenezia Archeological Field Work Camp

ArcheoVenezia Archaeological Field Work Camp

ArcheoClub d'Italia
Cannaregio, 1376/a, 30121 Venice Italy
Tel./Fax: ++39 (041) 710 515
E-mail: archeove@provincia.venezia.it
www.provincia.venezia.it/archeove/inglese/

Desc.: A project in the Venetian lagoon for the recovery of the island of Lazzaretto Novo is part of a general project entitled "For the rebirth of an island". There are excavation in the area of the *camere* and the *priorado* of the ancient lazzaretto (1468–1792) as part of an archaeology and history of public health project to verify the wall structures and the foundations present on the island. In-depth tests are verifying the wall structure and the foundations on the island.

Per.: 15–18th centuries and precedent periods.

Country: Italy.

Loc.: Island of Lazzaretto Nuovo (Venice Lagoon), Venice.

Travel: Train to Venice, then vaporetto (public boat) to the island.

Dur.: 10 days; August.

Age: Minimum 18.

Qualif.: No experience necessary.

Work: On-site training covers the correct use of instruments and tools, identification and retrieval of stratigraphic units (SU), examination and classification of finds (pottery, numismatics, glass fragments, anthropology), archaeological drawing, survey, and graphical reconstruction.

Lang.: Italian, French, English.

Accom.: Lodging with hot water showers. Board meals prepared by a cook with the volunteers.

Cost: EUR400 (approx.US$420). Boat pass for Venice costs about EUR30.

Applic.: Deadline for registration July 15.

See also:
ArcheoClub d'Italia

Ardudwy Early Landscapes Project

Department of History and Welsh History
University of Wales, Bangor Gwynedd LL57 2DG UK
Tel.: ++44 (1248) 382 156
Fax: ++44 (1248) 382 759
E-mail: r.a.johnston@bangor.ac.uk – john.roberts@heneb.co.uk
www.bangor.ac.uk/history/ardudwy

Desc.: The project is looking into the later prehistoric upland landscapes of northwest Wales, focusing on 1km^2 core area, roughly centred upon a settlement enclosure and ring cairn. Past excavation has revealed a range of features including hut circle settlement remains, platforms, and early field boundaries.

Per.: Prehistoric.

Country: United Kingdom.

Loc.: Northwest Wales. The study area is located on the mountainous western flanks of Snowdonia overlooking Cardigan Bay and the Lleyn Peninsula near Harlech.

Travel: Details provide upon application.

Dur.: 1 month; summer.

Age: Minimum 18.

Qualif.: Training will be provided but the project will be most suitable for those with some prior experience.

Work: Excavation and training. Participants should be familiar with, or prepared to work in, a rugged upland environment.

Lang.: English.

Accom.: Camping.

Cost: Approximately GB£75 (US$115). Includes food and accommodation.

Applic.: Contact the University or the Gwynedd Archaeological Trust at Ffordd y Garth, Bangor, Gwynedd LL57 5RT, UK.

ARKEOS

Service Archéologique du Douaisis
191 rue Saint Albin, 59 500 Douai France
Tel.: ++33 (3) 27 71 38 90
Fax: ++33 (3) 27 71 38 93.
E-mail: arkeos@wanadoo.fr
www.arkeos.org

Desc.:	The organisation is exploring remains of a Gallic and a Gallo-Roman settlement. A very large Gallo-Roman villa is now being examined. Some buildings, walls, and tombs are being excavated. Other work conducted by the organisation concerns medieval settlements.
Per.:	Late Hellic and Early Roman (1st century BC to 1st century AD).
Country:	France.
Loc.:	An industrial zone near Douai.
Travel:	Train from Paris to the meeting place in Douai. Volunteers are transported daily by van to the excavation site.
Dur.:	2 weeks.
Age:	Minimum 18.
Qualif.:	No experience necessary.
Work:	Excavation, documentation, mapping, etc.
Lang.:	French, English.
Accom.:	In a school dormitory.
Cost:	EUR25 (approx. US$27) participation fee. Room and board included Monday to Friday.
Applic.:	By ordinary mail, fax, or e-mail.

ASTOVOCT – Association Togolaise Des Volontaires Chretiens Au Travail

Rue de l'Hôpital, BP 97, Kpalimé Togo
Tel.: +228 410 715 or 064 828 or 057 583
Fax: +228 410 715
E-mail: astovoct@yahoo.com – sgastovoct@yahoo.fr
www.wcc-coe.org/wcc/links/liaison-dir/togo.html

Desc.: International workcamp focused on cultural awareness of African culture in Togo.

Per.: Modern/contemporay.

Country: Togo.

Loc.: Lom Kpalim.

Travel: Meet in Kpalim on the eve of the workcamp. Airport pick-up can be arranged. A letter of confirmation is required for this service.

Dur.: 3 weeks.

Age: 18.

Qualif.: This camp is open only to volunteers with a knowledge and skills in arts and would like to know African culture in its depth.

Work: The volunteers will produce T-shirts, clothes in Togolese style or fashion, and stationery. The volunteers will also present or perform theatre, and African dance and percussion.

Lang.: English and French are both required.

Accom.: Tent camping. Volunteers can sleep in the office of the association 1 day before and 2 days after the workcamp.

Cost: EUR160 (approx. US$170). Food, accommodation, and airport pick-up included.

Applic.: Contact the workcamp association of home country.

Notes: Bring a camera, paintbrushes, and white T-Shirts for Batik art. Volunteers can also bring school supplies and books to donate to the local library, clothes for distribution, and medicines (antibiotics, anti-inflammatories, pomades, etc.) to donate to the health clinics. Not all bankcards are accepted in Togo.

Baga Gazaryn Chuluu Survey

Center for the Study of Eurasian Nomads
577 San Clemente Street
Ventura, California 93001 USA
Tel./Fax: ++1 (805) 653 2607 or (510) 549 3708
E-mail: jkimball@csen.org
www.csen.org

Desc.: The American and Mongolian archaeologists have initiated a full-coverage pedestrian survey of a remote section of the desert-steppe zone of Middle Gobi province in Mongolia. Ancient petroglyphs can be discovered on the granite outcrops. Stone stelae, erected by early Turkic nomads, are located in the main valley running between the towering peaks. Volunteers assist archaeologists from US and Mongolian research institutions in beginning the survey and in conducting several small-scale excavations of burial and habitation sites dated to the Bronze and Early Iron Age (800–400 BC).

Per.: Upper Palaeolithic to 20th century AD: Neolithic, Bronze Age, Early Iron Age, Medieval.

Country: Mongolia.

Loc.: South central Mongolia, Middle Gobi province, approximately 30 miles (50km) north of the city of Mandalgov.

Travel: Meeting point arranged with application.

Dur.: 1–2 months. July to August.

Age: Minimum 20.

Qualif.: No experience required. Training will be provided by both American and Mongolian archaeologists.

Work: Fieldwork; ground survey, site mapping, use of GPS and GIS, settlement excavation, and artefact processing. Cultural excursions plus several jeep trips into the true sand Gobi of Mongolia to the south to collect ore samples and visit archaeological sites known from Mongolian research reports.

Lang.: English.

Accom.: Tent camping (no electricity). Bring a tent, sleeping bag, and mat.

Cost: US$1,200 for 4-week session, US$1,400 for 6-week session. All expenses at the site, 12 nights of lodging in an expedition rental in Ulaanbaatar, and transport to and from the site by either local bus or minivan included. Airfare not included nor any expenses in Ulaanbaatar beyond lodging. Personal insurance is not included but is recommended.

Applic.: On-line form. Mail application and deposit of US$300 (4-weeks) or US$500 (6 weeks) by April 15; final payments by May 25. Deadlines are strict to allow time for visa processing. A visa will not be granted until the entire contribution is paid. The organization will facilitate obtaining visas for all participants.

Notes: Challenging field conditions, a moderate workload (especially hiking), living in tents under semi-desert conditions, and a meat-oriented diet. Consult the website for clothing and equipment recommendations.

See also:
Center for the Study of Euarsian Nomads

Baikal Archaeology Project

Department of Anthropology, University of Alberta
Edmonton, Alberta T6G 2H4 Canada
Tel.: ++1 (780) 492 3879
Fax: ++1 (780) 492 5273
E-mail: andrzej.weber@ualberta.ca
http://baikal.arts.ualberta.ca/

Desc.: This field school is a joint venture between the University of Alberta and the Department of Archaeology, Irkutsk State University, Russia. The project will involve excavation of an early Bronze Age gravesite. The site, located directly on Lake Baikal, features good preservation of skeletal remains and grave goods characteristic of a hunting-gathering culture.

Per.: Bronze Age; 4000–6000 years ago.

Country: Russia.

Loc: Siberia (Lake Baikal region), 185 miles (300km) east of Irkutsk.

Travel: Participants typically rendezvous in Frankfurt. Details confirmed upon application.

Dur.: 7 weeks; June to August.

Age: Minimum 18.

Qualif.: Introductory University anthropology course.

Work: Excavation, documentation, data collection, topographic survey and identification, and removal and curation of skeletal material. Kitchen and camp duties on a rotating basis.

Lang.: English, Russian.

Accom.: Tent camping at the site. Participants must bring their own all-weather tent, with wind resistance being an important criterion. The field school may assist students in purchasing their tents in a bulk order through the University. Very simple living conditions (plenty of clean but cold lake water and a sauna once a week). All meals are provided at the camp.

Cost: Approximately US$450 for food. Airfare not included.

Applic.: Deadline February 15.

Notes: Contact Project Director Dr. Andrzej Weber for further information. Academic credit available through the University of Alberta. Additional tuition fees apply.

Ba'Ja Neolithic Project

Ex oriente e.V., Free University of Berlin
Huttenweg 7, D-14195 Berlin Germany
Tel.: ++49 (30) 795 9937 or 838 6747
Fax: ++49 (30) 795 9937
E-mail: hggebel@zedat.fu-berlin.de
www.vereine.freepage.de/ex-oriente

Desc.: This excavation project investigates a village that belongs to the earliest sedentary societies in the Near East. Terraced, well-preserved housing inhabited people that started to develop social stratification. Palaeontological research on the human impact on nature by over-population and resource conflict that likely terminated the occupation at this remote site.

Per.: Early Neolithic, 7th millennium BC.

Country: Jordan.

Loc.: Southern Jordan, 9 miles (14km) north of Petra.

Travel: By airplane to Amman International airport; taxi to base camp.

Dur.: 4–5 weeks; April to June.

Age: Minimum 18.

Qualif.: Excavation experience is valuable. Mental and physical strength; good health, good head for heights, heat tolerance, cultural tolerance in Muslim social environment.

Work: Basic training in excavations techniques provided; assisting archaeologists; cleaning and registering finds; camp management. Harsh conditions of expedition life to be expected.

Lang.: English.

Accom.: Very basic dig camp (sleeping on air mattresses in sleeping bags on the rocks). Sparse 2-bedroom houses at base camp.

Cost: US$500 for 4 weeks. Food, accommodation, and local transport related to the dig included. Visas, insurance, and travel not included.

Applic.: Informal explanation of interest and experience to project director.

Baldan Baraivan

Cultural Restoration Tourism Project (CRTP)
410 Paloma Avenue, Pacifica, California 94044 USA
Tel.: ++1 (508) 347 7390
Fax: ++1 (508) 347 7471
E-mail: alexandra@crtp.net
www.crtp.net

Desc.: Baldan Baraivan is a Buddhist monastery situated in the Siberian-Mongol steppes. It was once a thriving centre of religious education and culture (one of the most important in Mongolia) but was destroyed by government forces in the 1930s. Only the ruins of the main building, the "Yellow Temple", survive. The project aims to restore the site and surrounding areas. Participants may also share in the rituals being observed by the monks currently studying at the site.

Per.: Late 17th century to the 1930s.

Country: Mongolia.

Loc.: 300km east of the capital city of Ulaan Bataar in Khentii Province.

Travel: Specific details provided upon application approval.

Dur.: 1 week minimum; May to September.

Age: Minimum 18.

Qualif.: No experience necessary but must be willing to live and work in camping conditions.

Work: Excavation and documentation Monday to Saturday; participants only work half days on Saturday.

Lang.: English.

Accom.: Participants live in traditional Mongolian gers (round felt and wood tents) or personal tents. All meals are included and prepared by a Mongolian cook with the help of volunteers.

Cost: US$1,120 (tax-deductible in full) per week. Airfare not included. Early registrants receive discounted fees.

Applic.: On-line form or contact the organisation directly.

Notes: Contact Alex Cleworth for further information. Academic credit available with approval from home university. Additional tuition fees apply.

Bamburgh Research Project

Bamburgh Castle, Bamburgh
Northumberland NE UK
Tel.: ++44 (1904) 330 727
E-mail: paulgething@bamburghresearchproject.co.uk
www.bamburghresearchproject.co.uk

Desc.: The project is centred on the Bamburgh Castle and is dedicated to using the most modern field techniques, implemented by experienced field archaeologists, to provide training for students and volunteers alike. There are many sites being excavated including an early medieval cemetery, deep strat, multi-period within the castle, and a medieval port; there is also a comprehensive survey programme and a fully functioning media department dedicated to filming the archaeological process.

Per.: Multi-period; early Medieval to modern.

Country: United Kingdom.

Loc.: Bamburgh Castle, 50 miles (80km) north of Newcastle on the northeast coast.

Travel: Nearest reailway station is Berwick on Tweed, 15 miles (24km) from Bamburgh on the main East coastline. Regular bus service from Berwick to Bamburgh. Pick-up available at Berwick with prior notice. Youth or wheelchaired volunteers may be picked up in Newcastle with prior arrangement.

Dur.: July to September.

Age: All ages.

Qualif.: No experience necessary.

Work: Excavation, training, field walking, and test pitting.

Lang.: English.

Accom.: Fully equipped campsite. Volunteer must bring own tent and personal items.

Cost: GB£95 (approx. US$145) per week. Tuition, travel to and from the site daily, food, and camp space included.

Applic.: Limited placements available.

Banstead

North Downs Plateau Archaeology Research Group
(Surrey Archaeology Society)
Green Curve, Banstead Surrey SM7 1NS UK
Tel.: ++44 (1737) 356 039
E-mail: stellahill@nutwood66.fsnet.co.uk

Desc.: Banstead is a research excavation on a downland hilltop site, dominated by a Neolithic or Bronze Age settlement containing very large quantities of flint tools. Several palaeoliths and a Mesolithic pit containing axe production waste are also present. Bronze Age and Iron Age artifacts have been discovered. The site appears to have later been occupied by a late Roman farmstead, before being influenced by the nearby Medieval manor house and church. Further work will concentrate on the later prehistoric aspects of the site, together with investigations of the Medieval church.

Per: Multi-period; Neolithic, Bronze Age, Iron Age, Roman, Medieval.

Country: United Kingdom.

Loc.: Great Meadow, Banstead, Surrey.

Travel: Request instructions.

Dur.: Sundays, all year.

Age: Minimum 18.

Qualif.: No experience necessary.

Work: Research, excavation, and training.

Lang.: English.

Accom.: None. Volunteers arrive on site only on Sundays.

Cost: GB£10 (approx. US$ 15) per year.

Applic.: Contact the organisation.

Belize Valley Archaeology Reconnaissance Project

Belize

E-mail: archaeology@bvar.com

www.bvar.org

Desc.: The Caracol and Baking Pot projects involve students in all aspects of the investigations, from the excavation of prehistoric Maya architecture to the illustration of the artefacts recovered from the site. The project is directed by Dr. Jaime Awe who also directs investigations in several cave sites in the area, and his preliminary exploration of Actun Tunichil Muknal was featured in a 1993 National Geographic Explorer documentary film titled "Journey through the Underworld".

Per.: Classic and Post-Classic Maya.

Country: Belize.

Loc.: San Ignacio in the Cayo District of Western Belize, about 72 miles (116km) west of Belize City.

Travel: Pick-up at Belize International airport.

Dur.: 2–4 weeks; June to August.

Age: Minimum 18.

Qualif.: Good health for high physical, emotional, and mental demands.

Work: Extensive training in archaeological field techniques: survey, reconnaissance, excavation, analysis, and GPS.

Lang.: English; Spanish useful.

Accom.: Camps are basic, without electricity or running water.

Cost: US$1,750 for 1-month Field School; US$950 for 2-week Field Research. Camp facilities, weekday meals, and transportation to and from the site included. Travel to and from Belize and incidental expenses not included.

Applic.: On-line form.

Notes: Academic credit available through Sonoma State University; see www.sonoma.edu/people/poe/bvar/.

See also:

Western Belize Regional Cave Project

Ben Lawers Archaeological Field School

The National Trust for ScotlandWemyss House, 28 Charlotte
Square, Edinburgh Scotland EH2 4ET UK
Tel.: ++44 (131) 243 9470
Fax: ++44 (131) 243 9301
E-mail: conservationvolunteers@nts.org.uk – jwills@nts.org.uk
www.thistlecamps.org.uk/benlaw.htm

Desc.: The National Trust for Scotland owns around 12,000 acres of
the southern slopes of Ben Lawers above Loch Tay in
Perthshire. The remains of prehistoric and medieval
archaeological sites attest the area displays extensive
evidence for past human activity. The most numerous traces
of settlement belong to the last 400 years and form one of the
best preserved and well documented landscapes of its type
in Scotland. The Field School is investigating the Medieval
and later rural settlements and associated structures.

Per.: Medieval and later.

Country: United Kingdom.

Loc.: Southern slopes of Ben Lawers above Loch Tay in Perthshire.

Travel: Pick-up and drop-off in Edinburgh. The nearest train station
is in Crianlarich.

Dur.: 1–2 weeks; July to September.

Age: Minimum 18.

Qualif.: No experience necessary. Professional archaeologists
supervise and provide instruction in excavation techniques.

Work: Excavation.

Lang.: English.

Accom.: Meggernie Scout Centre in Glen Lyon. The Centre is a large
converted farmhouse with kitchen, dining/activity hall, showers,
and drying room.

Cost: GB£90 (approx. US$ 145) per week (GB£75 for students,
unwaged or retired people).

Applic.: Inquire for details.

Notes: Bring raingear and warm clothing.

See also:

Thistle Camps

Billown Neolithic Landscape Project

School of Conservation Sciences
Talbot Campus, Fern Barrow, Poole Dorset BH12 5BB UK
Tel.: ++44 (1202) 595 415
Fax: ++44 (1202) 595 478
E-mail: billown@bournemouth.ac.uk – consci@bournemouth.ac.uk
http://csweb.bournemouth.ac.uk/consci/text/arky_field_billown.htm

Desc.: This project involves the excavation of Neolithic features associated with a long mound, pit-circle, ceremonial site and middle to late Bronze Age structures forming part of a small settlement. Geophysical, topographic, and environmental surveys are carried out in the surrounding countryside.

Per.: Neolithic.

Country: United Kingdom.

Loc.: Castletown, Isle of Man.

Travel: Daily flights with Manx Airlines (Isle of Man, tel. ++44 (8457) 256256, www.manx-airlines.com) from many airports throughout the UK and Ireland. Rail direct to Douglas and car and passenger ferries (Isle of Man Steam Packet Company, tel. ++44 (8705) 523523, www.steam-packet.com). Travel Services of Douglas, tel.++44(345) 581407, www.isleofmantravel.com.

Dur.: 1 week for volunteers, 4 weeks for students; June to July.

Age: Minimum 18.

Qualif.: No experience necessary.

Work: Excavation and survey. Sunday to Friday; 8:45–17:30.

Lang.: English.

Accom.: Volunteers must make their own arrangements. Hotels and guesthouses are available in and around Castletown and nearby Port Erin, Peel, and Douglas but will necessitate personal transport. Further information with Manx Tourist Office, tel.++44 (1624) 686801, www.isle-of-man.com.

Cost: GB £80 (US$120) for generic volunteers per week. GB£575 for 4 weeks for students for validated course (including tutition, fees, examinations). Lunch and local transport are included.

Applic.: Deadline May 31 with full payment. Request forms via e-mail.

Notes: Academic credit available with approval from home institution.

Black Mountain

Northwest College, Anthropology Department
231 West 6th Street
Powell, Wyoming 82435 USA
Tel.: ++1 (307) 754 6131
E-mail: traveler@wsunix.wsu.edu
www.nwc.cc.wy.us/area/anthropology/2310wy.html

Desc.: Geoarchaeological and palaeo-environmental research in the Middle Rocky Mountains is emphasised as well as survey and documentation of historic and prehistoric sites in the Shoshone National Forest. The project is specifically trying to understand environmental change and hunter-gatherer response over the last 5,000 years. Additional field research is possible at the Platt site, a late Prehistoric Shoshone and Crow campsite.

Per.: Palaeo-Indian through late Prehistoric.

Country: United States.

Loc.: Near Cody, Wyoming, east of Yellowstone National Park.

Travel: Details provided upon application.

Dur.: 10 days to 6 weeks; June to July.

Age: Minimum 16.

Qualif.: No experience necessary for field school students or volunteers; the supervisory field laboratory position requires archaeological field school and laboratory experience.

Work: Excavation, research, and cultural resource management.

Lang.: English.

Accom.: Camping in variable conditions. Bring personal camping gear. Volunteers and students are responsible for themselves on the 4-day breaks between sessions.

Cost: US$278 per session. Food, lodging, and transportation during the 10-day session included. Airfare not included.

Applic.: Contact Judson Finely.

Notes: Academic credit available through Northwest College and the University of Wyoming.

Butser Ancient Farm

Nexus House, Gravel Hill, Waterlooville Hampshire PO8 0QE UK
Tel.: ++44 (7980) 563 872 or (23) 9259 8838
Fax: ++44 (23) 9259 8838
www.butser.org.uk

Desc.: This is a replica farm of what would have existed in the British Iron Age. Founded in 1972, it moved to its present site at Bascomb Copse in 1992. The farm has buildings, structures, animals, and crops of the kind that existed at that time. The museum functions as an open-air laboratory where research into the Iron Age and Roman periods goes on using the methods and materials that were available at that time and by applying modern science to ancient problems.

Per.: British Iron Age to Roman; 300 BC to 400 AD.

Country: United Kingdom.

Loc.: Petersfield.

Travel: Details provided upon application.

Dur.: 2–3 days minimum; May to October.

Age: Minimum 18.

Qualif.: No experience necessary.

Work: Assist in construction of a Roman Villa with mosaic floors. Training provided. Practical workshops include gathering herbs for simple medicinal recipes, and metalworking.

Lang.: English.

Accom.: No room or board provided.

Cost: No fees charged to volunteer. Practical workshops cost GB£30 (approx. US$45) per day.

Applic.: Telephone the Project Director Rick Wilgoss.

Cahuachi Consolidation – Proyecto Nasca

Centro Italiano Studi e Ricerche Archeologiche Precolombiane
Via delle Grazie 6,   25122 Brescia   Italy
Tel.: ++39 (030) 377 3738 or 377 3486
Fax: ++39 (030) 377 3739
E-mail: animasalva@tin.it
www.geocities.com/proyectonasca/

Desc.: The Italian Centre for Study and Research of Pre-Columbian Archaeology is a non-profit cultural association dedicated to the study and research on pre-Columbian American sites. The project takes the first steps in the consolidation of the Cahuachi site. Excavations within a 25km square site have been undertaken over the past 20 years. The phase of restoration is now being undertaken at the Nasca's ceremonial centre of Cahuachi.

Per.: Pre-Columbian; 4000 BC to 900 AD.

Country: Peru.

Loc.: Nasca, Peru.

Travel: Details provided upon application.

Dur.: 1 month minimum; December and January.

Age: Minimum 18.

Qualif.: Basic experience required.

Work: Excavation in 5x5 m sectors called "quadricole", drawings, photographs materials storage, cataloguing and preparation. The first 10 days are 7:00–13:00; 14:30–16:30. The subsequent days are 6:30–13:30 for fieldwork and 15:00–17:30 for laboratory.

Lang.: English, Spanish, Italian.

Accom.: Tent camping at a campsite in the desert. Volunteers must provide their own tents.

Cost: US$790. (US$40 must be paid by June 15, the remainder upon arrival.) Airfare not included.

Applic.: On-line form. Deadline November 25.

Notes: Academic credit available with approval from home university. Additional tuition fees apply.

Canterbury Archaeological Trust Ltd.

Whitefriars Office
c/o 92a Broad Street, Canterbury, Kent CT1 2LU UK
Tel.: ++44 (1227) 76 53 64 or 46 20 62
Fax: ++44 (1227) 78 47 24
E-mail: cat.whitefriars@virgin.net – admin@canterburytrust.co.uk
www.canterburytrust.co.uk

Desc.: Canterbury Archaeological Trust (CAT) was established in 1976. Between 2000 and 2004 CAT is engaged in a series of major excavations at the 'Whitefriars' in the heart of the historic city of Canterbury. Archaeologists expect to find multi-period evidence and in particular more of the Whitefriars friary, from which the area takes its name. Canterbury is well known for its cathedral but the city has many other historic buildings still standing for the visitor to explore.

Per.: Late Iron Age, Roman, Anglo-Saxon, Norman, Medieval and post-Medieval to modern.

Country: United Kingdom.

Loc.: Canterbury, Kent, southeast England.

Travel: Train, bus connections from the port of Dover, 14 miles (23km) away, and London, 56 miles (90km) away. Canterbury has 2 rail stations: East and West. The site is 5 minutes walk away from Canterbury East rail station and directly opposite the bus station. Canterbury West rail station is 15 minutes walk.

Dur.: The project is running from July 2003 to January 2004.

Age: Minimum 16.

Qualif.: No experience is necessary. Basic training provided.

Work: Excavation and site recording depending upon volunteer ability. Washing finds as appropriate.

Lang.: English.

Accom.: Either youth hostel in town or campsite 3 miles out of town.

Cost: No project fee. Room and board not included.

Applic.: Write or e-mail Whitefriars site directors, Alison Hicks and Mark Houliston, to enquire for when volunteers will be taken.

Notes: Bring weather-appropriate clothing, steel-toed boots, and personal trowel (or buy a trowel at the project).

Carnuntum

Archaeologisches Museum Carnuntum
Hauptstrafle 1, A-2404 Petronell-Carnuntum   Austria
Tel.: ++43 (2163) 28 82 15
Fax: ++43 (2163) 28 84
E-mail: franz.humer@noel.gv.at
www.carnuntum.co.at

Desc.:   Carnuntum is the largest archaeological site in Austria. After centuries of demolition the former capital of the Roman province, Pannonia Superior, is now being systematically excavated. The objective is to rescue, study, and present this site in a sensitively restored manner using modern monument preservation techniques while at the same time making sensible economic use of this resource. The excavations of a part of the civilian town in Petronell are combined with reconstruction, scientific publications, and inclusion of the visitors to the archaeological fieldwork.

Per.:   Roman, 1–5th centuries AD.

Country: Austria.

Loc.:   Villages of Petronell-Carnuntum and Bad Deutsch-Altenburg, Province of Lower Austria, 25 miles (40km) east of Vienna.

Travel: Train or bus.

Dur.:   6 weeks

Age: Minimum 18.

Qualif.:   Satisfactory academic grade and interest in archaeology and history.

Work: Excavation, documentation, mapping, etc.

Lang.:   German, English.

Accom.: None provided. Various accommodation available in the villages.

Cost: No direct project fee. Food, lodging, and insurance not included.

Applic.:   By ordinary mail, fax, or e-mail.

Notes: Bring work clothes and gloves.

Castell Henllys Training Excavation

Department of Archaeology, University of York
The King's Manor, York YO1 7EP, UK
Tel.: ++44 (1904) 43 39 01
Fax: ++44 (1904) 43 39 02
E-mail: ppe101@york.ac.uk
www.york.ac.uk/depts/arch/staff/sites/henllys/castell_henllys.htm

Desc.: This project is investigating the site of an Iron Age inland promontory fort and adjacent Romano-British farmstead that has some evidence for post-Roman activity. Much of the fort has been examined, but work continues on the main defences, which have uncovered unexpected evidence for ritual activity and iron working. Further investigations will be undertaken on the defences and on the farmstead lying just outside the main fort.

Per.: Iron Age and Roman.

Country: United Kingdom.

Loc.: The valley of the Gwaun, a tributary of the River Nevern that enters the sea at Newport, 5 miles (8km) from the site.

Travel: Details provided upon application.

Dur.: 2 weeks; July to August.

Age: Minimum 16.

Qualif.: No experience necessary.

Work: Excavation.

Lang.: English.

Accom.: Tent camping with toilets and showers. Tents available to rent if required. Students help with campsite duties on a rotation basis.

Cost: GB£155 (approx. US$ 230) per week for first 2 weeks; GB£110 per each subsequent week. Tuition, campsite, and food included.

Applic.: Contact Dr. Harold Mytum, Director.

Cathedral Camps

16 Glebe Avenue, Flitwick, Bedfordshire MK45 1HS UK
Tel.: ++44 (1525) 716 237
E-mail: admin@cathedralcamps.org.uk
www. cathedralcamps.org.uk

Desc.: Maintenance, conservation, and restoration of cathedrals and their surroundings all over the country.

Per.: Various.

Country: United Kingdom.

Loc.: Various locations in the UK.

Travel: Details provided upon application.

Dur.: 1 week; July to September.

Age: Minimum 16; most volunteers are aged 17–25.

Qualif.: No experience necessary.

Work: Maintenance and restoration of cathedrals and gardens. Workday is 8:30–17:30, 4–5 days per week.

Lang.: English.

Accom.: Camping.

Cost: A contribution of approx. GB£60 (approx. US$90) to cover camp costs, board, and lodging.

Applic.: For further details and an application form contact Shelley Bent at the above address.

CCIVS – Coordinating Committee for International Volunteers

1 rue Miollis, 75015 Paris France
Tel.: ++33 (1) 45 68 49 36
Fax: ++33 (1) 42 73 05 21
E-mail: ccivs@unesco.org
www.unesco.org/ccivs/

Desc.: This international non-governmental organisation plays a coordinating role in the sphere of voluntary service. Historical monuments and archaeological sites have been maintained, restored and preserved by volunteers. The actions and projects concerning cultural heritage preservation involve non-qualified persons and young people, from any background. These activities, led by professionals, also aim at initiating, training, and developing restoration techniques. CCIVS organises, in co-operation with the cultural division of UNESCO, numerous work camps for the preservation of cultural heritage.

Per.: Modern/contemporary.
Country: Over 100 countries.
Loc.: Various.
Travel: Details provided with specific project.
Dur.: Typically 3–4 weeks but longer terms are available; year round.
Age: Inquire for programs for volunteers under 18.
Qualif.: No experience necessary for workcamps.
Work: Projects may involve landscaping, reconstruction and restoration of buildings, etc., in a workcamp situation.
Lang.: Local language of the member organisation.
Accom.: Ranges from tent camping to hostels to hotels.
Cost: Varies with each member organisation.
Applic.: Contact member organisation directly. See website for links.
Notes: CCIVS produces several publications on volunteer service. Contact them for the list of publications and ordering.
See also:
UNESCO

Center For The Study of Eurasian Nomads

577 San Clemente Street
Ventura, California 93001 USA
Tel/Fax: ++1 (805) 653 2607 or (510) 549 3708
E-mail: jkimball@csen.org
www.csen.org

Desc.: The Center was established to preserve archaeological remains and to promote ethnographic research on the nomadic (and sedentary) cultures who lived or are currently living in the vast steppe lands that stretch from southern Russia through Kazakhstan, southern Siberia, western Mongolia, and northern China. Although the contemporary nomads are limited to specific regions, the steppes as a whole are extremely rich in archaeological remains dating from 4000 BC and earlier.

Per.: Various.
Country: Throughout Eurasia.
Loc.: Varies with project.
Travel: Details provided with each project.
Dur.: 2 weeks to 2 months; June to August.
Age: Minimum 18.
Qualif.: No experience necessary.
Work: Excavation and survey.
Lang.: English.
Accom.: Camping.
Cost: Dependent upon project.
Applic.: On-line form.
See also:
Baga Gazaryn Chuluu Survey
Golden Hills Khazar Excavations

Chantiers Jeunesse

4545, Avenue Pierre-De Coubertin, PO Box 1000
Branch M, Montreal, Québec H1V 3R2 Canada
Tel.: ++1 (514) 252 3015 or toll free in NA 1 (800) 361 2055
Fax: ++1 (514) 251 8719
E-mail: cj@cj.qc.ca
www.cj.qc.ca

Desc.: The goals of Chantiers Jeunesse (Mouvement Québecois des Chantiers Jeunesse) are to support and strengthen the development of the autonomy of young people. Workcamps encourage community involvement, initiate social involvement, and encourage intercultural communication and understanding between people from different countries and cultures. Most exchanges are between Quebecois and European volunteers.

Per.: Various.

Country: Throughout Europe and North America.

Loc.: Various.

Travel: Details provided with specific workcamp.

Dur.: 3–6 weeks.

Age: 16–25.

Qualif:: No experience necessary.

Work: Construction, reconstruction, and community development.

Lang.: French, English.

Accom.: Typically camping or hostel.

Costs: CAD$10 application fee, CAD$60 participation fee. Extra fees for Mexico (CAD$270), former Soviet Union (Lithuania, Estonia, Belarus, Ukraine, Russia) countries (CAD$125), and Turkey (CAD$80). Food, accommodation, transportation from home to workcamp site, recreational activities, and a minibus for local trips included. Personal expenses, transportation, medical insurance, passport, and visa cost not included.

Applic.: International volunteers must contact a workcamp organisation in their country of residence. See www.alliance-network.org. Deadline end of February (summer projects) or June (fall).

Notes: Canadian citizens or permanent residents with permanent residence in Quebec.

Chinese Young Volunteers Association

All China Youth Federation
NO.10,Qianmen Dongdajie,Beijing,100051,China
Tel.: ++86 (10) 67 01 81 32 or 85 21 20 99
Fax: ++86 (10) 67 01 81 31 or 67 03 18 37
E-mail: acyf@public2.bta.net.cn – cyva@163.net
www.acyf.org – www.zyz.org.cn

Desc.: This a national organisation engages volunteers in work for the public good and the social security. It is a member organisation of the All-China Youth Federation and the Coordinating Committee for International Voluntary Service (CCIVS) of the UN. Its main purposes are to eliminate poverty, to protect the environment, to provide medical services, to disseminate science and technology, to promote social development, to set up inter-relationships of reciprocal help, affection, and social ethics. In 1998 this project commenced with the Chinese government to renovatethe Dai Temple.

Per.: The Qin (221-226 BC), Han (206 BC-220 AD), Tang (618-907), and Song (960-1279) dynasties.

Country: China.

Loc.: The town of Tai'an; the main access to the holy Taishan Mountains.

Travel: Details provided upon application.

Dur.: 3–4 weeks.

Age: Minimum 18.

Qualif.: No experience necessary.

Work: Reconstruction, renovation.

Lang.: Chinese; possibly English.

Accom.: Rustic house, 4 per room. The food is local fare.

Cost: Inquire for details.

Applic.: Apply through the Coordinating Committee for International Volunteers (see listing).

Notes: This project is not offered annually. Contact CYVA for other opportunities.

See also:

CCIVS – Coordinating Committee for International Volunteers

Circumpolar Ethnographic Field School
University of Northern British Columbia (UNBC) Anthropology Program
3333 University Way, Prince George
British Columbia V2N 4Z9 Canada
Tel.: ++1 (250) 960 5643 Fax: ++1 (250) 960 5545
E-mail: michel@unbc.ca
http://anthro.unbc.ca

Desc.: This ethnographic study will allow students to spend time in Russia learning how to do anthropological research in a field setting. Most of the time will be spent in the capital of the Komi Republic (the city of Syktyvkar) with more than a month in on the tundra with Izhma reindeer herders. The UNBC field school is in partnership with the Syktyvkar State University.

Per.: Contemporary.

Country: Russia.

Loc.: Komi Republic in the city of Syktyvkar and a northern Komi village in the Izhma region.

Travel: Details provided upon application.

Dur.: 3 months; May to August.

Age: Minimum 18.

Qualif.: Oriented to anthropology students but those from other disciplines may apply.

Work: Training in Russian-language and ethnographic field methods. Individual research projects undertaken for credit.

Lang.: English (accreditation through TOEFL or equivalent).

Accom.: Basic lodging.

Cost: Approximately CAD$6,000 for Canadian citizens and permanent residents. Tuition, living costs, airfare, and spending money included. The cost of a Russian visa and travel medical insurance is not included. The estimated cost for foreign students is US$5,500.

Applic.: Deadline February 28. See the website for details.

Notes: Academic credit available through UNBC. For more information contact Michel Bouchard, anthropology instructor and field school coordinator.

Club du Vieux Manoir

Ancienne Abbaye du Moncel
60700 Pontpoint, France
Tel.: ++33 (3) 44 72 33 98
Fax: ++33 (3) 44 70 13 14
E-mail: secretariat@clubduvieuxmanoir.asso.fr
http://cvmclubduvieuxmanoir.free.fr

Desc.: The objectives of the organisation are to develop cultural and leisure activities in order to protect, restore, promote, and revitalise the architectural heritage and its relationship with the current cultural and social life. Its goals are to protect and renovate historical monuments and threatened sites; open the restored monuments to the public; create and manage museums in order to make the local cultural heritage accessible; and publish historical, archaeological, and cultural tourism studies. Works are mostly on castles, villas, and forts.

Per: Middle Ages to modern.

Country: France

Loc.: The regions of Hautes Alpes, Aisne, Oise, and Indre.

Travel: Exact information is given on the website for each project.

Dur.: Usually 15 days for summer activities; for permanent sites or activities not during the summer the duration can be arranged.

Age: Minimum 14–18, depending on the project.

Qualif.: No experience necessary. Motivation to protect cultural heritage.

Work: Masonry and general restoration work, archaeological excavations, cleaning and maintaining vegetation, mapping, public education, tourist promotion, and cultural interpretation.

Lang.: French.

Accom.: Tent camping.

Cost: EUR28 (approx.US$30/GB£18) for membership fee and food.

Applic.: On-line form to be filled out in French and sent in with a photo and the payment of the membership and boarding fees.

Notes: The organisation has activities year round, such as guided weekend visits to monuments or painting courses, etc.

Colonial Landscape of St. Christopher

Department of Archaeology, University of Bristol
43 Woodland Road, Clifton, Bristol BS8 1UU UK
Tel.: ++44 (117) 954 6060 Fax: ++44 (117) 954 6001
E-mail: Dan.Hicks@bris.ac.uk
www.bris.ac.uk/Depts/Archaeology/fieldschools/fieldschool/
stkitts/stkitts.htm

Desc.: The project looks at the complex sequence activities surrounding the manufacture of sugar, dating back to the 1690s. The remains of a well-preserved large 17th century enclosure is being examined further through landscape survey and open-area excavations. The field school introduces the principles and practice of historical archaeology and provides a unique introduction to that of the Caribbean.

Per.: Prehistoric to 20th century.

Country: St. Kitts.

Loc.: Eastern Caribbean.

Travel: Meet at St. Kitts Basseterre airport for pick-up.

Dur.: 3 weeks; July.

Age: Minimum 18.

Qualif.: University students.

Work: Excavation, survey, and lectures.

Lang.: English.

Accom.: Basic lodging.

Cost: GB£1,240 (approx.US$ 1,850). Food, accommodation, tuition, and transport included. Airfare not included.

Applic.: Deadline March 31. On-line form to print and fax or post with a 1-page CV, and a statement of interest to Dan Hicks, Project Director. E-mail ahead to announce intention to apply. Print out 2 copies of the recommendation forms and pass to 2 referees for them to complete and fax or post.

Notes: Academic credit available through the University of Bristol with approval with home institution.

See also:

Historical Archaeology in Bermuda

Combined Caesarea Expeditions

Department of History, University of Maryland, College Park
College Park, Maryland 20742-7315 USA
Tel.: ++1 (301) 405 4353
Fax: ++1 (301) 314 9399
E-mail: Caesarea@umail.umd.edu
www.digcaesarea.org

Desc.: This amphibious research project combines excavation of the terrestrial remains of the ancient city of Caesarea Maritima with underwater investigation of the site's ancient harbour. Excavations have uncovered the ancient city's streets, private dwellings, aqueducts, baths, circus, stadium, theatre, religious shrines, and the artificial harbour, formed of giant breakwaters extending far out into the sea.

Per.: Roman; 22–10 BC.

Country: Israel.

Loc.: Caesarea.

Travel: Transportation to and from the airport is not available unless part of a group. Meeting point to be determined.

Dur.: 4–8 weeks; May to July.

Age: Minimum 18 unless accompanied by a parent of senior relative.

Qualif.: No experience necessary for ground digs. Volunteers must be at least secondary school graduates and be in good health. SCUBA certified for harbour excavations and must bring their certification cards to Israel.

Work: Excavation, recording, processing and field analysis of finds.

Lang.: English.

Accom.: Beit Gil kibbutz accommodates 2 people per room with air-conditioning and private bath. Sunday to Thursday only.

Cost: US$250–425 per week depending upon season and whether scuba is included. Room and board Sunday to Thursday included. Weekend and personal excursion costs not included.

Applic.: On-line forms (specific form for divers). Money order or certified cheque only, made out to the "UM Foundation/Caesarea Fund".

Notes: This project is not available in 2003 but will resume in 2004.

Compagnons Batisseurs

National Secretariat
2 rue Molière, 37000 France
Tel/Fax: ++33 (2) 47 61 32 10
E-mail: compabat@club-internet.fr
www.compagnons-batisseurs.org

Desc.: This non profit organisation was born 50 years ago aimed at helping a population hard hit by the damage of World War II. It has been putting solidarity into practice by means of workcamps in reconstruction and restoration as well as promoting peace and better understanding between people from all corners of the globe.

Per.: Various.

Country: France.

Loc.: Mainly in the regions of Bretagne, Centre, Midi Pyrénées, and Provence Alpes Côtes d'Azur, and abroad throughout Europe.

Travel: Details provided upon application to specific project.

Dur.: Each stage is 2–6 days; summer.

Age: Minimum 18.

Qualif.: No experience necessary.

Work: Workcamps in masonry, brickwork, painting, carpentry, or other skills applied to restoration and recontruction.

Lang.: French or language of host country.

Accom.: Typically group camping.

Cost: EUR180–600 (approx.US$200-650), depending upon duration.

Applic.: On-line form.

Concordia

Heversham House
20-22 Boundary Road, Hove BN3 4ET UK
Tel.: ++44 (1273) 42 22 18
Fax: ++44 (1273) 42 11 82
E-mail: info@concordia-iye.org.uk
www.concordia-iye.org.uk

Desc.: Most Concordia workcamps are environmental or renovation projects. Through Concordia there are also opportunities for long-term voluntary service through the European Voluntary Service and other programmes.

Per.: Various.

Country: Over 60 countries worldwide.

Loc.: Most of the time, camps are in small isolated villages and there is not necessarily a car available on the camp.

Travel: Specific details provided for each workcamp.

Dur.: 3 weeks.

Age: Minimum 20.

Qualif.: No particular skills required.

Work: Workcamps in building restoration and conservation. work time is about 6 hours a day

Lang.: French, English, German.

Accom.: Self-catered basic accommodation. A common room for sleeping and eating. Sleeping may be on the floor or in tents (varies with each workcamp). Bring a sleeping bag and mat.

Cost: EUR115–300 (approx.US$125–320) plus EUR16 for membership, depending on the project. Food and accommodation included. Travel and personal expenses not included.

Applic.: Consult website for appropriate contact.

Notes: Volunteers must join the Supporters' Network. Concordia also has offices in France and Germany (consult website). Bring seasonal clothing, working clothes, shoes, gloves, etc.

See also:
Alliance of European Voluntary Service Organisations
UNESCO

Cornell Halai and East Lokris Project

Department of Classics, 120 Goldwin Smith Hall
Cornell University, Ithaca, New York 14853 USA
Tel.: ++1 (607) 255 3354 or 255 8328
Fax: ++1 (607) 254 8899
E-mail: jec13@cornell.edu
http://halai.fac.cornell.edu/chelp/home.htm

Desc.: The ancient acropolis of Halai, in the present seaside town of Theologos, Greece, was located near major land and sea routes in antiquity, and its well preserved remains are easily accessible today.

Per.: Neolithic, Archaic, Hellenistic, Bronze Age, Classical, Late Roman or Byzantine.

Country: Greece.

Loc.: Halai is located in the seaside town of Theologos, about 60 miles (100km) north of Athens, in Lokris (a district of the larger province of Phthiotis).

Travel: About 2 hours by car from Athens. Buses to Malesina will go to Theologos.

Dur.: 6 weeks; June to July.

Age: Minimum 18.

Qualif.: Volunteers to work with architecture (particularly with experience with Autocad) and small finds.

Work: Surface survey, excavation, mapping, and recording surface features.

Lang.: English.

Accom.: Participants live either in Theologos, Tragana or Vivos.

Cost: Volunteers normally provide for their own travel and receive room and board while participating.

Applic.: Contact the project by mail or e-mail with a brief description of previous experience.

Notes: As a preliminary to the study season, there will probably be 2 workcamps at the site arranged through Volunteers for Peace (www.vfp.org.)

Cotravaux

11 Rue de Clichy, 75009 Paris France
Tel.: ++33 (1) 48 74 79 20
Fax: ++33 (1) 48 74 14 01

Desc.: Cotravaux coordinates French workcamps. Its role is to promote voluntary work and community projects concerning environmental protection, monument restoration, and social projects. The organisation offers many workcamps in different regions of France. Many of the organisations members of Cotravaux work with foreign partners.

Per.: Various.

Country: France.

Loc.: Various.

Travel: Enquire with the organisation of choice.

Dur.: 2–3 weeks; year round but mostly June to October.

Age: Minimum 18.

Qualif.: No experience necessary.

Work: Excavation or reconstruction. Enquire with the organisation of choice.

Lang.: English, French.

Accom.: Typically tent camps.

Cost: Volunteers must pay for their own transportation to the camps. Room and board included (some camps require a daily contribution).

Applic.: Contact Cotravaux by fax or mail to obtain the list of partner workcamps in France or other specific countries.

Notes: A list of Cotravaux member organisations can be obtained through the website of Jeunesse et R0construction (www.volontariat.org).

See also:

Jeunesse et Réconstruction

Crow Canyon Archaeological Center

23390 CR K, Cortez, Colorado 81321 USA
Tel.: ++1 (970) 565-8975 or toll free in NA 1 (800) 422 8975
Fax: ++1 (970) 565-4859
E-mail: Marketing@crowcanyon.org
www.crowcanyon.org

Desc.: This organisation offers individuals the opportunity to become involved in archaeology through a wide variety of programs for adults, youths, and school groups. The Crow Canyon Archaeological Center is dedicated to involving the public in the study of archaeology and Native American cultures. Volunteers may participate in long-term research on the ancestral Pueblo Indians by working alongside professional archaeologists in excavation and laboratory work.

Per.: Basketmaker through Pueblo periods in the Southwest.

Country: United States.

Loc.: Cortez, Colorado.

Travel: Details provided upon application.

Dur.: 1 week; July to August.

Age: Minimum 18, except family excavation and week-long programmes for middle school and high school students provide a good introduction to the archaeology of the Southwest. An intensive 3-week summer field school is available for older teens.

Qualif.: No experience necessary.

Work: Excavation, artefact analysis, and lab programmes.

Lang.: English.

Accom.: Room and board provided on campus

Cost: US$700–900 per week. Room and board included. Airfare not included.

Applic.: On-line form.

Notes: Academic credit available through the Colorado State University. Additional tuition fees apply. The organisation also organises international archaeological vacations.

CVE – Caribbean Volunteer Expeditions

Box 388, Corning, New York 14830 USA
Tel.: ++1 (607) 962 7846
E-mail: ahershcve@aol.com
www.cvexp.org

Desc.: Caribbean Volunteer Expedition members measure and document historical plantations, windmills, and other structures to help local Caribbean agencies keep a record of their architectural heritage. Projects examples are the Historic Restoration in San Salvadore, Bahamas and the Salvage Archeology Project in San Salvadore, Bahamas.

Per.: Various.

Country: Throughout the Caribbean.

Loc.: Various.

Travel: Details provided upon application.

Dur.: Typically 1 week.

Age: Minimum 18.

Qualif.: No experience necessary. Volunteers may perform architectural surveys and drawings, mapping, and plan development, stabilize ancient ruins, restore historical buildings, and create visitor centers, help to develop and prepare exhibits and interpretive material, work on the conservation and cataloguing of collections and artifacts, prepare exhibit areas and improve public access.

Work: Most days are in the field for about half of the day.

Lang.: English.

Accom.: Local hotels, houses, or campgrounds.

Cost: Varies with each expedition. Volunteers pay for airfare, food and housing, plus a small administrative fee to CVE.

Applic.: Phone or e-mail the organisation.

CVG – Conservation Volunteers Greece

Omirou 15, GR – 14562 Kifissia
Athens Greece
Tel.: ++30 (1) 623 1120
Fax: ++30 (1) 801 1489
E-mail: cvgpeep@otenet.gr
www.cvgpeep.gr

Desc.: Summer work camps in Greece. These projects usually take place in remote areas of Greece in co-operation with Forestry Departments, Local Authorities, Cultural Associations, etc. Intercultural exchanges and conservation work allow young people to contribute to a hosting community.

Per.: Various.

Country: Greece.

Loc.: Depending upon project; usually remote areas.

Travel: Details provided with specific projects.

Dur.: 2–3 weeks; fixed dates are provided for every project; summer.

Age: Minimum 18.

Qualif.: No experience necessary.

Work: Cultural heritage projects involve restoration of traditional buildings, ancient cobbled-stone footpaths, and help in archaeological digs. Work is 5–6 hours/day, 6 days/week.

Lang.: English.

Accom.: Facilities are modest. Hosting is usually in schools and community or youth centres. Volunteers should bring along a sleeping bag and sleeping mat. Household chores involved.

Cost: Approximately EUR120 (approx. GB£80/US$130).

Applic.: On-line Volunteer Exchange Form. This is also provided by Alliance of European Voluntary Service partner organisations (see listing).

CVS-BG – Cooperation for Voluntary Service Bulgaria

Plachkovitca str. Nr. 12 fl.2,
1407 Sofia Bulgaria
Tel./Fax: ++359 (2) 62 81 47
E-mail: cvs-bg@bluelink.net
www.bluelink.net/cvs-bg/

Desc.: This cooperation is between 3 organisations, ECO-CLUB 2000, Green Balkans Sofia, and Pro International Bulgaria, who have agreed to work together organizing international volunteer projects. Workcamps are available in archaeology, architectural renovation and reconstruction of cultural and historical monuments

Per.: Various.

Country: Bulgaria.

Loc.: Various.

Travel: Volunteers are responsible to arrive at the workcamp location independently. A month before beginning of the camp, volunteers are sent an Infosheet with project details.

Dur.: 2–4 weeks.

Age: Minimum 18.

Qualif.: No experience necessary.

Work: Usually 6 hours per day.

Lang.: English.

Accom.: Basic housing with hot water and separate rooms. Usually volunteers prepare the food.

Cost: Vary with each camp, costs are moderate and cover room and board.

Applic.: On-line form plus membership fee. Visa assistance will be provided if necessary. Apply at lease 2 months in advance.

Cypress Hills Archaeological Project

Department of Archaeology
University of Calgary, Calgary, Alberta T2N 1N4 Canada
Tel.: ++1 (403) 220 7629 or 580 0205
Fax: ++1 (403) 282 9567 or 893 3987
E-mail: gaoetela@ucalgary.ca
www.scape.brandonu.ca

Desc.: This project is designed to give adult members of the public an opportunity to participate in the excavation of a deeply stratified archaeological site.

Per.: Prehistoric; 7,250 years ago.

Country: Canada.

Loc.: The excavations take place at the Stampede site, located in Elkwater, Alberta, a small community in Cypress Hills Interprovincial Park in the southeast corner of the province. Closest city is Medicine Hat.

Travel: Arrive at Calgary International airport. Travel may be by bus or car (request instructions from the project).

Dur.: Minimum 2 days; May to August.

Age: Minimum 16.

Qualif.: No experience necessary.

Work: Excavation. Daily from 9:00–16:30, but participants do not work for no more than 5 consecutive days.

Lang.: English; some French and possibly German.

Accom.: No accommodation. Numerous campsites are available in the park. To reserve contact the visitor centre at ++1 (403) 893 2248 or GR Management Ltd at ++1 (403) 893 3782.

Cost: Free. Camping fees range from CAD$11–24 per night although special rates may be available for those who plan longer stays.

Applic.: Phone, mail, or e-mail to request an application package with all the relevant information. State any restrictions or requirements. Volunteers are asked to fill in a waiver form prepared by personnel at Cypress Hills Interprovincial Park.

Notes: From May 1 through August 31 the mailing address for the project is Cypress Hills Archaeological Project, PO Box 12, Elkwater, Alberta, Canada T0J 1C0.

Czech American Archaeological Field School in Premyslovice Neolithic Village

College of DuPage
Well Blvd, Glen Ellyn, Illinois 60187-6599 USA
Tel.: ++1 (630) 942 2022
E-mail: staeck@cdnet.cod.edu – www.cod.edu/people/faculty/
staeck/czech_american_archaeological_field_school.htm

Desc.: This project studies the origins of the Czech people, culture, and state. Students participate in ongoing archaeological excavations exploring the Hana Valley, complete with hill forts, most with Neolithic components, as well as sites with Bronze Age, Celtic, Medieval, and Early Modern components. The site also lies near a main, large, walled site (Rmiz) and just slightly further form 3 known burial complexes

Per.: 4000 BC to the post-Soviet Block era.

Country: Czech Republic.

Loc.: Project base in Premyslovice, eastern Czech Republic (Moravia), 3 hours east of Prague.

Travel: Group purchase of tickets from O'Hare to Prague arranged.

Dur.: 1 month; June to July.

Age: Minimum 18.

Qualif.: No experience necessary.

Work: Excavation.

Lang.: English.

Accom.: Premyslovice town's chateau. Hostel-style accommodations with hot water. Meals in local restaurant.

Cost: US$2195 plus administrative fee of US$420. Group travel within the Czech Republic plus 3 meals per day Monday to Friday Included. Airfare and optional tuition and weekend excursions not included.

Applic.: On-line form and US$100 deposit. Application deadline February 1, formal deadline March 1, and thereafter if space permits. Copy of formal identification and remaining payment due by June 1.

Notes: Contact Dr. John P. Staeck, Director, Czech-American Archaeological Field School. Further details on website.

Duensberg Project

Pro International
Bahnhofstrasse 26A, 35037 Marburg Germany
Tel.: ++49 (6421) 65277
Fax: ++49 (6421) 64407
E-mail: pro-international@lahn.net
www.campinformation.info

Desc.: The Duensberg is a hill with a celtic ring fort, located on the northern periphery of the settlement area of celtic culture. This project involves working in areas of archaeological importance to help excavate and preserve the site. Excavations are at different places on the site including settlement remains and a wooden water-basin of Celtic period.

Per.: 1st century BC and Roman.

Country: Germany.

Loc.: About 50 miles (80 km) north of Frankfurt am Main, near Giessen.

Travel: Giessen train station; Frankfurt/Main or Frankfurt-Hahn airports.

Dur.: 2 weeks; July.

Age: 16–30.

Qualif.: No experience necessary.

Work: Excavation and field survey.

Lang.: English.

Accom.: Tent camping in the forest at the excavation site. Bring a sleeping bag and mat. Toilets washing facilities are available. Volunteers prepare meals and clean.

Cost: No project fee. Includes accommodation and food. Volunteers pay travel-costs, personal expenses, partial costs for leisure trips, excursions, and other activities of the group.

Applic.: Partner organisation is LYVS – League of Youth Voluntary Service: 40 Karl Marx Street, Minsk 220030, Belarus. Tel. ++37 (517) 263 3544; fax: 263 7554. E-mail: lyws@user.unibel.by. – www.alliance-network.org/f_members/ lyvs.htm

See also:
Pro International

Early Man in India

Earthwatch International
3 Clock Tower Place, Suite 100
Box 75, Maynard, Massachusetts 01754 USA
Tel.: ++1 (978) 461 0081 or toll free in NA 1 (800) 776 0188
Fax: ++1 (978) 461 2332
E-mail: info@earthwatch.org – www.earthwatch.org

Desc.: India's rich Stone Age past that is being investigated through ongoing excavations at Attirampakkam, of the richest Palaeolithic sites in southeast Asia. Discovery of stone tools and other artifacts prove the inhabitation of hundreds of thousands of years of human habitation. The finds here could place India within the context of migratory routes taken by early man out of Africa.

Per.: Palaeolithic.

Country: India.

Loc.: Attirampakham, Tamil Nadu, South India.

Travel: Specific meeting point provided upon application.

Dur.: 2 weeks; January to March.

Age: Inquire with project for minimum age restrictions.

Qualif.: No experience necessary.

Work: Excavation, and recording and archiving artefacts.

Lang.: English. Local languages are useful.

Accom.: Double rooms in houses with Indian-style toilets, irregular electricity, and cold water.

Cost: US$1,495 (approximately GB£995). Room and board included.

Applic.: On-line form to e-mail, fax, or post. Select project and dates of preference. Reserve placement by submitting completed form with deposit of US$250. Full payment required 90 days in advance of project start date.

See also:
Earthwatch Institute

Earthwatch Institute

3 Clock Tower Place, Suite 100
Box 75, Maynard, MA 01754 USA
Tel.: ++1 (978) 461 0081 or toll free in NA 1 (800) 776 0188
Fax: ++1 (978) 461 2332
E-mail: info@earthwatch.org
www.earthwatch.org

Desc.:	Earthwatch Institute is the world's oldest, largest, and most respected organisation directly involving the public in scientific field research. Members of the public are sent into the field to work side-by-side with leading scientists. These teams of volunteers will collect data and work as expedition members.
Per.:	Various.
Country:	Over 45 countries throughout North, Central, and South America, Asia, Europe Africa, Asia, Australia and Antarctica.
Loc.:	Various.
Travel:	Set meeting points are established for each project. Usually at the nearest international airport.
Dur.:	3 days to 3 weeks; year round.
Age:	Minimum 18; minimum 16 with some projects.
Qualif.:	No experience necessary.
Work:	Various aspects of field and laboratory work.
Lang.:	English or local language.
Accom.:	Anything from tent camping to hotels. Facilities range from complete with hot water to cold water and pit toilets.
Cost:	US$80–2,695. Room and board included.
Applic.:	On-line form to e-mail, fax, or post. Select project and dates of preference. Reserve placement by submitting completed form with deposit of US$250. Full payment required 90 days in advance of project start date.

See also:
Ancient Nomads of Mongolia
Early Man in India
Easter Island Cultures

Easter Island Cultures

Earthwatch International
3 Clock Tower Place, Suite 100
Box 75, Maynard, Massachusetts 01754 USA
Tel.: ++1 (978) 461 0081 or toll free in NA 1 (800) 776 0188
Fax: ++1 (978) 461 2332
E-mail: info@earthwatch.org – www.earthwatch.org

Desc.: How and why the Easter Islanders exhausted their resources is still in debate. Early studies of Easter Isand concentrated almost entirely on the smashed stone heads 'moai' and the largest ceremonial sites. In the past couple of decades scholars have been investigating the remains of the ancient society and trying to understand the social evolutions that brought this culture to its demise.

Per.: Prehistory through to the Ice Age; 1400–1800 AD.

Country: Chile.

Loc.: The town of Hanga Roa on Easter Island.

Travel: Specific meeting point provided upon application.

Dur.: 2 weeks; October to December.

Age: Minimum 18.

Qualif.: No experience necessary.

Work: Survey of house sites, test pits and excavation in gardens, laboratory processing.

Lang.: English.

Accom.: Double rooms in houses with full bath facilities.

Cost:: US$2,495 (approximately GB£1,760). Room and board included.

Applic.: On-line form to e-mail, fax, or post. Select project and dates of preference. Reserve placement by submitting completed form with deposit of US$250. Full payment required 90 days in advance of project start date.

See also:
Earthwatch Institute

Eco-Archaeological Park Pontecagnano Faiano

Legambiente
Via Salaria 403, 00199 Rome Italy
Tel.: ++39 (06) 8626 8324/5/6
Fax: ++39 (06) 8626 8319
E-mail: legambiente.vol@tiscali.it
www.legambiente.com/canale8/campi

Desc.: The Eco-Archaeological Park covers 22 hectares extending from the city of Pontecagnano to the surrounding hills. Particularly in the summer there are entertainment activities, music and theatre shows, and exhibitions with young artists and local organisations. In the Park you can find a vilanovian settlement dated back to the Iron Age, an Etruscan city, and the Roman colony of Picentia. The centre of the city is object of excavations made by the University of Naples.

Per.: Iron Age and later.

Country: Italy.

Loc.: Pontecagnano, near Salerno, South of Naples, Italy.

Travel: By bus or train from Naples and Salerno.

Dur.: 2 weeks.

Age: Minimum 18.

Qualif.: No experience necessary.

Work: Maintenance and cleaning of the Park, reclamation of some areas, aesthetic improvements with wall paintings.

Lang.: Italian.

Accom.: In a structure in the park.

Cost: EUR166 (approx.GB£110/US$180) plus membership fee.

Applic.: Contact the organisation.

See also:

Legambiente

Elderhostel

11 Avenue de Lafayette
Boston, MA 02111-1746
Tel.: ++1 (978) 323 4141 or toll free in NA 1 (877) 426 8056
Fax: ++1 (617) 426 0701 or toll free in NA 1 (877) 426 2166
E-mail: Registration@elderhostel.org
www.elderhostel.org

Desc.: Elderhostel is a not-for-profit organisation dedicated to providing extraordinary learning adventures for people 55 and over. Elderhostel offers projects in collaboration with academic institutions to provide educational travel opportunities exploring the archaeology and anthropology of various cultures past and present.

Per.: Various.

Country: Worldwide.

Loc.: Various.

Travel: Details provided upon application. Projects in the US and Canada require participants to provide their own transportation to the programme site.

Dur.: 1 week; year round.

Age: Minimum 55.

Qualif.: No experience necessary but useful skills are welcomed.

Work: Accompanying field archaeologists and/or tribal members on daily expeditions to locate and record sites or artefacts or rock art via sketching, measuring, photographing, mapping. etc.

Lang.: English.

Accom.: Hotels, motels, or conference centre facilities.

Cost: About US$100 per day in the US and Canada. Registration, accommodations, meals, lectures, field trips, and other extracurricular or social activities included. Most international programmes include roundtrip airfare from the US.

Applic.: On-line form, regular mail, using the registration form in the Elderhostel catalog, or by telephone.

Notes: Hearing impaired individuals can call toll free in NA 1 (877) 426 2167.

El Pilar Archaeological Reserve for Maya Flora and Fauna

BRASS El Pilar Program
420 Settlers Valley Drive, Pflugerville, Texas 78660 USA
Fax: ++1 (805) 893 2790 (University of California)
E-mail: ford@alishaw.ucsb.edu – CWernecke@compuserve.com
www.arts.cornell.edu/arkeo/Fieldwork/ElPilar.html
www.lsweb.sscf.ucsb.edu/projects/pilarweb/

Desc.: Advanced projects in a number of areas including archaeology, ecology, plant and wildlife biology, history, agriculture, and community development.

Per.: 450 BC to 1000 AD.

Country: Belize.

Loc.: Cayo District, north of San Ignacio, on the western border.

Travel: Details provided upon application.

Dur.: 2 weeks, April to June.

Age: Minimum 18.

Qualif.: Volunteers and students in good physical shape may apply. Experience is preferred, but not required.

Work: Ceramics, drafting, computer work, photography, or fieldwork may be involved.

Lang.: English.

Accom.: Modern accommodations with bathroom and showers.

Cost: US$2,500. Included lodging, meals (Monday to Saturday), and local commute. Travel to Belize and Sunday meals not included.

Applic.: On-line form. Deadline end of February.

Notes: Coordinated with ISBER/MesoAmerican Research Center at the University of California, Santa Barbara, California 93106 USA. Dr. Anabel Ford, Director, Dr. Clark Wernecke, Associate Director.

Excavations at Capernaum

Jerusalem Center for Biblical Studies
85 Country Oak Drive, Humboldt, Tennessee 38343 USA
Tel.: ++1 (731) 824 2577
Fax: ++1 (731) 824 2611
E-mail: cpagejcbs@aol.com
www.jcbs.org – www.jerusalem-center.org

Desc.: Mentioned frequently in all 4 gospels, Capernaum was pivotal in the ministry of Jesus (he had personal relationships with at least 4 families there) and became a principal local in the development of Jewish Christianity, starting from the 1st century. Situated on the northwestern shore of the Sea of Galilee, Capernaum has been excavated most recently (1978–82) and foundations of large villas and a significant ceramic and coin record were uncovered. The long-term goal is to reach the foundations of the remains from the Roman/Herodian period, in hopes of learning more about the possible relationship between Jesus and the aristocracy of Capernaum.

Per.: Herodian-Byzantine, Roman-Ummayad.

Country: Israel.

Loc.: Capernaum, 7 miles (11km) north of Tiberias on the Sea of Galilee).

Travel: Details provided upon application. E-mail travel queries to: aknowles@travelwithus.com.

Dur.: 2–3 weeks; October.

Age: Minimum 18.

Qualif.: No experience necessary.

Work: Excavation.

Lang.: English.

Accom.: Royal Plaza Hotel in Hammat Tiberas; very close to Sea of Galilee; double occupancy.

Cost: US$2,299 (2 weeks); US$2,799 (24 days). Airfare from the US included.

Applic.: Deadline July 31. Contact Charles R. Page.

See also:
Excavations at Kursi-Gergesa

Excavations at Kursi-Gergesa

Jerusalem Center for Biblical Studies
85 Country Oak Drive, Humboldt, Tennessee 38343 USA
Tel.: ++1 (731) 824 2577 Fax: ++1 (731) 824 2611
E-mail: cpagejcbs@aol.com
www.jcbs.org
www.jerusalem-center.org

Desc.: Kursi was apparently an important pilgrimage site for early Christians; the gospels of Matthew and Mark indicate that the ministry of Jesus was introduced into the Gentile world from there. A Byzantine bath complex complete with drain pipes, underground heating system and pools, plus artefacts that date to the Byzantine and early Islamic periods have been recently discovered. Previous excavations have also revealed a 5th-century chapel paved with 3 layers of mosaics. Further excavation coninues to the north and east, in search of remains of additional rooms or perhaps what may have been an adjoining inn for pilgrims.

Per.: Late Roman-Early Islamic, Byzantine, Ummayad.

Country: Israel.

Loc.: Kursi on the eastern shore of the Sea of Galilee.

Travel: Details provided upon application. E-mail travel queries to: aknowles@travelwithus.com.

Dur.: 2–3 weeks; April to May or August to September.

Age: Minimum 18.

Qualif.: No experience necessary.

Work: Excavation.

Lang.: English.

Accom.: Royal Plaza Hotel in Hammat Tiberas; very close to Sea of Galilee; double occupancy.

Cost: US$2,299 (2 weeks); US$2,799 (24 days). Airfare from the US included.

Applic.: Deadline February 17 for spring session; June 30 for summer session. Contact Charles R. Page.

See also:
Excavations at Capernaum

Falerii – Via Amerina

Gruppi Archeologici d'Italia
Via degli Scipioni 30/A, 00192 Rome, Italy
Tel./Fax: ++39 (06) 39 73 44 49
E-mail: gainaz@tin.it – gaiedit@tin.it – gaistampa@tiscalinet.it
www.gruppiarcheologici.org

Desc.: The Roman street called Via Amerina and the tombs in the necropolis of the nearby city of Falerii Novi comprise this monumental site, which is among the most important giving historical evidence of the Agro Falisco.

Per.: Roman; 3rd century BC to 3rd century AD.

Country: Italy.

Loc.: Between Civita Castellana and Nepi, in the Province of Viterbo, about 40 miles (60km) north of Rome.

Travel: Details provided upon application. Participants must arrive Monday at 18:00 and leave Sunday at 10:00.

Dur.: 1–2 weeks.

Age: Minimum 18.

Qualif.: No experience necessary.

Work: Excavation, survey, and documentation for a larger project encompassing the whole layout of Via Amerina, in order to create an environmental-archaeological park in the area.

Lang.: Italian, English.

Accom.: In Casale Montemeso. Rooms with bunks and shared bathrooms.

Cost: EUR215 (approx.US$230) per week; EUR335 (approx. US$350) per 2-week-session.

Applic.: Participants must be members of the Gruppi Archeologici d'Italia. Membership fee of EUR 32 (approx.US$35, includes insurance and subscription to the magazine *Archeologia*) can be paid at a local office or at the National office at the above address.

Notes: Bring work boots, gloves, and clothes, a water bottle, hat, and sleeping bag.

See also:
Gruppi Archeologici d'Italia

Farnese – Rofalco

Gruppi Archeologici d'Italia
Via degli Scipioni 30/A, 00192 Rome, Italy
Tel./Fax: ++39 (06) 39 73 44 49
E-mail: gainaz@tin.it – gaiedit@tin.it – gaistampa@tiscalinet.it
www.gruppiarcheologici.org

Desc.: The Etruscan settlement of Rofalco is on a spit of tuff (a mineral deposit) dominating the valley of the Olpeta. It was protected by the rugged nature of the area and by powerful walls with lookout towers. The programme of the Archaeological Campaign of research is part of a project that aims to excavate the numerous monumental evidences of that area.

Per.: Etruscan; 4th to 3rd centuries BC.

Country: Italy.

Loc.: Selva del Lamone (forest of Lamone), near Farnese in the Province of Viterbo, about 40 miles (60km) north of Rome.

Travel: Details provided upon application. The sites are easily reachable by bus or train from Rome. Participants must arrive Monday at 18:00 and leave Sunday at 10:00.

Dur.: 1–2 weeks; August.

Age: Minimum 18.

Qualif.: No experience necessary

Work: Excavation, documentation, survey, etc.

Lang.: Italian, English.

Accom.: At the primary school of Farnese. Rooms with bunks and shared bathrooms.

Cost: EUR198 (approx.US$215) per week; EUR 302 for 2-weeks.

Applic.: Participants must be members of the Gruppi Archeologici d'Italia. Membership fee of EUR32 (includes insurance and subscription to the magazine *Archeologia*) can be paid at a local office or at the National office at the above address.

Notes: Bring work boots, gloves, and clothes, a water bottle, hat, and sleeping bag.

See also:
Gruppi Archeologici d'Italia

Field School in East-Central Europe

The University College of the Cariboo
Kamloops, BC V2C 5N3 Canada
E-mail: europe@cariboo.bc.ca
www.cariboo.bc.ca/europe/field_course.htm

Desc.: This excursion offers the opportunity to make contact with the Roma (Gypsy peoples). Destinations include Presov, a largely rural society still relatively untouched by Western values. The focus here will be on the sizable population of Gypsies who live dispersed in dozens of poverty-stricken rural settlements. As well, in the Ukrainian Transcarpathia region, Uzhgorod is attractive but isolated small city and a multi-ethnic melting pot of Ukrainians, Roma, Hungarians, Russians, Slovaks, and Rusyns.

Per.: Modern.

Country: Czech Republic, Slovakia, Ukraine.

Loc.: Prague, Presov, Svinia, and Vilshinki (a cosmopolitan metropolis, a small city, an isolated mountain village, and an ethnic ghetto).

Travel: Local transportation rather than chartered buses.

Dur.: 4 weeks; May.

Age: Minimum 18.

Qualif.: No experience necessary. Non-students accepted space permiting.

Work: Independent field research.

Lang.: English.

Accom.: Basic hotels and student residences with 2–4 beds per room or billeting in private homes.

Cost: Inquire for current season. Costs include tuition, airfare, course-related travel in Europe, shared accommodation, and meals in Vilshinki. Visa fees, course material, insurance, and remaining meals not included.

Applic.: Submit official course application. Detailed information will be provided. Contact Dr. David Scheffel. See also the Svinia Project at www.roma.sk.

Notes: Academic credit available.

FIYE – International Youth Exchange Foundation

Nowy Swiat 18 / 20 lp.116
00-373 Warszawa Poland
Tel.: ++48 (602) 64 31 27
Fax: ++48 (22) 812 0348
E-mail: fiye@fiye.org
www.fiye.org

Desc.: These camps involve working in areas of archaeological importance to help excavate and preserve sites; intercultural exchanges between participating countries, focusing on similarities and differences in lifestyle, cultural events, and icons; or the organisation of and involvement in specific cultural events including historic, religious, and artistic festivals.

Per.: Various.

Country: Worldwide.

Loc.: Various.

Travel: Details upon application.

Dur.: 2 weeks up to 12 months.

Age: 18–25.

Qualif.: No experience necessary.

Work: Includes cultural work, environment preservation, activities with children, construction and renovation, education and intercultural exchanges.

Lang.: English or language of host country.

Accom.: Basic accommodation but varies with project.

Cost: Inquire with host organisation.

Applic.: Select a project through the website and contact the host organisation.

Footsteps of Man

Archaeological Cooperative Society "Footsteps of Man"
Piazzale Donatori di Sangue 1, 25040 Cerveno BS Italy
Tel.: ++39 (0364) 433 983
Fax: ++39 (0364) 434 351
E-mail: orme@rupestre.net – fossati@numerica.it
www.rupestre.net/orme/

Desc.: This centre of research and study of rock art and member of the International Federation of Rock Art Organizations, undertakes annual archaeology fieldwork in Paspardo, Valcamonica. The project involves research on the site, with excursions to find as yet undiscovered engraved rocks; analysis of damage to the rock surfaces and conservation problems; drawing the engravings with plastic sheets; and catalogue the engravings. Studies will be put on the Internet.

Per.: Neolithic.

Country: Italy.

Loc.: Paspardo and Valcamonica, (Brescia province) Northern Italy. The site is Paspardo and other areas in Valcamonica.

Travel: Meeting point at the bus stop of Ceto-Cerveno in Valcamonica. Meeting time to be confirmed prior to arrival. Bus from the Garibaldi metro station in Milan or train from the National Railway station in Brescia to the station of Ceto-Cerveno.

Dur.: Minimum 7 days; July to August.

Age: Minimum 16.

Qualif.: Archaeologists, scholars, students, and enthusiasts welcome.

Work: Excursion, analysis, drawing, cataloguing.

Lang.: English and Italian; French and Spanish also spoken.

Accom.: Houses in Paspardo with dormitories, showers, and kitchen.

Cost: EUR45 (US$48)/day (EUR315 for 7-day minimum stay), paid upon arrival. Accommodation, food, and transport to the work site included. Reading materials provided at an additional cost.

Applic.: On-line form. Send deposit of EUR50 (for 1 week) or EUR100 (for 2 weeks) through bank transfer (request bank information).

Notes: Bring work clothes and gloves, gym shoes, sleeping bag, and personal insurance. Anti-tetanus vaccination recommended.

Giurdignano Project – Megalithic Garden of Europe

Legambiente
Via Salaria 403, 00199 Rome Italy
Tel.: ++39 (06) 8626 8324/5/6
Fax: ++39 (06) 8626 8319
E-mail: legambiente.vol@tiscali.it
www.legambiente.com/canale8/campi

Desc.: At the Southern tip of Apulia, the heel of Italy, Giurdignano has one of the largest amounts Italian of dolmen and menhir. It is a sort of rupestrian museum, full of cult places as the Saint Salvatore Abbey, built in the rock, the Basilica delle Centoporte Abbey and ancient olive oil presses.

Per.: Medieval; 10th century.

Country: Italy.

Loc.: Giurdignano near Lecce, southeastern Italy.

Travel: Train to Lecce then Guardignano.

Dur.: 2 weeks.

Age: Minimum 18.

Qualif.: No experience necessary.

Work: Cleaning the necropolis near the Centoporte Abbey and restoring the dry walls. The activities are co-ordinated by the University of Lecce.

Lang.: Italian.

Accom.: In a school.

Cost: EUR166 (approx US$175) plus membership fee.

Applic: Legambiente Head Office.

See also:
Legambiente

Golden Hills Khazar Excavations

Center for the Study of Eurasian Nomads (CSEN)
577 San Clemente Street
Ventura, California 93001 USA
Tel./Fax: ++1 (805) 653 2607 or (510) 549 3708
E-mail: jkimball@csen.org
www.csen.org

Desc.: The far east of Europe was once ruled by Jewish kings who presided over numerous tribes, including their own tribe: the Turkic Khazars. The Khazars were an advanced civilization with one of the most tolerant societies of the medieval period. It hosted merchants from all over Asia and Europe.

Per.: Medieval; 9th–10th century AD; 650–1016.

Country: Russia.

Loc.: The Khazar fortress is in the lower Don River region, about 70km east of Rostov-na-Don in the North Black Sea region.

Travel: Meeting point at Rostov-on-Don International airport.

Dur.: 2 weeks; June to July.

Age: Minimum 18.

Qualif.: Excavation experience helpful but not necessary.

Work: Excavations and excursions. Workday is 7:00–13:00, excursions and other activities in the afternoon.

Lang.: English. Russian is very useful.

Accom.: Tents in a well-organised field camp.

Cost: US$1,100. Airport pick-up, lodging, meals, lectures, excursions, museums, local commuting, camp doctor, and interpreters included. Travel and insurance not included.

Applic.: On-line form. US$250 deposit due with application April 15; US$850 due May 15. Deadlines are imperative for the Russian Visa application and processing. No invitations for visas will be issued until full contribution is received in the CSEN office.

Notes: Bring personal small tools, such a trowel, small scoops, and several small brushes, film, a camera, and writing materials for notes. Rain gear may be necessary.

See also:
Center for the Study of Eurasian Nomads

Gordon's Lodge Fieldschool

PO Box 18953, London W14 0YZ UK
Tel: ++44 (1908) 374 926
E-mail: countyarchaeologicalservices@btinternet.com
www.archaeological.training.btinternet.co.uk

Desc.: The medieval element comprises the remains of a substantial limestone building or buildings. The precise location of any Romano-British features have yet to be confirmed by excavation, but Roman pottery and a number of types of Roman roof tile have been recovered. Aerial photographs suggest the possible presence of Bronze Age enclosures, house platforms, burials, and possibly also Iron Age enclosures.

Per.: Prehistoric to late Medieval; 11th to 14th centuries.

Country: United Kingdom.

Loc.: Near Grafton Regis, between Milton Keynes and Northampton, about 60 miles (95km) northwest of London. It is situated on farmland on the Buckinghamshire/Northamptonshire border, close to the historic village of Grafton Regis.

Travel: The fieldschool is easily accessible from junction 15 of the M1 motorway and is about 7 miles (11km) from Milton Keynes railway station. Pick-up at the station may be arranged.

Dur.: 4 days; June to August.

Age: Minimum 18.

Qualif.: No experience necessary. Fieldwork experience welcome.

Work: Excavation, recording, and planning, section drawing, surveying and levelling, and post excavation analysis.

Lang.: English.

Accom.: Camping available on site; a list of local B&Bs can be provided.

Cost: GB£30 (approx.US$45) per day; GB£135 (US$200) per session or GB£200 (US$300) for 2 sessions. Tuition included. Food and accommodation not included. A limited number of places at a concessionary rate for those studying archaeology at degree level are available.

Applic.: Contact Pat Lawrence.

Gruppi Archeologici d'Italia

National Office
Via degli Scipioni 30/a
00192 Rome, Italy
Tel./Fax: ++39 (06) 39 73 44 49
E-mail: gainaz@tin.it – gaiedit@tin.it – gaistampa@tiscalinet.it
www.gruppiarcheologici.org

Desc: This Association was founded in 1965 and its aim is to contribute to the protection and the safeguard of the Italian cultural heritage, together with other institutions. It is a member of the National Volunteering Centre and promoter and founder of the "European Forum of Associations for Cultural Heritage" and of Koinè "Federation of the archaeological associations in the Mediterranean basin". The Association, that has around 100 offices, contributed to the realisation of many projects, thanks to the direct engagement of the members.

Per: Various.

Country: Italy.

Loc.: South-central Italy.

Travel: Details provided upon application.

Dur.: 2 weeks; summer.

Age: Minimum 15 for some camps; minimum 17 for others.

Qualif.: No experience necessary.

Work: Evaluation, cleaning, and excavation with archaeological documentation, land reconnaissance, and underwater observation. During the camp, volunteers will attend other activities, such as training, conferences, meetings, etc.

Lang.: Italian, English

Accom.: Local structures with bunks and shared bathrooms.

Cost: EUR350–400 (approx. US$ 380-430) per camp plus membership fee of EUR32 (approx.US$35, includes insurance and subscription to the magazine *Archeologia*).

Applic.: By telephone, fax, or e-mail.

Notes: Bring work boots and clothes, gloves, water-bottle, hat, and sleeping bag, as well as identification documents, membership card, health certificate, and anti-tetanus vaccination certificate.

GSM – Genclik Servisleri Merkezi
Youth Services Centre
Bayindir Sokak 45/9, Kizilay 06650 Ankara Turkey
Tel.: ++90 (312) 417 1124
Fax: ++90 (312) 425 8192
E-mail: gsm@gsm-youth.org
www.gsm-youth.org

Desc.: Workcamps are organized by GSM in cooperation with municipalities, universities, and local initiatives in various sectors including culture and renovation. GSM is a member of the Alliance of European Voluntary Service Organisations, UNESCO/CCIVS, YDC (Youth for Development and Cooperation), YEN (Youth Express Network), WAY (World Assembly of Youth), and the Mediterranean Youth Forum.

Per.: Various.

Country: Turkey.

Loc.: Various.

Travel: Volunteers must arrange their own transfer to and from the camp.

Dur.: 2 weeks.

Age: Minimum 18.

Qualif.: No experience necessary.

Work: Renovation 5–6 hours per day; 5–6 days per week.

Lang.: English.

Accom.: Student dorms, camp houses, pensions, hotels, or tents. Meals provided either in a restaurant, cafeteria, or at the camp by a cook or by self-catering.

Cost: Inquire regarding camp costs and membership fees.

Applic.: Contact organisation via e-mail.

Notes: The organisation has a limited amount of insurance against illnesses and accidents. Volunteers are recommended to have their own insurance in their own countries.

Hebrew University of Jerusalem
Institute of Archaeology
Mount Scopus Jerusalem 91905 Israel
Tel.: ++972 (2) 588 2403/4
Fax: ++972 (2) 582 5548
E-mail: velvart@h2.hum.huji.ac.il – info@h2.hum.huji.ac.il
www.hum.huji.ac.il/archaeology

Desc.: The Institute of Archaeology, established at the Hebrew University in 1926, is the oldest university department of archaeology in Israel. Research activity of the Institute is based on the archaeological excavations carried out at an average of 15 sites each year, many of them in cooperation with the Israel Antiquities Authority or with museums, universities, and research institutes in Israel and abroad.

Per.: Prehistory to Middle Ages.

Country: Israel.

Loc.: Various.

Travel: Details provided with each project.

Dur.: 1–6 weeks; June to September, depending upon project.

Age: Minimum 18.

Qualif.: No experience necessary.

Work: Survey, excavation, laboratory work, archiving, etc.

Lang.: English, Hebrew.

Accom.: Usually in a kibbutz, but may vary.

Cost: Approximately US$300 per week, but cost varies with each project.

Applic.: Each project is linked through the University website. Contact the project directly to apply.

See also:
Kfar Hahoresh
Ramat Hanadiv
Sha'ar Hagaolan
Tel Hazor

Heidelberg College Experiential Archaeological Program

Center for Historic and Military Archaeology
Heidelberg College, Tiffin, Ohio 44883 USA
Tel.: ++1 (419) 448 2327 or 448 2070 Fax: ++1 (419) 448-2236
E-mail: dbush@mail.heidelberg.edu – mpratt@mail.heidelberg.edu
www.heidelberg.edu/~dbush/
www.johnsonsisland.com

Desc.: This learning programme is available to all Northwest Ohio and Michigan area primary and secondary schools to be conducted at the Johnson's Island Civil War Military Prison Site. Students participate in an actual archaeological study and discover materials related to the daily activities of the prisoners and learn how scientists search for patterns in material culture to help explore human existence.

Per.: Modern.

Country: United States.

Loc.: Johnson's Island, located in Sandusky Bay, Lake Erie, approximately 3 miles (5km) from Sandusky.

Travel: Transportation is the responsibility of the sending school.

Dur.: 1 day; September to November and March to June.

Age: 5th- to 12th- grade students.

Qualif.: Teachers are given a manuscript that covers what their students should learn prior to the site excavation.

Work: Explore the plow zone ($2m^2$), collect field specimens, scrape the soil with trowels, and screen it, and identify and bag all recovered cultural material.

Lang.: English.

Accom.: 20–25 students on site during the excavation but students are not housed overnight. Portable toilets are on site.

Cost: US$325 per field day per group of students (20–25 students).

Applic.: Limited opportunities available.

Notes: Interested adults are accepted to volunteer in the spring and fall. There are 2 Teacher Workshops and Adult Digs (15 day experiences) in July. Contact Dr. David Bush, Site Director.

See also:
Heidelberg College Summer Undergraduate Field School

Heidelberg College Summer Undergraduate Field School

Center for Historic and Military Archaeology
Heidelberg College, Tiffin, Ohio 44883 USA
Tel.: ++1 (419) 448 2327 or 448 2070 Fax: ++1 (419) 448-2236
E-mail: dbush@mail.heidelberg.edu – mpratt@mail.heidelberg.edu
www.heidelberg.edu/~dbush/
www.johnsonsisland.com

Desc.: The historic Johnson's Island Civil War Prison site was chosen as the Union depot of captured Confederate officers in late 1861. The Federal Government leased the island for $500 a year and built a prison designed to hold 2,500 prisoners who left behind an extensive historical and archaeological record. Journals, letters, autographs, maps, and other documents give vast insight into what prison life was like, as well as the personal conflicts and hardships encountered among families and friends during the Civil War.

Per.: Modern.

Country: United States.

Loc.: Johnson's Island, located in Sandusky Bay, Lake Erie, approximately 3 miles (5km) from Sandusky.

Travel: Specific details provided with application.

Dur.: 5 weeks; early June to July.

Age: Minimum 18.

Qualif.: No experience necessary. The program is designed for undergraduate college students or adults interesting in gaining intensive field experience.

Work: Laboratory work preparing the recovered cultural materials (artefacts). Transcribing copies of historical documents.

Lang.: English.

Accom.: None.

Cost: US$2,220 plus a laboratory fee of US$75 (subject to change).

Applic.: Academic credit available with approval from home university.

Notes: Contact Drs David Bush and Michael Pratt.

See also:
Heidelberg College Experiential Archaeological Program

Helike Archaeological Excavations

The Helike Society
Poste Restante, 25003 Diakopton Achaia Greece
Tel.: ++30 (2) 6910 82348 or (2)10380 8850
(in the USA) ++1 (212) 769 5230
E-mail: eliki@otenet.gr – soter@amnh.org
www.geoprobe.org/helike/volunteers.html

Desc.:	Helike was the principal city in the region of Achaea. Numerous cores and trial trenches have been dug locating remains of the Roman town and traces of earlier occupations.
Per.:	Classical and Early Helladic.
Country:	Greece.
Loc.:	Helike; near the villages Rizomylos and Nikolaiika, about 4 miles (7km) southeast of Aigion, southwest shore of Gulf of Corinth.
Travel:	Details from Athens to Nikolaiika provided upon application.
Dur.:	2–4 weeks; July to August.
Age:	Minimum 18.
Qualif.:	No experience necessary. Instruction is provided but participants are advised to do prior reading on the region and the history of ancient Greece.
Work:	Excavation, survey, processing, recording, and geoarchaeology; Monday to Friday.
Lang.:	English.
Accom.:	Hotel Poseidon Beach (2 persons per room), in the village of Nikolaiika. Meals will be at the hotel or a nearby taverna.
Cost:	US$460 or EUR460 per week plus US$50 (EUR50) application fee. Room, meals, and some project expenses included. US$150 (EUR150) cancellation fee prior to May 15, no refund after.
Applic.:	On-line form to print and mail no later than May 15. Upon acceptance, the total costs must be submitted.
Notes:	A physician's note is required by May 15. Health and accident insurance is the responsibility of the volunteer. A tetanus shot is recommended. Academic credit available through Rutgers University-Newark. Additional tuition fees apply (tel.) ++1 (212) 769 5230 or (e-mail) soter@amnh.org.

Herstmonceux

International Study Centre at Herstmonceux Castle
Hailsham, East Sussex, BN27 1RN UK
Tel.: ++44 (1323) 834 444 or in NA ++1 (613) 533 2815 or toll
free (800) 733 0390
Fax: ++44 (1323) 834 499 or in NA ++1 (613) 533 6453
E-mail: castle@business.queensu.ca – www.queensu.ca/isc/

Desc.: The original castle was built in the 15th century but dismantled and rebuilt in the 20th century, when it was used by the Royal Greenwich Observatory. The estate is now owned by Queens University, Kingston, Ontario. The excavation is not funded but run totally by volunteers with help from the County Archaeologist and professional archaeologists who give their time when possible.

Per.: Post Medieval

Country: United Kingdom.

Loc.: Remote countryside of Herstmonceux, East Sussex; the nearest railway station is Polegate.

Travel: No transport provided. Details on how to arrive provided upon application.

Dur.: 1 week; July to August.

Age: Minimum 18.

Qualif.: No experience necessary.

Work: Research excavation on part of range of agricultural brick buildings

Lang.: English.

Accom.: Tent camping or B&B.

Cost: GB£25 (US$37) per week to dig. GB£15 (US$22) per week for tent. GB£14.50 per night at B&B.

Applic.: E-mail for further information.

Historical Archaeology in Bermuda

Department of Archaeology, University of Bristol
43 Woodland Road, Clifton, Bristol BS8 1UU UK
Tel.: ++44 (117) 954 6060
Fax: ++44 (117) 954 6001
E-mail: Dan.Hicks@bristol.ac.uk
www.bris.ac.uk/depts/archaeology/fieldschools/fieldschool/bermuda/

Desc.: Bermuda was among the first permanent English settlements in the New World. Admiral George Somers of the Virginia Company of London established the town of St. George in 1612 and Bermuda was at the time called Somers Islands. St. George remained the capital until 1815, after which time development in the town was relatively lacking. Excavations have been carried out at 3 sites to reveal well-preserved 17th- and 18th-century structural remains. The field school is run in parallel with the Bermuda National Trust Archaeology Camp.

Per.: Modern; 17th–18th centuries.

Country: Bermuda.

Loc.: In the town of St George

Travel: Participants are met at the Bermuda airport by project staff.

Dur.: 3 weeks; winter.

Age: Minimum 18.

Qualif.: No experience necessary.

Work: Full training in field survey and stratigraphic excavation.

Lang.: English.

Accom.: Basic lodging.

Cost: To be confirmed but will be inclusive of all administration, tuition, accommodation, food, and transport (except airfare).

Applic.: Deadline August 15. On-line form to print and fax or post with a 1-page CV, and a statement of interest to Dan Hicks, Project Director. E-mail ahead to announce intention to apply. Specific recommendation forms (2) are required by fax or post.

Notes: Academic credit available through the University of Bristol with approval with home institution.

See also:
Colonial Landscape of St. Christopher

Hofstadir

Center for Viking and Medieval Studies
PO Box 1016, Blindern N-0315 Oslo Norway
E-mail: fieldschool@mellomalder.uio.no
www.geo.ed.ac.uk/nabo/hofstadir2000.html

Desc.: The project at Hofstadir, an early Viking settlement, is in collaboration with the Institute of Archaeology (Fornleifastofnun íslands) and the North Atlantic Biocultural Organization (NABO). The project aims to promote Icelandic archaeology, encourage students to develop a research interest in the archaeology of the North Atlantic, and provide an insight into the technical and theoretical issues particular to the archaeology of Iceland and its North Atlantic context. The project involves training in the field, with an emphasis on techniques of excavation and analytical methods particular to Icelandic conditions, environmental archaeology, and the use of historical records in archaeological interpretation.

Per.: Viking and later medieval periods.

Country: Iceland.

Loc.: Myvatn, northeast Iceland.

Travel: Fly to Akureyri, northern Iceland.

Dur.: 4 weeks; July to August.

Age: Minimum 18.

Qualif.: Preference will be given to those who already have specialised or intend to specialise in North Atlantic archaeology. Both graduate and undergraduate participants are accepted but all should have had prior coursework in archaeology and some fieldwork experience.

Work: Excavation. Monday to Friday, 8:00–17:00 with coffee and lunch breaks. Hands-on experience in finds processing and data computerisation will be given in the evenings, lectures and seminars on Saturday mornings, and field trips on Sundays.

Lang.: English.

Accom.: Modern boarding school with dorm-style double rooms, hot showers, flush toilets, electricity (220V), and kitchen. Supplies found in nearby towns. Food is basic; strict vegetarians or severely lactose-intolerant students will not be easily accommodated.

Cost: Room and board provided free and there is currently no charge for academic instruction owing to fellowship support from funding agencies. Students pay their own airfare to Akureyri and for personal expenses.

Applic.: Deadline April 1. Send application with CV, references, and a statement of interest. An information package is sent to successful applicants by June 1. Europe applications must be directed to Dr. Christian Keller at the above address. North American applications must be directed to Dr. T.H. McGovern at the Northern Science and Education Center, Department of Anthropology (NORSEC), Hunter College CUNY, 695 Park Ave New York, New York 10021. E-mail: nabo@voicenet.com.

Notes: Academic credit available through the City University of New York with approval from home institution (contact NABO@voicenet.com for details). EU-citizens must bring EU health form E-111 stamped by their local social services. All participants must carry personal travel insurance.

Home and Hearth in the Bronze Age

UREP – University Research Expeditions Program
University of California
One Shields Avenue, Davis, California 95616 USA
Tel.: ++1 (530) 757 3529 Fax: ++1 (530) 757 3537
E-mail: urep@ucdavis.edu
www.urep.ucdavis.edu

Desc.: The Szazhalombatta Archaeological Expedition (SAX) is a multinational archaeological investigation into the household archaeology of the Hungarian Bronze Age, a time of technological innovation in the introduction of metal for tools and weapons, such as swords, and horses.

Per.: Bronze Age.

Country: Hungary.

Loc.: West central Hungary, near Szazhalombatta, about a 1-hour drive south of Budapest along the Danube (longer by bus).

Travel: Meeting point in Szazhalombatta to be arranged. The team travels to the site in rental cars.

Dur.: 2 weeks; August.

Age: Minimum 18.

Qualif.: Archaeology, botany, geology, entomology experience useful.

Work: Excavate, screen, photograph, prepare soil samples, artefacts, and flotation residue for the lab, and record tallies.

Lang.: English and Hungarian.

Accom.: Local hotel in shared rooms or suites with private showers and toilets. The site is furnished with tents for shade and storage, a water tank for hand washing, and portable toilets. Meals are at the hotel and local restaurants.

Cost: US$1,785. Room and board and transport to the site included. Personal expenses and travel not included.

Applic.: Apply directly to the University. Include US$200 deposit.

Notes: Expedition requirements will be moderately physical. Participants will be provided with excavation equipment.

See also:

UREP– University Research Expeditions Program

Horizon Cosmopolite

3011 Notre-Dame West
Montreal, Quebec H4C 1N9 Canada
Tel.: ++1 (514) 935 8436
Fax: ++1 (514) 935 4302
E-mail: cosmopolite@sprint.ca
www.horizoncosmopolite.com

Desc.: The workcamps of this organisation offer the chance for youth of different nationalities to unite to work on a common project. Often the projects are related to the conservation of historic buildings or to the environment.

Per.: Various.

Country: Throughout Europe; Asia, and North America.

Loc.: Various.

Travel: Details provided upon application.

Dur.: 2–3 weeks; summer or late fall (some camps are year round).

Age: 18–30.

Qualif.: No experience necessary.

Work: 5 days per week, typically 6–8 hours per day.

Lang.: English with local languages useful.

Accom.: In a tent, house, school, or community centre, depending on the camp. Volunteers take turns with chores and meals.

Cost: CAD$225 (approx. US$ 150) enrolment fees for 1 workcamp. Each additional workcamp is CAD$100. Participation fees usually cost between CAD$40–250 for 2–3 weeks and vary depending on the country, the length of stay, the type of project, and the general conditions of the workcamp. Room and board included. Insurance, transportation, and visas not included.

Applic.: Send a CV, a letter of interest, and registration fee. Enrolment is 3 months prior to departure; 2–3 weeks are needed to confirm applications. Following confirmation pre-departure logistics (vaccinations, visas, insurance, plane tickets, day of training, participant guide, etc.) will be advised.

Humayma Excavation Project

University of Victoria, Department of Greek and Roman Studies
Victoria, British Columbia V8W 3P4 Canada
Tel.: ++1 (250) 721 8519
Fax: ++1 (250) 721 8516
E-mail: jpoleson@uvic.ca
http://web.uvic.ca/~jpoleson/Humayma/Volunteerinfo.html

Desc.: Excavation at this Nabataean through Early Islamis site in Jordan has been an ongoing project for the past 12 years. The focus of the work is on the early 2nd-century Roman fort and its adjacent civilian settlement (vicus). The fort is well preserved and among the very few of this period known in the Middle East. It has already yielded impressive architectural remains and artefacts.

Per.: Roman; 2nd–4th century.

Country: Jordan.

Loc.: Jordan's southern desert, 50 miles (80km) north of Aqaba.

Travel: Details provided upon application.

Dur.: 6 weeks; June to July.

Age: Minimum 18.

Qualif.: Excavation experience preferred but not essential.

Work: Excavation.

Lang.: English.

Accom.: Teacher's dorms at a regional high school with electricity and running cold water. Team members share double rooms. Food is basic.

Cost: CAD$1,000 (approx. US$ 660). Room and board included. Airfare not included.

Applic.: Deadline December 15.

Notes: Contact Dr. John Peter Oleson. Academic credit available through the University of Victoria. Additional tuition fees apply.

Idalion Expedition

Lycoming College, AC Box 3
Williamsport, Pennsylvania 17701 USA
Tel.: ++1 (570) 321 4283
E-mail: johnson@lycoming.edu – susanritamorris@yahoo.com
www.lycoming.edu/arch/cyprusdig.htm

Desc.: The ancient city of Idalion, Cyprus, was a centre for the copper trade, the city also housed the ancient cult of the Great Mother and her consort, later known as Venus and Adonis. Excavations focus on the Sanctuary of Adonis and the domestic and industrial complex in the Lower City.

Per.: Late Bronze Age to Roman; 7th–12th centuries BC.

Country: Cyprus.

Loc.: Dhali, 1 hour and 20 minute drive from the beach and 20 minutes from the capital of Nicosia. Taxis and buses available.

Travel: Details provided upon application.

Dur.: 6 weeks for students; 2 weeks for volunteers; June to July.

Age: Minimum 18.

Qualif.: No experience necessary.

Work: Field work, lectures, on-site excavation, pottery processing, field note taking, and illustrating. Artefacts are processed at the dig house. Sunday to Thursday, 6:00–12:00 and 16:00–19:00. Students attend after-dinner lectures 1–2 times a week.

Lang.: English.

Accom.: Dhali village dig houses, walking distance from the site, or at an elementary school. Meals on working days provided.

Cost: US$400 per week or US$2,000 for full 6 weeks for volunteers. US$3,276 for students (for tuition plus project costs). Field trips, accommodation, and weekday meals included. Airfare and transportation not included. All costs are subject to change.

Applic.: Deadline for students April 15; for volunteers May 20.

Notes: Academic credit available through Lycoming College. Contact the Office of Admissions at spencerj@lycoming.edu.

Iklaina Archaeological Project

University of Missouri-St. Louis
8001 Natural Bridge Road, St. Louis, Missouri 63121-4499 USA
Tel.: ++1 (314) 516 6241
Fax: ++1 (314) 516 7235
E-mail: cosmopoulos@umsl.edu
www.iklaina.org

Desc.: This project studies the emergence of complex society and statehood in ancient Greece. Its purpose is to investigate the site of Iklaina, one of the district capitals of the ancient kingdom of Pylos, in southwest Peloponnese, Greece. The exploration includes intensive surface surveys and interdisciplinary studies, that may lead to a full scale excavation.

Per.: Mycenaean era and Greek Bronze Age; 1600–1100 BC.

Country: Greece.

Loc.: Pylos, in southwest Peloponnese.

Travel: Students must arrive at Pylos, Greece independently. Contact the project for further instruction.

Dur.: 3 weeks; May to June.

Age: Minimum 18.

Qualif.: The course is designed as an introductory course. No background knowledge necessary and no prerequisites.

Work: Survey and field experience in related disciplines, such as ceramics, lithics, geophysical, and faunal analyses, as well as topographic and museum studies.

Lang.: English.

Accom.: In a hotel in the coastal town of Pylos, in double rooms (single room supplement possible). Classes will be held in a classroom at the hotel.

Cost: US$1,390. Accommodation, most meals, site visits, all travel within Greece, and archaeological support included. Airfare, insurance, tuition (for credit or auditing), and personal expenses not included.

Applic.: A non-refundable deposit of US$200 is required by March 15. Applications (including deposits) will be accepted later if space permits. Balance of travel costs due by May 1.

INEX Slovakia – Association for International Youth Exchange and Tourism

Prazská 11, 814 13 Bratislava
Tel.: ++421 (2) 52 62 42 31
Fax: ++421 (2) 52 49 47 07
E-mail: inexsk@stonline.sk
www.inex.sk

Desc.: INEX Slovakia offers several workcamps in various sectors. One of their archaeological camps is Lukácovce where the volunteers are able to work with archaeologists, uncovering a site from the Great Moravian Age, from the 8th century AD. This archaeological research is being undertaken by the University of Trnava. The project has 2 elements: working on the aforementioned dig and adjacent to the dig site there is a restoration project of a manor house that was built in the 15th century by the Knights' Templars. After the reconstruction there will be a Centre for Helping Children, folk art, and ceramics at the manor.

Per.: Medieval; 8–15th centuries.

Country: Slovakia.

Loc.: The village Lukàcovce lies close to the city of Nitra.

Travel: Fly to Bratislava; connections are usually through Prague. From the Central Bus Station in Bratislava (Autobusova stanica Mlynske Nivy) take a bus to Nitra (a bus should leave approximately every 30 minutes). From Nitra take a bus to Lùkácovce.

Dur.: 3 weeks; July, but may vary.

Age: Minimum 18.

Qualif.: No experience necessary.

Work: Archaeological work varies year to year but may include survey, excavation, and archiving; work on the manor house involves reconstruction and maintenance.

Lang.: English.

Accom.: In a building, but volunteers must bring a mat, sleeping bag, and blanket. Showers with hot water are available.

Cost: The partner organisation (see application below) determines any costs that may apply. INEX will not charge any additional fees.

Applic.: Interested volunteers must apply through the partner organisations that are in the Alliance of Voluntary Organisations or SCI.

Notes: Volunteers must provide their own insurance. Bring a sleeping bag, mat, flash lamp, raincoat (weather in the summer changes quickly), cutlery, working clothes, and working shoes. Besides international workcamps taking place mainly in summer months, INEX also organises trainings for present and future camp leaders, summer camps for children and for students, study visits, and other youth activities. INEX Slovakia is a member of the Alliance of European Voluntary Service Organizations (see listing), an official partner of Service Civil International (see listing) and successfully co-operates with organisations associated in Youth Action for Peace (see listing). All activities of INEX Slovakia are supported by the Ministry of Education of the Slovak Republic.

Ironbridge Gorge Museum Trust

The Wharfage, Ironbridge
Telford, Shropshire TF8 7AW UK
Tel.: ++44 (1952) 58 30 03
Fax: ++44 (1952) 58 80 16
www.ironbridge.org.uk

Desc.: Volunteers are required at this World Heritage site for demonstrations of exhibits, site maintenance, and street festivities. Other opportunities to volunteer are available at the Museum's other sites in the valley. The Iron Bridge is universally recognised as a potent symbol of the Industrial Revolution. It was built in 1779.

Per.: 18th century.

Country: United Kingdom.

Loc.: Spanning the River Severn at Ironbridge in Shropshire.

Travel: Details provided upon application.

Dur.: 2 weeks; April to October.

Age: Minimum 18.

Qualif.: Some historical background is a plus, although training, equipment, and supervision are provided.

Work: Museum curation and public education.

Lang.: English.

Accom.: No accommodation available. Volunteers are given a luncheon voucher for a full day's volunteering, plus free entry to other Trust sites.

Cost: Museum insurance covers all volunteers.

Applic.: Applications accepted year round to the Volunteer Co-ordinator, Blists Hill Victorian Town, at the above address.

Notes: Alternative contact is Janice Fletcher, at The Ironbridge Institute, Ironbridge Gorge Museum, Coalbrookdale, Telford, Shropshire TF8 7DX. Tel: ++44 (1952) 43 27 51, fax: ++44 (1952) 43 59 37, or e-mail: ironbridge@bham.ac.uk.

Ischia di Castro

Gruppi Archeologici d'Italia
Via degli Scipioni 30/A, 00192 Rome, Italy
Tel./Fax: ++39 (06) 3973 4449
E-mail: gainaz@tin.it – gaiedit@tin.it – gaistampa@tiscalinet.it
www.gruppiarcheologici.org

Desc.: The restoration campaign of the medieval town of Castro, encompasses the reconstruction and the cleaning of the facades of the buildings of the Piazza Maggiore and the preparation of self-guided interpretation tours. Similar activities are planned in the Medieval Settlement of Castellardo, a fortified town built on the area of Lombard castle destroyed in the mid-15th century.

Per.: Medieval.

Country: Italy.

Loc.: Villages of Castro and Castellardo in the Province of Viterbo, about 40 miles (60km) north of Rome.

Travel: Details provided upon application. Participants must arrive Monday at 18:00 and leave Sunday at 10:00.

Dur.: 1–2 weeks.

Age: Minimum 18.

Qualif.: No experience necessary

Work: Excavation, documentation, survey, etc.

Lang.: Italian, English.

Accom.: Mulino di Ischia di Castro, in bunks with shared bathrooms.

Cost: EUR198 (approx. US$215) per week; EUR302(approx. US$320) for 2-week session.

Applic.: Participants must be members of the Gruppi Archeologici d'Italia. Membership fee of EUR32 (US$35, includes insurance and subscription to the magazine *Archeologia*) can be paid at a local office or at the National office at the above address.

Notes: Bring work boots, gloves, and clothes, a water bottle, hat, and sleeping bag.

See also:
Gruppi Archeologici d'Italia

Israel Foreign Ministry

www.israel.org/mfa/
(search for "archaeological excavations")

Desc.: There are many Universities and organisations throughout Israel listed through the Ministry. Many archaeologists enlist volunteers to help on their digs, as volunteers are highly motivated and wish to learn and gain experience.

Per.: Various.

Country: Israel.

Loc.: Various.

Travel: Contact project of interest for details. Volunteers are responsible for their own travel arrangements to and from Israel.

Dur.: Various.

Age: Minimum 18.

Qualif.: Usually, no previous experience is necessary. Some expeditions offer credit courses from sponsoring institutions. Informal lectures covering the history and archaeology of the site are often supplemental.

Work: The work is often difficult and tedious including digging, shoveling, hauling baskets of earth and sherds, cleaning pottery sherds and more. The work schedule at an excavation is organized according to the conditions at the site; typically the dig begins before dawn and ends after noon with a rest period after lunch. The afternoons and early evenings may be devoted to lectures, cleaning and sorting of pottery and other finds, or they may be free.

Lang.: English, Hebrew.

Accom.: May range from sleeping bags in the field, to rooms in hostels or kibbutzim, to 3-star hotels near a site. Excavations conducted in or near a city often require volunteers to find their own accommodations. Volunteers who require kosher food should inquire in advance.

Cost: There is usually a registration fee and a charge for food and lodging, although on some excavations these are free. All charges listed are in US dollars.

Applic.: Any questions, comments, registration, or requests for additional information must be directed to the contact person indicated for each project, and not to the Israel Foreign Ministry. When applying to the director of an excavation you should indicate any previous studies you may have in archaeology or related fields, such as anthropology, architecture, geography, surveying, graphic arts; or experience in excavation work, pottery restoration or photography.

Notes: Volunteers should have comfortable, sturdy, weather appropriate clothing for heavy work. Work-gloves, sleeping bag, canteen, and towels are often required. Volunteers must arrange for medical and accident insurance in advance. Even in instances when accident insurance is provided, it is strongly advised that volunteers come fully insured, as the insurance offered is minimal. The Israel Ministry of Interior regulations require that passports of all volunteers (other than Israeli) be stamped with a volunteer visa (B4). This request should be made by the volunteer at the point of entry into Israel.

See also:

Northern "Sea Peoples" Excavation Project

Sha'ar Hagolan – Archaeological Excavations and Neolithic Art Centre

Tell es-Safi / Gath Archaeological Project

Tel Hazor Excavation Project

JAC – Joint Assistance Center

PO Box 6082, San Pablo 94806-0082 California USA
Tel.: ++1 (510) 464 1100
Fax: ++1 (603) 297 3521
E-mail: jacusa@juno.com
www.jacusa.org

Desc.: The international volunteer programmes of JAC are intended to provide opportunities to see India and learn about its people and their concerns while travelling. Projects can be cultural exchanges or workcamps in rural villages or individuals can establish individual programmes for study purposes.

Per.: Contemporary.

Country: India.

Loc.: Various.

Travel: Pick-up arranged at New Delhi International Airport possible.

Dur.: 1–4 weeks to 3 months; year round. An individual schedule is devised 30 days in advance of arrival in India

Age: Minimum 18.

Qualif.: No experience necessary.

Work: See list of programmes on the website or contact JAC with study proposals.

Lang.: English. Long-term project require basic Hindi.

Accom.: Tent camping or bamboo, thatch, and mud plaster huts. Bring sleeping bag and mat. Possibly portable toilets. Accommodation are safe and secure though not comfortable from Western standards. Simple vegetarian food by self-catered meals in camps.

Cost: US$150–550, plus US$50 non-refundable application fee. Room, board, administration costs, airport pick-up, and orientation included. International and local travel not included.

Applic.: On-line form. All fees have to be made at least 30 days before the departure date. Applicants outside the United States must enclose 3 International Reply Coupons.

Notes: Volunteers must abstain from consuming alcohol and non-vegetarian items and avoid smoking and non-prescription drugs.

Jeunesse et Réconstruction

10 rue de Trévise, 75009 Paris France
Tel.: ++33 (1) 4770 1588   Fax: ++33 (1) 4800 9218
E-mail: info@volontariat.org
www.volontariat.org

Desc.: Jeunesse et Réconstruction is a volunteer organisation active since 1948. Its main objectives are to favour the cultural exchange among young people from different countries, who work together as volunteers to help in social, environmental, agricultural, or cultural heritage protection projects. Jeunesse et Réconstruction has many reconstruction and cultural heritage preservation projects all over France, usually in association with local communities.

Per.: Multi-period.

Country: France.

Loc.: Various.

Travel: Pick-up may or may not be offered from main bus or train station or airport.

Dur.: 2–3 weeks; summer.

Age: Minimum 18; Junior programmes for 15–18.

Qualif.: No experience necessary.

Work: Reconstruction, plaster work, maintenance, gardening, masonry, painting, etc.

Lang.: French or language of host country.

Accom.: Tenting or basic lodging. Bring a sleeping bag.

Cost: Volunteers must add to the cost of the workcamp chosen (usually below EUR200) to cover food and accommodation, a EUR 30.50 application fee and EUR 23 for insurance.

Applic.: On-line form to e-mail or post with payment. Applicants who are not French, or not living in France, may only apply directly to Jeunesse et Réconstruction if no partner-organisation exists in applicant's home country.

Notes: Foreigners belonging to the European Union must bring the E111 form (for refunding medical expenses).

Judith River Dinosaur Institute

Box 429 Malta, Montana 59538 USA
Tel./Fax: ++1 (406) 654 2323
E-mail: nmurphy@ttc-cmc.net
www.montanadinodigs.com

Desc.: The Stegosaurus is amongst the most rare of the dinosaurs in North America; this project represents an opportunity for volunteers to work the first stegosaurus ever found in Montana.

Per.: Jurassic and late Cretaceous.

Country: United States.

Loc.: Judith River, near Great Falls, Malta, Montana.

Travel: Volunteers must arrive independently in Malta. Transportation beween motel and field provided.

Dur.: 1 week; July.

Age: Minimum 18.

Qualif.: Experienced amateurs are preferred. This project is for the more seriously interested and not just the casual vacationer.

Work: Field exploration, recording and mapping finds, interpretation and taphonomy, and excavation (jacketing and removal).

Lang.: English.

Accom.: Lodging is not included in the costs. A list of accommodations in Malta can be found at the Malta, Montana Chamber www.2chambers.com/montana2 or call ++1 (406) 654 1776.

Cost: US$750–850 per week (subject to change). Lunches, field tools, transportation to the site, and instruction provided. Meals (other than lunch in the field) and travel not included.

Applic.: On-line form to mail with a check for half of the fee as a deposit The deposit is refundable only if notification is received no less than 90 days prior to the applied for start date.

Notes: Rugged terrain and hot climate; participants must be in good physical condition.

Kalat Project

Chapter of Campobello di Licata, Archeoclub d'Italia
c/o Centro Polivalente, Via Trieste 1, 92023 Campobello di Licata, Italy
Tel.: ++39 (0922) 88 35 08
Fax: ++39 (0922) 88 35 08
E-mail: campi@kalat.org
www.kalat.org

Desc.: Archaeological, cultural, and natural heritage project in Western Sicily, at one of the most interesting archaeological areas in Italy. The area was for centuries occupied by Greeks, Romans, Normans, Swabians, Angevins, and Aragoneses and is rich in monuments and archaeological sites. Historical pathways for the creation of tourist itineraries are proposed.

Per.: Neolithic to Byzantine, Islamic, and late Middle Ages.

Country: Italy.

Loc.: Campobello di Licata, near Agrigento, Sicily.

Travel: Various train connections from Catania and Palermo to Campobello di Licata where the organisation can be called for pick-up. Request directions to arrive by car.

Dur.: 1 week; August.

Age: Minimum 18.

Qualif.: No experience necessary.

Work: Survey, archaeological research, mapping, public education, environmental recovery, tourist promotion, and cultural exchange.

Lang.: Italian, English.

Accom.: Hostel in Via Edison in rooms with 8 places.

Cost: Request information from the project.

Applic.: On-line form. Confirmation of booking will be made upon the receipt of the curriculum and pre-payment of half of the participation quota. The remainder is paid upon arrival.

Notes: Bring long trousers, boots, hat, flask, torch, sheets, and necessary toiletries.

Kendal Camp

IIWC of IPPA CJ Indonesia / IPPA Secretariat in Australia
School of Archaeology and Anthropology
ANU, Canberra ACT 0200, Australia
Tel.: ++61 (2) 6125 3120 Fax : ++61 (2) 6125 2711
E-mail: ippa@anu.edu.au
http://arts.anu.edu.au/arcworld/ippa/ippa.htm

Desc.: This is a cultural workcamp for immersion in the rural life of a small community in Indonesia. The theme of the workcamp is agricultural and participants will be involved in the planting and harvesting of a traditional rice crop.

Per.: Contemporary.

Country: Indonesia.

Loc.: Kendal, the capital town of Kendal regency, which lies approximately 18 miles (29 km) away from Semarang westward on the road to Jakarta

Travel: Details provided upon application.

Dur.: 10 days; March.

Age: Minimum 18.

Qualif.: No experience necessary.

Work: Plant and harvest rice in the village rice field and renovating a small irrigation system.

Lang.: English.

Accom.: Tent camping.

Cost: US$150.

Applic.: Contact workcamp association of home country. UNESCO can advise on the necessary contacts.

Notes: Bring cutlery and sleeping bag. This project may not be offered annually. Contact UNESCO (see listing) for other opportunities in Indonesia.

See also:
UNESCO

Kfar HaHoresh Archaeology & Anthropology Field School

Institute of Archaeology, The Hebrew University of Jerusalem
Mount Scopus Jerusalem 91905 Israel
Tel.: ++972 (2) 588 2403/4
Fax: ++972 (2) 582 5548
E-mail: goring@h2.hum.huji.ac.il
www.hum.huji.ac.il/archaeology/

Desc.: The Early Neolithic cultures of this region are the earliest agricultural societies in the world. The Kfar HaHoresh excavations reveal it is a unique mortuary and cult centre serving neighbouring lowland village communities. Finds include many human skeletons and secondary burials sealed under lime-plastered surfaces. There is evidence for extensive lime-plaster manufacture at the site; an experimental program of this early pyrotechnology is being conducted on-site.

Per.: Early Neolithic; 7000 BC.

Country: Israel.

Loc.:. In the Nazareth Hills of Lower Galilee, northern Israel.

Travel: Details provided upon application.

Dur.: 3 weeks; June to August.

Age: Minimum 18.

Qualif.: No experience necessary.

Work: Excavation, recovery, recording, and artefact analysis.

Lang.: English.

Accom.: Kibbutz Kfar HaHoresh in 2–3 person shared rooms. Meals are in the kibbutz dinning room.

Cost: US$1,200 for a 3-week session plus US$150 non-refundable registration fee. Additional tuition fees apply.

Applic.: Deadline mid-May. Request an application via e-mail.

Notes: Academic credit available through the Rothberg International School, Hebrew University.

See also:

Hebrew University of Jerusalem

Koobi Fora Field School

Rutgers Study Abroad, The State University of New Jersey
102 College Avenue, New Brunswick
New Jersey 08901-8543 USA
Tel.: ++1 (732) 932 0485
E-mail: jwharris@rci.rutgers.edu
www-rci.rutgers.edu/~mjr/index1.html

Desc.: This palaeoanthropology field school is conducted by research staff at the National Museums of Kenya and faculty from Rutgers University. Students learn the basic principles and field methods on location at the site was made famous by Richard Leakey and his colleagues in the 1970s for finds of ancient hominids. The programme involves hands-on introductory training in all the disciplines of palaeoanthropology: palaeontology, archaeology, geology, taphonomy, and ecology.

Per.: Palaeolithic.

Country: Kenya.

Loc.: On the eastern shore of Lake Turkana, northern Kenya; 1 week at Laikipia on the slopes of Mount Kenya.

Travel: Details provided upon application.

Dur.: 6 weeks; June to July.

Age: Minimum 18.

Qualif.: Undergraduate and graduate students may apply, regardless of background or discipline.

Work: Excavation, survey, mapping, artefact analysis, identification, 1-week session studying savannah landscapes and ecology.

Lang.: English.

Accom.: Basic lodging.

Cost: US$4,401 for New Jersey residents; US$5,361 for out-of-state residents. Costs subject to inflation and exchange rates. Room, board, and transportation included. Airfare not included.

Applic.: On-line form plus 2 letters of recommendation and a check or money order for US$20 application fee made payable to Rutgers Study Abroad. Mail to the attention of Jack Harris, Director. An information package is sent upon application .

Notes: Academic credit available with approval from home institution.

Körös Regional Archaeological Project

Department of Anthropology, Florida State University
1847 West Tennessee Street, Tallahassee, Florida 32306-4531 USA
Tel.: ++1 (850) 644 7021
Fax: ++1 (850) 644 4283
E-mail: wparkins@mailer.fsu.edu – yerkes.1@osu.edu
www.anthro.fsu.edu/koros/

Desc.: The prehistory, history, and culture of Hungary and Eastern Europe investigating the social and economic changes that occurred as farming, herding, and metal working. Students also will participate in seminars led by the faculty and visiting scholars and complete an independent research project.

Per.: Early Copper Age (Tiszapolgár Culture, 4,500 BC)

Country: Hungary.

Loc.: Small town in Békés County in southeastern Hungary, near the Romanian border.

Travel: By train; group travel to be arranged.

Dur.: 6 weeks; June to July.

Age: Minimum 18.

Qualif.: Juniors and seniors in good academic standing with a strong interest in archaeology.

Work: Excavation field school.

Lang.: English.

Accom.: Village hostel with kitchen, electricity, showers, and sleeping quarters with bedding and meals provided.

Cost: Funding from the National Science Foundation Research Experiences for Undergraduates (REU) Sites programme enables participants to receive a stipend that covers academic costs, program excursions, room and board, and airfare. Educational materials and personal expenses not included.

Applic.: Download from the website the application form and return completed with application fee of US$100 to Dr. William Parkinson at the above address. Deadline early March.

Notes: Pre-departure orientation meetings are required passports, travel, insurance, country specifics, and related topics.

KwaZulu Field Project

KwaZulu Natal Museu, Institute for CUltural Resource Management,
237 Loop Street, Private Bag 9070, Peitermaritzburg 3200 South Africa
Tel.: ++27(33) 345 1404 Fax: ++27 (33) 345 0561
E-mail: ganderson@nmsa.org.za
www.nmsa.org.za
www.kwazulu.net/Tourism/Museum/

Desc.: The Institute for Cultural Resource Management offers a field school in KwaZulu-Natal, South Africa. The field school offers 2 excavations along the beach dune cordons of KwaZulu-Natal and a rock art trip to the Drakensberg. The first excavation site consists of several stratified shell middens, with well preserved faunal remains and ostrich egg shell beads. This is the 1st Stone Age site to be excavated in these dune systems. The 2nd site is a village settlement that extends for about 500m. The site includes pits, fireplaces, central cattle byre, and other features associated with these villages.

Per.: Late to early Stone Age.

Country: South Africa.

Loc.: 25 miles (40km) north Richards Bay.

Travel: Pick-up at Durban International airport.

Dur.: 2 weeks followed by 5-day field trip; season to be determined.

Age: Minimum 18.

Qualif.: No experience necessary.

Work: Excavation, mapping, section drawings, sorting.

Lang.: English.

Accom.: Inquire with project.

Cost: US$1,000 (subject to change and exchange rates). Accommodation, subsistence, transport to and from Durban International airport, 3 supervisors in the field (or 1 supervisor for every 3 students) included.

Applic.: Inquire for details.

Notes: The rock art field trip is over a 5-day period and only available to those who have undertaken the 2-week excavation period.

Lamanai Archaeological Project

Lamanai Field Research Center (LFRC)
PO Box 63, Orange Walk District, Belize
Tel.: ++1 (954) 415 2897
E-mail: LauraHoward1900@aol.com – research@lamanai.org
www.lamanai.org/Arch.htm

Desc.: Participants are introduced to ancient Maya material culture, the management of these resources, and community involvement with archaeological database and cultural resource management strategies as they pertain to Maya archaeology. Biological research is being carried out at the Lamanai Field Research centre and participants may take field excursions such as identification of medicinal plants, canoeing, and night-spotlight safaris.

Per.: Pre-Classic to Historic Maya; 1500 BC to 1875 AD.

Country: Belize.

Loc.: Belize, near the town of Orange Walk.

Travel: Details provided upon application.

Dur.: 2 weeks; February to July.

Age: Minimum 18.

Qualif.: No experience necessary.

Work: Process, sort, and analyse artefacts including ceramics, lithics, and small finds, laboratory work, community development, lectures, and tours. Access to the extensive Lamanai collection for examination and reference. Excavations not involved.

Lang.: English.

Accom.: Fully screened, thatch-roof cabana at Lamanai Outpost Lodge shared with a maximum of 2 other students. Cabanas have private bathrooms with hot showers, towels, sheets, electricity, ceiling fan, purified drinking water, room-cleaning, and laundry service. On-site laboratory and well-equipped lecture hall.

Cost: Inquire for full costs.

Applic.: Contact Project Director Laura Howard.

Notes: Academic credit available with approval from home University.

Legambiente

Via Salaria 403, 00199 Rome Italy
Tel.: ++39 (06) 862 681 or 8626 8324
(for SCUBA activities ++39 (06) 8626 8400)
Fax: ++39 (06) 8626 8319
E-mail: legambiente.vol@tiscalinet.it
www.legambiente.com

Desc.: This organisation combines the protection of the environment with the restoration and enhancement of cultural Heritage. Current projects include restoration and protection camps in small islands near Sicily, underwater archaeology and ecology camps in Sicily, ecological research in the Italian Alps, archeological study in southern Italy and many others.

Per.: Various.

Country: Italy.

Loc.: Various.

Travel: Details provided with each project.

Dur.: 10–20 days; year round.

Age: Minimum18. Special programmes available for those under 18.

Qualif.: No experience necessary.

Work: Manual labour; restoration, renovation, cleaning, etc.

Lang.: Italian, English.

Accom.: Various accommodations from schools, houses, convents, etc.

Cost: EUR150–350 (approx US$ 170–380), plus membership fee.

Applic.: Contact the Volunteer office of Legambiente for further information and application forms.

See also:
Eco-Archaeological Park Pontacagnano Faiano
Giurdignano Project – Megalith Garden of Europe
Paestum Project – Between Environment and History
San Giorgio Convent
Walls of Verona

Limpopo River Valley Archaeology Field School

School of Geography, Archaeology and Environmental Studies
University of the Witwatersrand
Private Bag 3, PO Wits 2050, Johannesburg South Africa
E-mail: suttonm@science.pg.wits.ac.za
www.wits.ac.za/archaeology/fieldschool/

Desc.: This field school tours 3 famous palaeoanthropological sites near Johannesburg—Sterkfontein, Swartkrans, and Kromdraii, to learn about cave, fossil, palaeo-environment, and archaeological site formation processes. Visits to the Iron Age sites of Mapungabwe included.

Per.: Palaeolithic, early to middle Stone Age, Acheulean, Iron Age; 3.31 million years BP to 1000–1300 AD.

Country: South Africa.

Loc.: Limpopo River, along the northern border of South Africa.

Travel: Pick-up at the Johannesburg International Airport or the University.

Dur.: 1 month; July to July.

Age: Minimum 18.

Qualif.: This is an advanced level field school involving prerequisites.

Work: Excavation techniques, data recording, use of the total station EDM for on-site recording, introduction to lithic analysis, and hominid fossil recognition. Seminars and practical exercises.

Lang.: English.

Accom.: Small hotel close to the University and Pontdrift farmers' hall, with ablution facilities in the valley. Camp cots are provided for sleeping in the hall or volunteers may pitch their own tent outside. The area is remote with weekly trips once a week to Messina for supplies.

Cost: US$2,500. Airport pick-up, transportation, registration, tuition, lodging, and meals included. Airfare not included.

Applic.: On-line form, US$1,000 deposit to confirm placement. Deadline May 1. Tourist visa required. Register as an occassional student with 2 reference letters.

Notes: There is a small risk of Malaria in Messina. The site is 1 hour from the hospital; medical conditions must be made known.

Lubbock Lake Landmark

Museum of Texas Tech University
Box 43191 Lubbock, Texas USA
Tel.: ++1 (806) 742 2481 or 742 1117
Fax: ++1 (806) 742 1136
E-mail: eileen.johnson@ttu.edu
www.museum.ttu.edu/lll/

Desc.: Lubbock Lake, a 300-acre archaeological and natural history preserve, is a national historic and state archaeological landmark and on the national register of historic places. Current excavations focus on the Palaeo-Indian and Late Holocene records. Exhibits in the interpretive centre and guided tours of the excavation areas are open to the public.

Per.: Clovis through Historic periods; 9500 BC to 1930 AD.

Country: United States.

Loc.: Lubbock, Texas; less than 20 miles (30km) from Lubbock International airport.

Travel: Transportation from Lubbock International airport or Lubbock bus station to the project is provided.

Dur.: 9 weeks if from US, 6 weeks if from abroad; June to August.

Age: Minimum 18.

Qualif.: No experience necessary.

Work: Ecxavation. Volunteers have the opportunity to assist with special programmes and tours for the public. Crew members are expected to help with daily kitchen and camp chores.

Lang.: English.

Accom.: Room and board provided. Lodging is in 6-person tents with wooden floors, electricity, and showers.

Cost: No direct fees. Airfare, travel, hand tools and personal field supplies, insurance, and personal expenses not included.

Applic.: Contact the Project Director, Dr. Eileen Johnson. Academic credit available with approval from home university.

Notes: Major equipment and field supplies provided. Proof of health and accident insurance and current tetanus shot required. A field kit is available for purchase US$40.

Ma'ax Na Archaeology Project

New England Archaeology Institute
Department of Sociology and Anthropology
7000 College Station, Bowdoin College, Brunswick, ME 04011 USA
Tel.: ++1 (207) 725 8402
E-mail: eleanormking@earthlink.net
www.neai.org

Desc.: Ma'ax Na (meaning "Monkey House") seems to have occupied a prominent position in the larger Three Rivers archaeological region. The project investigates this large Mayan site and its environs to ascertain the configuration and limits of the ceremonial core and the number, location, and relationship of surrounding residential groups.

Per.: Classic Maya.

Country: Belize.

Loc.: The field camp is adjacent to the Rio Bravo Field Station in the centre of the Bolsa Verde conservation area.

Travel: Volunteers arrive at Belize International airport for pick-up.

Dur.: 3–4 weeks; May to June.

Age: Minimum 18.

Qualif.: No experience necessary but previous study is useful.

Work: Excavation , site mapping, interpretation of Mayan architecture, reconnaissance survey methods, processing techniques for stone tools, ceramics, bone, and shell, artefact curation and analysis, illustration, and lectures.

Lang.: English.

Accom.: The field station is a large building with upstairs dorm rooms with bunk beds and a large laboratory. Tent platforms with roofs also available. Kitchen, dining area, showers, and latrines.

Cost: US$1,595. Room and board, all travel within Belize, and heavy field equipment included. Airfare and exit tax not included.

Applic.: Request an application package via e-mail or regular post.

Notes: Bring a field notebook, trowel, tape measure, sting-line level, root clippers, a small backpack, and canteen.

Malta University

Foundation for International Studies
University Building, St Paul Street, Valletta VLT 07 Malta
Tel.: ++356 (21) 230 793 or 237 547 or 234 121/2
Fax: ++356 (21) 230 538 or 230 551
E-mail: summerabroad@um.edu.mt
www.um.edu.mt/studyabroad/

Desc.: At Tas-Silg, previous excavations have revealed underground tombs, an early prehistoric megalithic temple, and a Phoenician conversion of this temple, which continued to expand to include monumental altars, gateways, and porticos, at times utilising features of the original prehistoric temple.

Per.: Stone Age, Neolithic, Punic, Roman, Early Christian.

Country: Malta.

Loc.: Msida, near the capital city, Valletta.

Travel: Participants are met at the airport.

Dur.: 2–6 weeks; June to July.

Age: Minimum 18.

Qualif.: No experience necessary. The fieldwork sessions have a 2-week course prerequisite; students who have already attended similar courses in their home universities may be exempt.

Work: 40 hours of lectures on Mediterranean, Maltese, and Field Archaeology; field trips; excavation, and finds processing.

Lang.: English.

Accom.: Apartments (2 people in twin room) in an annex of a hotel with shower, toilet, and fully equipped kitchen.

Cost: US$750–2,365 depending upon programmes and services, which include study tours/site visits, excavation supervision, transport between the University and the excavation site, accommodation, airport transfers. Registration deposit of US$250.

Applic.: Registration and payment in full is due May 16.

Notes: Participants must have adequate health and accident insurance coverge. An anti-tetanus inoculation is advised.

Mapping the Past

University of Cape Town, Department of Archaeology
Beattie Building, Private Bag Rondebosch 7701 South Africa
Tel.: ++27 (21) 650 2353
Fax: ++27 (21) 650 2352
E-mail: becky@beattie.uct.ac.za
www.uct.ac.za/depts/age/mapping/

Desc.: This is an internationally-renowned fossil site of gompothere *Anancus*. The project utilises the latest mapping, visualisation, and geomantic technologies and is aimed at palaeontologists, archaeologists, engineers, architects, scientists, and others interested in exploring alternative various technologies.

Per.: Miocene and Pliocene; 5–6 million years ago.

Country: South Africa.

Loc.: West Coast Fossil Park at Langebaanweg, about 60 miles (100km) from Cape Town, on the Atlantic coast of the Western Cape province.

Travel: Participants are picked up at Cape Town International airport.

Dur.: 3 weeks; June to July.

Age: Minimum 18.

Qualif.: Advanced undergraduate and graduate students, or those with strong anthropological or biological backgrounds. Training in the pertinent technologies is provided, however, proficiency with computers and windows-based programmes and a basic understanding of palaeontological principles are necessary.

Work: Digital mapping, data collection, and laboratory work. Students build and present a web-based publication of collected material (archived data, spatial maps, images). GIS, GPS, computer imaging, 3-D visualisation, data acquisition, storage, and manipulation, and web publishing techniques are utilised.

Lang.: English.

Accom.: Dorms at the University.

Cost: US$3,000. Tuition, accommodation, meals, airport transfers, transport, University facilities, and tours included.

Applic.: On-line form, transcripts, professors' references, and registration to UCT due March 1; US$1,000 due April 15.

Maya Archaeology at Minanhá

Department of Anthropology, Trent University
Peterborough, Ontario K9J 7B8 Canada
Tel.: ++1 (705) 748 1011 X-1325 or 748 1011 X-1453
Fax: ++1 (705) 748 1613
E-mail: giannone@trentu.ca
www.trentu.ca/anthropology/

Desc.: This project focuses on the investigation of ancient Maya socio-economic and socio-political integration, specifically testing potential models for the Maya state, within what was once among the most volatile regions of the Maya subarea.

Per.: Classic Maya; 100–1200 AD.

Country: Belize.

Loc.: X-ual-Canil, Vaca Plateau of west central Belize.

Travel: Details provided upon application. Transport into San Ignacio town on Friday and pick-up on Sunday evening provided.

Dur.: 1 month; May to July.

Age: Minimum 18.

Qualif.: No experience necessary.

Work: Excavation, site reconnaissance, survey, lectures, site tours, field trips, labs, artefact analysis, processing, and illustration. Monday to Friday. 25–30 minute hike to the site each day.

Lang.: English, Spanish useful.

Accom.: Tent camping at the Martz Farm, a Belizean run eco-resort about 3 miles (5km) from the site. Students supply their own camping gear, tents, and mats. No electrical power but abundant water.

Cost: US$1,400. Food, lodging, operational, administrative, and staff costs included. Fees are paid to the Project Director upon arrival in Belize. Transportation to and from Belize, weekend room and board, and personal expenses not included.

Applic.: US$100 application deposit. Separate Trent summer school application form due in early March.

Notes: Academic credit available through Trent University. Additional tuition fees apply.

Maya Research Program

Texas Christian University
Box 298760, 2800 South University Drive
Fort Worth, Texas 76129 USA
Tel.: ++1 (817) 257 5943
E-mail: mrp@tcu.edu
www.mayaresearchprogram.org

Desc.:	The Program strives to better understand the past and to inform the public about the Maya, preserve and protect Maya ruins, and assist those with similar goals. The major current project is the Blue Creek Archaeological Project studying the social, political, and economic relationships that constituted ancient Maya society.
Per.:	Classic Maya; 100–1200 AD.
Country:	Belize.
Loc.:	Blue Creek in northwestern Belize.
Travel:	Details provided upon application.
Dur.:	2–8 weeks; May to July.
Age:	Minimum 18.
Qualif.:	No experience necessary.
Work:	Excavation, survey, laboratory work.
Lang.:	English, Spanish useful.
Accom.:	Base station, about 3–4km from the site.
Cost:	US$1,250 per 2-week session; US$1,000 for each subsequent session. Food, accommodation, and project-related costs included. Transportation to and from Belize, airport departure tax, and personal expenses not included.
Applic.:	On-line form.
Notes:	The Harkrider Scholarship brings young scholars from Belize and other countries to the United States for advanced study and young US scholars to Latin America.

Midwest Archeological Center, National Park Service

Room 474, Federal Building
100 Centennial Mall North Lincoln, Nebraska 68508 USA
Tel.: ++1 (402) 437 5392 ext. 114
E-mail: Bruce_A_Jones@nps.gov – Mark_Lynott@nps.gov –
Dawn_Bringelson@nps.gov
www.cr.nps.gov/mwac/

Desc.: The Midwest Archeological Center (MWAC) has an active, growing volunteer programme. Past projects include investigations at Pea Ridge National Military Park in Arkansas and Wilson's Creek National Battlefield in Missouri, excavations at Hopewell Culture National Historical Park in Ohio, fieldwork in locations such as Cuyahoga Valley National Park in Ohio, Voyageurs National Park along the boundary waters in northern Minnesota, Wind Cave National Park in South Dakota, and Fort Union Trading Post National Historic Site in North Dakota, and assisting in the MWAC laboratory in the analysis of archaeological data from these and other places. Please note: all projects pending passage of annual appropriations bills.

Per.: Multi-period; early prehistoric to 19th and early 20th centuries.

Country: United States.

Loc.: Mainly within the Midwestern United States.

Travel: It is the responsibility of the volunteer to get to MWAC or the work area at the beginning of their stay, and MWAC may be able to provide transport between lodging and work site daily. This depends on project-specific conditions.

Dur.: Minimum 1 week for field projects, lower intensity commitment in the lab; year round.

Age: Minimum 18.

Qualif.: No experience necessary.

Work: Survey, inventory, excavation, and lab inventory, cataloging, or analysis.

Lang.: English.

Accom.: Depending on each project's funding, MWAC may be able to provide housing at or near the project site. Type of housing and available funding varies by project.

Cost: Project-dependent. Volunteers may be reimbursed for out-of-pocket expenses (such as room and board) if funds are available.

Applic.: On-line form. Individuals will be directed towards appropriate projects based upon their specified interests and available opportunities.

Notes: MWAC is currently in the process of planning for new and ongoing projects. Interested parties should contact MWAC directly for more information or visit their website (above) to complete a volunteer application form. Volunteers must attain proof of insurance and apply for a J-1 Visa from the US embassy or consulate in their home country. Consult the NPS Office of International Affairs web page for international volunteers (http://www.nps.gov/oia/topics/ivip.htm) for more information on the application process.

Moab Archaeological Resource Survey Excavation

Department of Anthropology, Box 87-2402
Arizona State University Tempe, Arizona 85287-2402 USA
E-mail: shsavage@asu.edu
http://archaeology.asu.edu/Jordan/index.html

Desc.: This project was established to collect settlement, archaeological, and environmental data from the western part of the Madaba Plain in the highlands of central Jordan. The general goal of the fieldwork is to gather settlement, ceramic, lithic, faunal, and botanical data from an area that appears to have contained a single cluster of sites (the red circle).

Per.: Early Bronze Age to Byzantine; 3600–2200 BC to 330–620 AD.

Country: Jordan.

Loc.: Khirbet Qarn al-Qubish in the city of Madaba; about 20 miles (30km) southwest of Amman, the capital of Jordan.

Travel: Details provided upon application.

Dur.: 5 weeks; July to August.

Age: Minimum 18.

Qualif.: Qualified students and non-credit volunteers interested in the archaeology and culture of Jordan and the Ancient Near East.

Work: Survey, excavation, mapping, processing excavated materials, keeping field records, attending evening lectures. Lab work includes obtaining radiocarbon dates, analysis of faunal and botanical remains, lithic and petrographic analysis of ceramics.

Lang.: English.

Accom.: Rented houses in Madaba, with up to 4 students per room. Bathroom and kitchen facilities are shared. Main meals will be prepared by a cook, or taken at one of the local restaurants.

Cost: US$2,000. Room, board, project travel in Jordan, and camp fees included. (US$3,000 for students includes course registration). Airfare, books and supplies, optional fieldtrips and personal expenses not included. Costs are subject to change.

Applic.: US$150 deposit plus US$1,000 installment due February 1.

The National Trust

The Estates Department
33 Sheep Street, Cirencester, Glos GL7 1RQ UK
Tel.: ++44 (1285) 65 18 18
Fax: ++44 (1285) 65 79 35
E-mail: volunteers@ntrust.org.uk
www.nationaltrust.org.uk

Desc.: The National Trust offers working holidays for non-professional individuals interested in an alternative vacation throughout the UK. The project may be an archaeological excavation, historical site preservation, or drywall reconstruction.

Per.: Various.

Country: United Kingdom.

Loc.: England, Wales, and Northern Ireland.

Travel: Details provided upon application.

Dur.: 1–2 weeks; year round.

Age: Minimum 18.

Qualif.: No technical skills are required but volunteers with archaeological experience are particularly welcome.

Work: Digging and clearing. Workday is usually 9:00–17:00, weather permitting. Teamwork taking turns cooking and cleaning.

Lang.: English.

Accom.: Trust base camp; farmhouse, cottage, or apartment specially converted for group use. Most base camps have a fully equipped kitchen, hot showers, and bunk beds.

Cost: GB£65 (approx. US$100) for holidays between June 27 and August 29; GB£54 for other dates. Travel and personal expenses not included. A supplementary charge of GB£5 per person is made on bookings from overseas to cover bank and administrative charges in the UK.

Applic.: On-line form or phone the Bookings Office at 0870 4292429, stating the choice of holiday. A Confirmation Pack is sent giving specific details about the holiday and other instructions.

Notes: Work permits and visas are the responsibility of the volunteer. Bring a sleeping bag, raingear, work clothes, boots, and gloves.

NICE – Never-ending International WorkCamps Exchange

2-4-2-701 Shinjuku, Shinjuku-ku, Tokyo 160-0022 JAPAN
Tel.: ++81 (3) 3358 7140
Fax: ++81 (3) 3358 7149
E-mail: in@nice1.gr.jp – nice@nice1.gr.jp
http://nice1.gr.jp

Desc.: Cultural exchanges and workcamps in various sectors including culture and renovation. There are, for example, a couple of workcamps that are aimed at maintaining the local cultural heritage of a Japanese traditional house. Volunteers help to maintain the roof made of reeds. One location is in Tonami, an area famous for beautiful scenery of the scattered houses and the local cultural heritage of the traditional Japanese reed-roofed houses; the other is in Yawata, among the most productive areas for rice and snowy in winter.

Per.: Various.

Country: Japan and East Asia.

Loc.: Tonami, near Toyama, 125 miles (200km) northwest of Tokyo or Yawata, near Yamagata, in northern Japan along the Japan Sea.

Travel: From Tokyo to Tonami is 10–11 hours by midnight bus or train, or from Osaka is 6–7 hours by train. From Tokyo to Yawata is 6 hours by fast train or 10–11 hours by midnight bus or regular train.

Dur.: 3 weeks; October to November.

Age: Minimum 18.

Qualif.: No experience necessary.

Work: Cutting and carrying reeds for the roofs and assisting the carpenters. Monday to Friday; 6–8 hours per day.

Lang.: English, Japanese.

Accom.: Basic facilities or tent camping.

Cost: Fees paid to sending workcamp organisation. Additional fees (US$100–200) in some workcamps may be required. Food, accommodation, and project support included. Travel not included. A membership fee covers monthly newsletters and insurance.

Applic.: Japanese volunteers may apply directly. Foreign volunteers must apply to a partner workcamp organisation of home country. For European residents contatct the Alliance of European Voluntary Service Organizations; for residents of other countries contact the Coordinating Committee for International Voluntary Service at UNESCO in Paris.

Notes: Cultural events organised may include activities such as the Taros potato soup party, a famous events in this Shonai area, or participants may visit schools to demonstrate the methods of making a thatched-reed roof.

See also:
Alliance of European Voluntary Service Organisations
Coordinating Committee for International Voluntary Service
UNESCO

Northern 'Sea Peoples' Excavation Project

Haifa University, Department of Archaeology
Mount Carmel 3I905 Israel
Tel.: ++972 (9) 891 0275 or (4) 824 0234
Fax: ++972 (4) 824 8128
E-mail: amitrom@012.net.il
http://assawir.haifa.ac.il/

Desc.:   This project is aimed at exploring the archaeology and the history of the "Northern (non-Philistine) Sea Peoples" Shardana and Sikulu and to establish the site's chronology and to find its fortification system. These tribes are known for been settled in the northern coast of Canaan in the 12th century BC. Tel Assawir was suggested to be a contact point between the coast controlled by the "Northern Sea-Peoples" and the Israelites who settled in the hill country. A preliminary survey recovered figurines, seals, pottery and stone objects. In conjunction with the project are 2 additional sites: El-Ahwat and Excavations at the Misliya Cave Mount Carmel. El-Ahwat, in Arabic "the walls", is a surprising discovery in the Biblical archaeology of a fortified site in central Israel. Exposed architecture influenced by the western Mediterranean Nuraghic style. The site was discovered during the survey of the hill country of Manasseh. Founded in the Iron Age it lived only about 50 years and then was abandoned, never to be settled again. The architecture found presumably connects the site with the buildings of Sardinia in the western Mediterranean. There, corridors and "tholoi" typified the Nuragic culture of Bronze and Iron Ages in the island; and similar constructions were unearthed on this site. Historically, it connected the place with the Shardana, one of the well-known "Sea peoples" tribes. The Shardnan were famous warriors and mercenaries. Originated at Sardinia, they said to be settled in Canaan together with the Philistines by pharaoh Ramesses III following his victory over the "Sea-peoples" (1180 BC). A view of the Misliya Cliff Mount Carmel has long been a global center of prehistoric research focusing on cultural adaptations, social complexity, ecological background to human evolution, the emergence of modern humans and the passage from hunting-gathering to agriculture. Misliya Cave offers a unique opportunity to unearth rich archaeological assemblages, animal bones, and human remains. This new project should shed important light on the enigmatic relationships between Homo sapiens and Neandertals in an area where, unlike other regions, they apparently share a common culture.

Per.: Bronze and Iron Ages.

Country: Israel.

Loc.: 8 miles (13km) east of Caesarea, at the entrance to the Wadi 'Ara pass.

Travel: From Jerusalem, Tel Aviv, or Haifa airports, take a bus to the Hadera central bus station for pick-up Sunday at 10:00 or take the hourly bus to the Kibbutz Barkai.

Dur.: 5 days (Sunday to Thursday), 4-week stay possible space permitting; July to August.

Age: Minimum 16.

Qualif.: No experience necessary.

Work: Excavation plus assignments, lectures, and guided bus tours. Monday to Thursday, 6:00–13:30 andSunday 12:00–18:30.

Lang.: English, Hebrew.

Accom.: Kibbutz Barkai, about 2 miles from the dig site. Rooms, with bathroom and kitchen, house 3–4 people; bedding provided. Meals in the dining room except breakfasts is at the site.

Cost: US$250 per workweek. Previous dig participants will receive a 5% discount. It is possible to stay at the Kibbutz on weekends for an extra US$35 per day (US$70 per full weekend). Accommodation, laundry; bedding, transportation to and from the site, participation in all activities of the dig, and dig tours included. Transfer from airport and back, health and other insurance, medical care, and personal expenses not included.

Applic.: On-line form. Contact the university for payment instructions.

Notes: Good health is necessary (in certain cases a medical certificate may be demanded). Consult website for what to bring.

North Pennines Heritage Trust

Nenthead Mines Visitor Centre
Nenthead, Alston,Cumbria. CA93PD UK
Tel.: ++44 (1434) 382 037 or 382 045
Fax: ++44 (1434) 382 294
E-mail: np.ht@virgin.net
www;npht.com

Desc.: Volunteers can take part in a variety of projects including the Diston Castle project and a series of smaller building conservation projects. Work ranges from field survey and building recording to fieldwork and post-excavation work. There are also opportunities in archive and research projects.
Per.: Medieval.
Country: United Kingdom.
Loc.: Nenthead, Cumbria.
Travel: Volunteers are responsible for their transport to the Trust.
Dur.: At volunteers' discretion; year round.
Age: Minimum 17.
Qualif.: No experience necessary.
Work: Survey, excavation, restoration, post-excavation, archiving, and research.
Lang.: English.
Accom.: Provided at the Trust bunk house with a kitchen, bathroom, lounge area, and washroom.
Cost: Volunteers must pay for their travel plus a limited contribution for food and accommodation.
Applic.: Contact the Trust for instructions.

Notre Dame Archaeology Field School

The University of Notre Dame, Department of Anthropology
Summer Sessions Office, Room 510 Main Building
Notre Dame, Indiana 46556-5602 USA
Tel.: ++1 (574) 631-7282 – Fax: ++1 (574) 631-6630
E-mail: Sumsess.1@nd.edu – Mark.R.Schurr.1@nd.edu
www.nd.edu/~mschurr/

Desc.: Three projects have been ongoing for several years. The Goodall Tradition Northwestern Indiana Hopewell, was a prehistoric Middle Woodland culture that inhabited northwestern Indiana between about 200 BC to 400 AD. The Historical Archaeology of Native American Strategies studies the Removal Period during the early 19th century (when the virtual extinction of Native American culture in the lower Great Lakes occurred) and the economic and political strategies that were used to resist removal. The Collier Lodge Site is one of the few remaining examples of the numerous hunting lodges that were once a prominent part of the local economy. Works are to stabilize and restore the lodge.

Per.: Prehistory to 19th century.

Country: United States.

Loc.: Northern Indiana.

Travel: Details provided upon application.

Dur.: 5 weeks; May to July.

Age: Minimum 18.

Qualif.: No experience necessary. Non-degree students do not have to meet regular admission requirements.

Work: Excavation, geophysical survey.

Lang.: English.

Accom.: Room and board is available on campus or participants can make their own arrangements.

Cost: Students are responsible for room, board, and some minor supplies. Van rides to and from campus to the site, all major field equipment, and most supplies are covered by a US$225 transportation and lab fee.

Applic.: Deadline May 27. Students and non-students may apply.

Ometepe Petroglyph Project

Culturelink
609 Aileen Street, Oakland California 94609 USA
Tel./Fax: ++1 (510) 654 8635
E-mail: suzannebaker@mac.com
http://culturelink.info/petro/

Desc.: The volunteer archaeological field survey of the Maderas half of the Nicaraguan, along the northern slopes of the Maderas volcano, where the project has recorded and mapped 73 archaeological sites. Almost 1700 petroglyph panels on 1400 boulders have been photographed, drawn, and catalogued as part of the survey. Isla Ometepe has been known since the 19th century to be relatively rich in pre-Columbian sites, artefacts, and a monumental sculptural tradition and to contain numerous petroglyphs. This project initiates systematic site inventory and petroglyph recording on the island.

Per.: Dinarte phase, early Polychrome; 2000–500 BC.

Country: Nicaragua.

Loc.: Island of Ometepe, the largest island on Lake Nicaragua.

Travel: Team members will meet at the International Airport in Managua and will be transported by bus and boat to the Island, then on to the town of Balgues where the hacienda is located.

Dur.: 2 weeks to 1 month; February to March.

Age: Minimum 18.

Qualif.: No experience necessary. Survey experience preferred.

Work: Field walking, survey, mapping, drawing and photographing the petroglyphs, collecting and washing diagnostic pottery, inking maps and drawings, and cataloguing and archiving data.

Lang.: English, Spanish.

Accom.: Hacienda. Dorm-style rooms, basic showers and plumbing.

Cost: US$350 per week. Accommodation, transport, and basic meals included. Consult project for further details.

Applic.: Deadline December 25.

Paestum Project – Between Environment and History

Legambiente
Via Salaria 403, 00199 Rome Italy
Tel.: ++39 (06) 8626 8324/5/6
Fax: ++39 (06) 8626 8319
E-mail: legambiente.vol@tiscalinet.it
www.legambiente.com/canale8/campi/

Desc.: The aim of this project is to manage the Torre a Mare Dunes Oasis, which goes from the sea to the walls of Old Paestum. In this ancient city Legambiente manages one of the towers with a laboratory of environmental education.

Per.: Grecian.

Country: Italy.

Loc.: Paestum Salerno.

Travel: By train from Naples or from Salerno.

Dur.: 7–10 days; year round.

Age: Minimum 18.

Qualif.: No experience necessary.

Work: Guardianship of the dunes' vegetation, welcoming visitors, managing 2 information boxes, environmental reclamation and care, manufacturing informative panels, and reclamation of a part of the walls.

Lang.: Italian.

Accom.: In the Legambiente Volunteers Centre in Paestum.

Cost: EUR200 (approx.US$215) plus membership fee.

Applic.: Inquire for instructions.

See also: Legambiente

Palaeoanthropology Field School in South Africa

Institute of Human Origins, Arizona State University
PO Box 874101, Tempe, Arizona 85287-4101 USA
Tel.: ++1 (480) 727 6580 Fax: ++1 (480) 727 6570
E-mail: human.origins@asu.edu – kaye.reed@asu.edu –
055kevin@chiron.wits.ac.za
www.asu.edu/clas/iho/field.htm

Desc.: The Makapansgat Valley is the site of 3 million years of human evolution, including the early *Australopithecus africanus* assemblage at the Limeworks Cave and the Middle Pleistocene locality of the Cave of Hearths. The valley is also the home of Buffalo Cave, which has yielded interesting Pleistocene fauna around 780,000 years old.

Per.: Pleistocene.

Country: South Africa.

Loc.: Makapansgat Valley

Travel: Details provided upon application.

Dur.: 5 weeks; July to August.

Age: Minimum 18.

Qualif.: Advanced undergraduate and graduate students, or those with strong anthropological or biological backgrounds. Ability to hike, conduct excavations, and withstand physical exertion. However, certain physical disabilities can be accommodated.

Work: Hominid fossil demonstrations; fieldtrips; excavation; fossil identification; excavation techniques; cave geology; ecology.

Lang.: English.

Accom.: Basic lodging.

Cost: US$4,500 per person. US$2,000 due April 1, remainder due May 1. Travel within South Africa, lodging, meals, insurance, and 6 credit hours from Arizona State University included. Airfare, passport/visa expenses, and vaccinations not included.

Applic.: On-line form. Send application with statement of purpose, copies of transcripts, and 2 recommendation letters from professors by e-mail, fax, or post. Deadline February 4. Applicants are notified by March 10 of their admission status.

Palaeo-World Research Foundation Expeditions

610 Tudor Drive, Winchester, Virginia 22603 USA
Tel.: ++1 (866) 678 0911 (toll free in NA).
Fax: ++1 (540) 678 0911
E-mail: paleo-world@paleo-world.com
www.paleo-world.com

Desc: The Foundation provides a unique hands-on educational opportunity to participate and explore the science of dinosaur palaeontology. China expeditions are also available through the PaleoDragon International Science Foundation dinosaur base in LuFong, China.

Per.: Palaeolithic.

Country: United States.

Loc.: Northeastern Montana, in the town of Jordan and the field expedition is within 35 miles (55km) of the town, on local ranches.

Travel: Fly into Billings, Montana, and then take the Greyhound bus (contact the local station for schedules and costs) to Miles City for pick-up or drive to Jordan and be met in town.

Dur.: 1 week; June to September. Dig-for-a-Day digs available.

Age: Minimum 18, unless with parents for a family dig.

Qualif.: No experience necessary.

Work: Survey, excavation, fossil preparation (plaster jacketing, casting, and moulding) and removal, and quarry mapping. Hiking, digging, and hauling within limits.

Lang.: English.

Accom.: There are 2 motels and several restaurants in town.

Cost: US$950 (full package) or US$650 (expedition only) plus deposit of US$250. US$1,900 (family up to 2 adults and 2 children under12; family not friends) plus US$400 deposit. Dig-for-a-Day is US$100 (adult), US$50 (12 and under), or US$250 (family).

Applic.: Registration and medical and liability forms must be filled and submitted along with the non-refundable deposit.

Notes: Student Grants are available for students working on a palaeontology related degree. See the website for details.

Passport in Time

Passport in Time Clearinghouse
PO Box 31315, Tucson, Arizona 85751-1315 USA
Tel.: ++1 (520) 722 2716 or toll free in NA (800) 281 9176
Fax: ++1 (520) 298 7044
E-mail: pit@sricrm.com
www.passportintime.com

Desc.: Passport in Time is a volunteer archaeology and historic preservation program of the USDA Forest Service. Volunteers work with professional archaeologists and historians on projects including archaeological. Past projects have included preservation of ancient cliff dwellings in New Mexico, excavations of prehistoric Indian villages or a 19th-century Chinese mining site in Hell's Canyon, Idaho, restoration of historical monuments or ancient art in Colorado, or survey for sites in remote wilderness areas.

Per.: Various.

Country: United States.

Loc.: Various.

Travel: Volunteers are responsible for travel to the project site.

Dur.: 4 days minimum; year round.

Age: Minimum 18.

Qualif.: No experience necessary.

Work: Excavation, rock art restoration, survey, archival research, historic structure restoration, gathering oral histories, or writing interpretive brochures.

Lang.: English.

Accom.: Camping; may be backcountry camping where volunteers are responsible for their own food and gear, or campsites with hook-ups for RVs, or volunteers may stay at local hotels and travel to the site each day. Some projects offer meals prepared by a camp cook, often for a small fee.

Cost: No fee to participate. No transport, food, or lodging provided. The projects vary in length from two days to two weeks

Applic.: On-line form.

Notes: Volunteers with disabilities may be accommodated.

Pella Volunteer Scheme

University of Sydney
NEAF, School of Archaeology A14, NSW 2006 Australia
Tel.: ++61 (2) 9351 2364/6394
Fax: ++61 (2) 9351 6392
E-mail: neaf@antiquity.usyd.edu.au – pella@antiquity.usyd.edu.au
http://acl.arts.usyd.edu.au/research/pella/

Desc.: The research is being conducted upon the Bronze Age Migdol Temple, as well as on the temple outbuildings, a Middle Bronze Age gate, and lovely Late Roman storehouses. The major ruin field at Pella covers an area of 10 hectares, although recent work by the Pella Hinterland Survey shows that the landscape was scattered with farmsteads, industrial installations and burials beyond the main areas of settlement.

Per.: Bronze Age to Late Roman.

Country: Jordan.

Loc.: Pella.

Travel: Details provided upon application.

Dur.: 9 weeks; January to March.

Age: Minimum 18. Inquire with project for family opportunities.

Qualif.: No experience or professional qualifications necessary.

Work: Excavation, sampling, and bagging artifacts. Part-time digging and working in the trenches and cleaning, sorting, and identifying artefacts. Training provided.

Lang.: English.

Accom.: Pella dig house, located in a compound on the main tell, with shared rooms (couples are accepted); all bedding provided; hot and cold running water, western-style bathing facilities; laundry; and mix of Arabic and Western food is provided.

Cost: AUS$3,200 (approx. US$1,940), subject to currency fluctuations. Transfers to and from the dig and full room and board included.

Applic.: On-line form. Approximately 45 volunteers accepted.

Notes: Optional trips to visit other tourist attractions in Jordan once a week are offered at a small additional cost for the hire of a coach, site charges, and lunch.

Piddington

Upper Nene Archaeological Society (UNAS)
Toadhall, 86 Main Road, Hackleton, Northampton NN7 2AD UK
Tel.: ++44 (1604) 870 312
Fax: ++44 (1933) 318 211
E-mail: unarchsoc@aol.com – unas@friendship-taylor.freeserve.co.uk
www.unas.org.uk – www.members.aol.com/unarchsoc/unashome.htm

Desc.: The Upper Nene Archaeological Society was formed in 1962 by several active local fieldworkers who wanted to share their knowledge of what they were finding out about the area's prehistoric and Roman past. The Society has since grown to over 150 members, mainly from Northamptonshire, but also from other parts of Britain and the world. An independent society and a registered charity, UNAS aims to promote study and interest in archaeology, the discovery and investigation of sites and the preservation of items of archaeological interest of all periods. The Piddington project is an excavation of a late Iron Age settlement and Romano-British villa.

Per.: Late Iron Age and Romano-British.

Country: United Kingdom.

Loc.: Piddington off B526 Northampton-Newport Pagnell Road.

Travel: Train from London Euston to Northampton, takes about 1:15 hours unless fast train is available.

Dur.: 2 weeks; August.

Age: Minimum 18. Special consideration may be given to very keen 15–17-year-old volunteers.

Qualif.: No experience necessary.

Work: Excavation.

Lang.: English.

Accom.: Accommodation can be arranged. Camping next to the site. Meals arranged.

Cost: GB£38(US$60) for members for 3 weeks; GB£45 for non-members; GB£30 and GB£35 respectively for 2weeks; GB£20 for 1 week only for members. Costs are subject to change.

Applic.: Include a self-addressed envelope or 2 IRCs with application.

Notes: Contact Roy or Liz Friendship-Taylor.

Poulton Research Project

27 Morton Road, Chester CH1 5NR
Tel.: ++44 (1244) 377092
Fax: ++44 (1244) 390091
E-mail: patricia@gorsuch.freeserve.co.uk
http://srs.dl.ac.uk/arch/poulton

Desc.: This is a long-term research investigation into the evolution of the historic, environmental, social, and economic landscape of Cheshire, in particular the hinterland of Chester. It is based on a medieval chapel associated with the lost Cistercian Abbey of Poulton together with its associated cemetery. The site has also provided positive evidence for the location of a Roman villa/farmstead/temple. The abbey site lies on another estate and a small trench has already yielded a finely carved spiral sandstone staircase blocked off by a 16th/17th-century brick wall. The Project is community based and welcomes volunteers and students as well as special needs groups.

Per.: Multi-period; Neolithic to 19th century.

Country: United Kingdom.

Loc.: 5 miles (8km)southwest of Chester, on the Welsh border.

Travel: Participants arrive to Chester via plane, train, bus, or car. They will be met in Chester and taken to their campsite or hostel.

Dur.: 2 days; July to August.

Age: Minimum 16. No upper restriction but must be physically fit enough to endure hard labour.

Qualif.: No experience necessary. Mainly university students.

Work: Excavation.

Lang.: English.

Accom.: None provided. Campsite or hostel nearby. Transport to and from the site is provided.

Cost: GB£100 (approx. US$150) per week or GB£20 (US$30) per day.

Applic.: On-line form. Accepted volunteers receive an information package, including site location maps and further details.

Notes: Contact Patricia Piercy.

Pro International

Bahnhofstrasse 26A, 35037 Marburg Germany
Tel.: ++49 (6421) 65277
Fax: ++49 (6421) 64407
E-mail: pro-international@lahn.net
www.campinformation.info

Desc.:	This organisation facilitates international workcamps for young people to exchange experiences and to learn more about other social, cultural, and political living conditions by working and living together in an international group.
Per.:	Various.
Country:	Worldwide.
Loc.:	Various.
Travel:	Detailed information is available on the website.
Dur.:	1–2 weeks.
Age:	16–26.
Qualif.:	No experience necessary
Work:	Reconstruction 5–6 hours per day; Monday to Friday.
Lang.:	English or language of host country.
Accom.:	Simple accommodation, in youth hostels, schools, huts, empty houses, or tents. Basic furniture, beds, mattresses, blankets, etc., and equipment for self-catering provided.
Cost:	No project fee. Includes accommodation and food. Volunteers pay travel-costs, personal expenses, partial costs for leisure trips, excursions, and other activities of the group.
Applic.:	On-line form. EUR65 registration fee is to be paid upon application. After application the placement is confirmed through the partner organisation. Detailed information about the camp and description, map, travel instructions, etc., will be made available.
Notes:	Owing to agreements with partner organisations in several hosting countries prospective volunteers from those countries are given the appropriate contacts.

See also:
Duensberg Project

Ramat Hanadiv Excavations

Institute of Archaeology, The Hebrew University of Jerusalem
Mount Scopus Jerusalem 91905 Israel
Tel.: ++972 (2) 588 2403/4
Fax: ++972 (2) 582 5548
E-mail: bentor@h2.hum.huji.ac.il
www.hum.huji.ac.il/archaeology

Desc.: The excavation of an ancient Herodian palace will focus on the reception hall, peristyle courtyard, and triclinium. The site contains a very rich assemblage of artefacts reflecting many facets of daily life at Ramat Hanadiv.

Per.: Early Roman.

Country: Israel.

Loc.: The southern edge of Mount Carmel, about 6 miles (10km) northeast of Caesarea.

Travel: Taxi from airport to Kefar Glickson. Alternatively, a combination of buses and trains is necessary (consult website for details).

Dur.: 1 week; July to August.

Age: Minimum 18.

Qualif.: No experience necessary.

Work: Exposing architectural remains, cleaning, and registering pottery and other artefacts. Monday to Friday, 5:30–13:00.

Lang.: English.

Accom.: Kibbutz Kefar Glickson, about 8km east of Ramat Hanadiv. Apartment-style suites with 2 bedrooms (sleeps 3–4), 2 bathrooms, and a kitchen; or the Youth Hostel with rooms that sleep 3–4 with a common bathroom and kitchen. Meals, project transport, bedding, and towels provided.

Cost: US$350 per week for the youth hostel, US$400, US$480, or US$640 per week for various rooms at the kibbutz.

Applic.: Contact the project by fax or e-mail.

Notes: Bring work clothes and gloves, sturdy shoes, and a flashlight. Volunteers must arrange their own health insurance.

See also:
Hebrew University of Jerusalem

Rempart

1, rue des Guillemites, 75004 Paris France
Tel.: ++33 (1) 42 71 96 55
Fax: ++33 (1) 42 71 73 00
E-mail: contact@rempart.com
www.rempart.com

Desc.:	Rempart, a union of conservation associations in France, organises short voluntary work schemes around the world. The projects are all based around restoration and maintenance of historic sites and buildings, from a glamorous French chateau to a garden in Vietnam.
Per.:	Various.
Country:	Worldwide.
Loc.:	Various.
Travel:	Details provided upon application.
Dur.:	2 weeks; year round.
Age:	Minimum 17 or 18.
Qualif.:	Some previous voluntary experience is required.
Work:	Restoration; usually 30–35 hours per week.
Lang.:	French.
Accom.:	Basic accommodations; varies with each camp.
Cost:	About GB£10 (US$16) per day. Includes food and lodging.
Applic.:	Contact the organisation.

Rochford Hundred Field Archaeology Group

63 Orchard Avenue, Hockley, Essex, SS5 5BA UK
Tel.: ++44 (702) 200 461
E-mail: rhfag@hotmail.com
www.fortunecity.com/victorian/villiers/1325/

Desc.: The aims of this group is to re-establish the tradition of independent fieldwork by unpaid volunteer archaeologists. It undertakes archaeological work either in its own name or in support of other local and under-resourced organisations.
Per.: Various.
Country: United Kingdom.
Loc.: Southeast Essex.
Travel: Details provided upon application.
Dur.: Day digs and organised excursions.
Age: Minimum 16.
Qualif.: No experience necessary.
Work: Excavation and survey. Training provided.
Lang.: English.
Accom.: None.
Cost: Annual membership subscriptions: GB£15 (US$22) or GB£10 for retirees and GB£5 for students/ unwaged.
Applic.: On-line form or contact directly.
Notes: Contact Annette Salmons

Royal Tyrrell Museum Day Digs & Volunteer Preparation Program

PO Box 7500, Drumheller, Alberta TOJ OYO Canada
Tel.: ++1 (403) 823 7707 Fax: ++1(403) 823 7131
Call toll free in Alberta 310-0000 or in NA 1 (888) 440 4240
E-mail: info@tyrrellmuseum.com
www.tyrrellmuseum.com

Desc.: The Day Digs give participants the chance to be a "Palaeontologist For A Day" assisting in on-going research by working with museum staff in an actual quarry, excavating dinosaur bones and discovering the different aspects of palaeontology. The Volunteer Preparation Program (VPP) undertakes the preparation of fossils from the park under the supervision and training of technicians and museum staff.

Per.: Late Cretaceous.

Country: Canada.

Loc.: Royal Tyrrell Museum, Drumheller Valley, Alberta, for Day Digs; Field Station of the Royal Tyrrell Museum, Dinosaur Provincial Park, near Brooks, Alberta, for Volunteer Preparation Program.

Travel: Calgary International Airport, bus transportation or car rental from Calgary to museum. No transport provided for VPP.

Dur.: Day Digs run daily 8:30–4:00; June to October. The VPP runs 1 day perweek and every other weekend from October to March.

Age: Minimum 10 for Day Digs (youth must be accompanied by an adult); 15 for VPP.

Qualif.: No experience necessary

Work: Excavation for Day Digs. Fossil preparation for volunteers.

Lang.: English.

Accom.: None. Hotels and B&Bs are present in the area.

Cost: CAD$90 (US$60) per adult; CAD$60 per youth (ages 10–15) for Day Digs. No charge for the Volunteer Preparation Program.

Applic.: On-line form or phone for Day Digs. Volunteers apply through the Head of Research of the museum.

See also:
Royal Tyrrell Museum Field Experience

Royal Tyrrell Museum Field Experience

PO Box 7500
Drumheller, Alberta T0J 0Y0 Canada
Tel.: ++1 (403) 823 7707   Fax: ++1(403) 823 7131
Call toll free in Alberta 310-0000 or in NA 1 (888) 440 4240
E-mail: info@tyrrellmuseum.com
www.tyrrellmuseum.com

Desc.: Work alongside Royal Tyrrell Museum scientists and technicians in an integrated field research programme in Alberta's world-famous badlands at the UNESCO World Heritage Site, Dinosaur Provincial Park. The Museum maintains a year-round interpretive centre and laboratory facility at the Park as well as a field camp.

Per.: Late Cretaceous and later.

Country: Canada.

Loc.: Dinosaur Provincial Park.

Travel: Calgary International airport, bus to Drumheller for pickup.

Dur.: 1–2 weeks; May to August.

Age: Minimum 18.

Qualif.: No experience necessary. Palaeontology students are welcome and limited bursaries are available. Good physical condition is required.

Work: Prospecting, excavation, and survey. Laboratory and museum work for specimen preparation and display.

Lang.: English.

Accom.: Permanent field station in the park with air-conditioned ATCO sleeping trailers with semi-private rooms, men's and women's bathrooms and showers, laundry room, and cookhouse and dining room; tenting at the other camp sites.

Cost: CAD$950 (US$620) per week. Includes room and board, and work-related supplies; 10% discount to previous participants.

Applic.: On-line form. Applications are accepted in February with CAD$300 (US$200) deposit. Balance due upon arrival.

Notes: Rainy days are often spent in the laboratory or the museum.

See also:
Royal Tyrrell Day Digs & Volunteer Preparation Program

Rural Ireland Lifeways Project

Centre for the Study of Rural Ireland
Campus Box 4660, Illinois State University
Normal, Illinois 61790-4660 USA
Tel.: ++1 (309) 438 2271 – E-mail: ceorser@ilstu.edu
www.internationalstudies.ilstu.edu/
www.ilstu.edu/~ceorser/field_school.htm

Desc.: This anthropologically based project specifically concentrates on the archaeology rural villages of Irish peasants during the 1750–1850 period and possibly earlier. Excavations have occurred on 3 tenant village sites in north County Roscommon and in County Sligo to retreive artefacts of the rural Irish home.

Per.: Modern; 18–19th centuries.

Country: Ireland.

Loc.: North County Roscommon and County Sligo.

Travel: Details provided upon application.

Dur.: 3–6 weeks; June to August.

Age: Minimum 18.

Qualif.: No experience necessary.

Work: Excavation.

Lang.: English.

Accom.: In Riverstown, a small town about 12 miles (20km) south of Sligo in a self-catering apartment or B&B. Students prepare their own lunches for the field but dinners are provided.

Cost: Approximately US$2,000 for 3 weeks and US$600 per each additional week. Instructional costs, room and board, project-related travel, and an international ID card included. Airfare and personal expenses not included.

Applic.: Deadline May 1. Contact the Office of International Studies for an application form at Campus Box 6120, Illinois State University, Normal, IL 61790-6120, tel. ++1 (309) 438 5365 or e-mail oisp@ilstu.edu.

Notes: Academic credit available through the Illinois State University. Non-ISU students must enroll in the University for the summer.

La Sabranenque

Rue de la Tour de l'Oume
30290 Saint Victor la Coste France
Tel.: ++33 (4) 6650 0505
Fax: ++33 (4) 6650 1248
E-mail: info@sabranenque.com
www.sabranenque.com

Desc.: Summer Volunteer sessions allow volunteers to join with La Sabranenque to take part in the on-going restoration of Mediterranean architecture projects. Volunteers work in the morning and the occasionally afternoon. Volunteer & Visit is a work programme on historic sites coupled with outings that offer the discovery of the towns, monuments, and countryside of Provence.

Per.: Medieval to 19th century.

Country: France, Italy.

Loc.: Various villages.

Travel: Details provided upon application.

Dur.: 2 weeks; June through September for Summer Volunteer sessions. 1 week; March, April, May, October for Volunteer & Visit.

Age: Minimum 18.

Qualif.: No experience necessary.

Work: Work varies depending on the project but most involve stone masonry. Other techniques used can include any stage of historic restoration, from clearing of rubble to roof-tiling, stone-cutting, flooring with tiles or wood, interior plastering, arch and vault construction, path paving, dry-stone walling, etc.

Lang.: English, French, or Italian.

Accom.: In stone houses in the beautiful old village that La Sabranenque has restored; 2 per room.

Cost: US$580 for 2-week period. Room, board, and project-related expenses included.

Applic.: Mail in form.

San Giorgio Convent

Legambiente
Via Salaria 403, 00199 Rome Italy
Tel.: ++39 (06) 8626 8324/5/6
Fax: ++39 (06) 8626 8319
E-mail: legambiente.vol@tiscalinet.it
www.legambiente.com/canale8/campi/

Desc.: The aims of this project are: stimulating the micro-economy of the Regional Park Sirente Velino and obtaining a partial self-sufficiency of the convent through the cultivation of biological products. The convent dates back to the 17th century and pathway net is from the transhumance zone.

Per.: 1600 AD.

Country: Italy.

Loc.: Goriano Valli, Tione degli Abruzzi municipality, Regional Park Sirente Velino, Abruzzi region Central Italy.

Travel: Rome to L'Aquila by train, then bus or train to Goriano Valli.

Dur.: 10 days to 1 month; year round.

Age: Minimum 18; project for teenagers from 15–17 available.

Qual.: No experience necessary. Experience with brickwork and gardening is an advantage.

Work: Convent and garden maintenance, pathway works, and cleaning of the park. Workday is 7 hours, 6 days per week.

Lang.: Italian.

Accom.: In the former convent, in bedrooms with 2–8 beds per room plus bathroom.

Cost: EUR200 (approx.US$215) plus membership fee.

Applic.: Inquire for instructions.

See also:
Legambiente

Saveock Mill

37 Queen St., Penzance
Cornwall TR18 4BH UK
E-mail: tmrowe@aol.com

Desc.: The aim of the project is to understand the human use of the valley from prehistory into the present day. The dig will be looking at the site of the original medieval farmhouse at Saveock and a unique site that includes stone lined drains, a water pit, a platform area that has the remains of a bowl furnace and flue within it and a casting pit.

Per.: Medieval to present.

Country: United Kingdom.

Loc.: In a river valley close to the city of Truro, Cornwall.

Travel: Details provided upon application.

Dur.: July to August.

Age: All ages welcome.

Qualif.: No experience necessary.

Work: Volunteers will be given instruction in all aspects of excavation from recording to finds work. The workweek is Monday to Friday. Experimental archaeology possibilities in nearby Cornish Celtic Village.

Lang.: English.

Accom.: Camping.

Cost: GB£180 (approx. US$270) per week. Food, camping, and tuition included.

Applic.: Contact Toni-maree Rowe.

SCI – Service Civil International

International Secretariat
St-Jacobsmarkt 82, B-2000 Antwerpen, Belgium
Tel.: ++32 (3) 226 5727
Fax: ++32 (3) 232 0344
E-mail: sciint@sciint.org
www.sciint.org

Desc.: SCI is a voluntary NGO founded in 1920 that aims to promote international understanding and peace. It provides volunteers for projects in the United States and Europe for communities that cannot afford labour. Every year more than 20,000 volunteers of all nationalities work in over 100 camps. SCI has operational relations with UNESCO and is a member of CCIVS, YFJ, AVSO, and UNITED for Intercultural Affairs.

Per.: Various.

Country: Western and Eastern Europe, United States, Australia.

Loc.: Various.

Travel: Details provided upon application to specific project.

Dur.: 2–3 weeks; mainly June to September. People with workcamp experience can volunteer for 3–6 months.

Age: Minimum 18 for Europe; minimum 16 for the United States.

Qualif.: No experience necessary.

Work: Reconstruction of cultural and historical buildings; workcamps.

Lang.: English. For other languages, inquire with local SCI office.

Accom: Typically tent camping or dormitories. Bring a sleeping bag.

Cost: US$65–300, depending upon country. Accommodation, food, and insurance included. Transportation not included.

Applic.: Standard application; no need to be a member.

Notes: See SCI Germany at www.sci-d.de; SCI-IVS USA at www.sci-ivs.org; IVS (International Voluntary Service is part of a wider international group in the British chapter of SCI) at www.ivsgbn.demon.co.uk; IVP Australia at www.ivp.org.au.

See also:
SCI Spain – Servicio Civil Internacional

SCI Spain – Servicio Civil Internacional

C/ Fomento, 18 Bajo 28012 Madrid Spain
Tel.: ++34 (91) 542 4263
Fax: ++34 (91) 559 2307
E-mail: oficina@ongsci.org
www.ongsci.org/
www.nodo50.org/siv/index1.html

Desc.: This is the Spanish Branch of Service Civil International (SCI); it organises workcamps in various sectors including archaeology and historical restoration.

Per.: Various; from prehistoric to modern.

Country: Spain and worldwide.

Loc.: Various.

Travel: Details provided upon application with specific project.

Dur.: 2–5 weeks.

Age: Minimum 18.

Qualif.: No experience necessary.

Work: Excavation or restoration 35–40 hours per week.

Lang.: Spanish.

Cost: Participants must be members of SCI Spain (membership EUR 25, approx. US$27) or of their national SCI branch. Participation fee for each workcamp is EUR 75 (approx.US$80).

Accom.: Mostly dormstyle accommodation (with bunkbeds) in schools, youth hostels, religious institutions. Occasionally volunteers lodge in campgrounds and must bring their own tent.

Applic.: Consult www.sciint.org for contact in home country. If a local national branch does not exist application must be made directly with SCI Spain.

See also:

SCI – Service Civil International

Sedgeford Archaeological and Historical Research Project

Dove House, 32 School Road
Heacham, Norfolk PE31 7DQ UK
Tel.: ++44 (1485) 570 414
E-mail: mcmackie@globalnet.co.uk
www.sharp.org.uk

Desc.: This is among the largest and best-appointed projects for volunteer excavators in the country, setting out to investigate the entire history and origins of this delightful Norfolk village. The project takes a democratic approach and tries to ensure that everyone understands what is going on and can take part in the process of investigation.

Per.: Middle Saxon to early Medieval.

Country: United Kingdom.

Loc.: Sedgeford, Norfolk.

Travel: Heathrow or Gatwick International airport; train to London King's Cross or Liverpool Street; bus or taxi to Sedgeford. Extensive details on how to arrive by car, bike, or foot on website. Further details provided upon application.

Dur.: 1 week; July to August.

Age: Minimum 18; families may be possible.

Qualif.: No experience necessary.

Work: Excavation, training, research.

Lang.: English.

Accom.: Camping with toilets, hot water showers, and laundry facilities. B&B's available. Catered meals.

Cost: GB£125–140 (approx. US 180–210) per week; student rate GB£95–110. Full subsistence (tent, facilities, meals) included; GB£50 for project only; no camping or meals. Cost range dependant upon dates.

Applic.: On-line form. Payment deadline March 1 for spring, June 1 for summer season. Contact Chris Mackie, SHARP Enrolment Secretary, 19a Neville Road, Heacham, King's Lynn, PE31 7HA UK, tel.: ++44 (1485) 570 452.

Notes: Several subjects of investigation available with this project.

Semirechie and South Kazakhstan Archaeological Camp

Institute of Archaeology of Almaty, ISP—International Scientific Projects
Tole Bi 21, Suite 31, 480100 Almaty, Kazakhstan
Tel.: ++7 (3272) 91 73 38 or 91 82 93
Fax: ++7 (3272) 91 61 11
E-mail: ispkz@nursat.kz
www.cincpac.com/afos/posts/986.html

Desc.: In the region of south Kazakhstan and Semirechie (the land of the "Seven rivers" stretching along the piedmonts of the Tianshan from the Talas valley to the Djungarian Gate and where the modern towns of Taraz, Bishkek, and Almaty are situated) 4 camps are organised: Balasas; The Petroglyphs of Chu-Ili Mountians; Koilyk; and Otrar.

Per.: Multi-period; Bronze, Iron, and Middle Ages.

Country: Kazakhstan.

Loc.: Balasas is a valley of the Dzungarian mountains, 250 miles (400km) northeast of Almaty. The Chu-Ili Mountains are in a semi-desert landscape southwest of Balkhash Lake, Tamgaly. Koilyk is situated on the piedmonts of the Dzungarian mountains, 375 miles (600km) northeast of Almaty (Semirechie) near to the Lepsy River. The Otrar oasis covers an area of 200km^2 of medieval remains; the main town is Otrar.

Travel: Details provided upon application.

Dur.: 15 days to 1 month; July to October.

Age: Minimum 18; students under 18 in school groups possible.

Qualif.: Volunteers and archaeology students welcome.

Work: Survey, excavation, and lectures.

Lang.: English.

Accom.: Student hotel in Almaty , tents in the field, or country houses in Koilyk-Antonovka.

Cost: US$250 per week. Transport, food, tent lodging, and lectures included. US$30 administration fee for foreigners.

Applic.: Contact the project for details.

Notes: Anti-tetanus recommended. Valid passport and visa required.

Sha'ar Hagolan
Archaeological Excavations and Neolithic Art Centre

Institute of Archaeology, The Hebrew University of Jerusalem
Mount Scopus Jerusalem 91905 Israel
Tel.: ++972 (2) 588 2403/4   Fax: ++972 (2) 582 5548
E-mail: msgarf@pluto.mscc.huji.ac.il – MICMIL@aol.com
www.hum.huji.ac.il/archaeology/

Desc.: The Neolithic village of Sha'ar Hagolan is an important prehistoric art centre in Israel for the study of the function and use of art objects in the Neolithic period. The emphasis is on the discovery of artefacts in the site (houses, rooms, courtyard, graves, etc.) plus other aspects of the material culture, which indicate a long-distance exchange network, connecting remote areas in the ancient Near East; and animal bones and botanical remains to reconstruct the economy of this ancient agricultural community.

Per.: Neolithic (8000–7500 years ago).

Country: Israel.

Loc.: Sha'ar Hagolan is 1 mile (1.5km) south of the Sea of Galilee in the Jordan Valley. The closest town is Tiberias.

Travel: Buses run from the airport to the central bus station in Tel-Aviv and onwards to Tiberias, then local taxi to Kibbutz Sha'ar Hagolan.

Dur.: 3–6 weeks (1 term or full season); June to August.

Age: Minimum 18.

Qualif.: No experience necessary. Field training and lectures provided.

Work: Excavation, sieving, washing, cleaning, sorting, and recording the objects, workshops and lectures. Workdays are Monday to Friday. Excavations are under sunshades but good health is required as the work is in the heat and involves lifting and carrying buckets weighing up to 45 pounds (20kg).

Lang.: English.

Accom.: Kibbutz Sha'ar Hagolan (10-minute walk from the site) has air-conditioned rooms, 4 standard beds per room. Sheets, blankets, and pillows provided but not towels. Running water, hot showers (24 hours a day), electricity, conventional sanitation, a small kitchen with a refrigerator, and coffee/tea facilities. Free laundry once a week.

Cost: US$1,100 for full season (6 weeks), US$600 for 1 term (3 weeks). US$50 registration fee sent directly to Dr. Michele Miller. Payment for room and board upon arrival. Credit cards welcome. Weekends at the kibbutz are free of charge.

Applic.: On-line form.

Notes: Bring medical and accident insurance documentation, work clothes and shoes (not sandals), towels, sunscreen, and personal items. A local supermarket sells basic needs. Academic credit available through the Rothberg International School of the Hebrew University of Jerusalem with additional fees.

See also:

Hebrew University of Jerusalem

Silchester Roman Town Life Project

Reading University, Department of Archaeology
Whiteknights, PO Box 227, Reading RG6 6AB UK
Tel.: ++44 (118) 931 6255
Fax: ++44 (118) 931 6718
E-mail: a.s.clarke@reading.ac.uk
www.silchester.rdg.ac.uk

Desc.: A major long-term excavation of a Roman town, run as a training dig for Reading University. Excavations are looking at approximately a third of a single *insula*, in the heart of the commercial and industrial quarter of the town.

Per.: Late Iron Age to sub-Roman.

Country: United Kingdom.

Loc.: Halfway between Reading and Basingstoke.

Travel: See website for specific details.

Dur.: July to August.

Age.: Minimum 16.

Qualif.: The field school is suitable for both beginners and those with some experience.

Work: Urban excavation; volunteering and training.

Lang.: English.

Accom.: Camping with running water and hot showers. Volunteer must bring own tent.

Cost: GB£200 (approx.US$300) per 6-day week. Food and campsite facilities included. Tent and personal items not included.

Applic.: Apply to the Department of Archaeology, Reading University.

Notes: Contact Amanda Clarke

Sino American Field School of Archaeology

SAFSA and the Museum of Asian Art
4206 - 73rd Terrace East, Sarasota, Florida 34243 USA
Tel./Fax: ++1 (941) 351 8208
E-mail: fmfsafsa@Juno.com
www.geocities.com/fmfsafsa/

Desc.: In 1990, the Fudan Museum Foundation in collaboration with Xi'an Jiaotong University and the Archaeological Research Institute of Shaanxi Province, established the Sino-American Field School of Archaeology (SAFSA). The Education Commission of Shaanxi Province, China, and the Society of Professional Archaeologists, USA, accredited the school. Since about 1906 China was closed to foreign archaeologists; SAFSA was the first foreign group that had a permit to excavate in Xi'an together with Chinese archaeologists. Participants have the opportunity to establish future scholarly collaboration with Chinese specialists. The basic principle of the school is not only the summer archaeological practice, but also a good will gesture toward the Chinese people.

Per.: Prehistory through Tang; 1000 BC to 907 AD.

Country: China.

Loc.: Shaanxi Province; mainly salvage excavations near Xi'an.

Travel: Individual flight from participants' home. Flights must be arranged for all participants arrive on the same day at Shanghai-Pudong airport. Departure to home is from Beijing.

Dur.: 1 month; July to August.

Age: Minimum 17.

Qualif.: Open for students from seniors of high school, college/university students, teachers, professors, and a limited number of interested adults.

Work: Excavation practicum, restoration, and the study of Chinese cultural history with guest lectures from Chinese specialists.

Lang.: English.

Accom.: Hotels.

Cost: US$3,795 participation fee. Roundtrip from JFK New York, air travel from Shanghai to Xi'an to Beijing, tuition and textbook, room and board (3 meals per day, double occupancy lodging), excursions, and tour (Beijing, Shanghai, and nearby areas) included. Deduct US$1,100 from the participation fee if flying independently.

Applic.: Request application form from Dr. Alfonz Lengyel, American Director, and return it with a passport photocopy and US$200 down payment for registration fee. First half of the participation fee due April 1, second half due May 15 by cashier's check payable to Fudan Museum Foundation – Safsa. Participation is limited to 15.

Notes: Academic credit available through Xi'an Jiaotong University with approval from home institution. Participants are responsible for their own sickness, accident and travel insurance. Consult with appropriate health authorities about vaccination requirements in China.

Slavia Project

Rybitwy 12, Lednogora, 62-261, Poland
Tel.: ++(61) 427 4968
Fax: ++(61) 427 5020
E-mail: fieldwork@poczta.onet.pl
www.slavia.org

Desc.: Excavations continue at the early medieval stronghold town of Giecz, whose interior structures include a very well preserved 11th-century stone church, with the only known passage crypt in Poland. Human bone deposits here are found in 2 ossarium layers. Students will excavate an associated, exterior cemetery site used from the second half of the 11th century to the end of the 12th century. Grave offerings include knives, decorative heads, rings, coins, amber and bone artifacts and articles yet to be found. Skeletal preservation is excellent. Beneath the cemetery lie the remains of an earlier tribal settlement, dating to the 8th–10th centuries.

Per.: Early Medieval; 9th–11th centuries AD.

Country: Poland.

Loc.: The contemporary village of Giecz, Wielkopolska.

Travel: Details provided upon application.

Dur.: 2 weeks; July to October.

Age: Minimum 18.

Qualif.: No experience necessary.

Work: Excavation, drawing, record keeping, artefact analysis and handling, mapping and surveying, lectures, and tours.

Lang.: English, Polish.

Accom.: Within the Giecz stronghold. Food is local cuisine; vegetarians can be accommodated.

Cost: Approx. US$470 per week. Room and board, transportation within the country, instruction, field trips, admission fees, and equipment included. Airfare not included.

Applic.: Contact Project Director Dr. Marek Polcyn for details.

Notes: Academic credit available through the Adam Mickiewicz University, Poznan.

SMELT Low Birker

Michigan Technological University, Department of Social Sciences
1400 Townsend Drive, Houghton, Michigan 49931 USA
Tel.: ++1 (906) 487 2113 or 487 2160
Fax: ++1 (906) 487 2468
E-mail: smelt@up.net – ceblair@mta.edu
www.social.mtu.edu/smelt/

Desc.: Since 1988 SMELT has sought to explore issues relating to early, large scale primary production, principally relating to wrought iron through a mix of experimentation and excavation. SMELT was founded as an experimental archaeology project designed to look at how tall shaft furnaces might have operated in the European Iron Age. Replica furnaces have been fired and utilised to compare the ground level and below ground level remains to those known from European sites.

Per.: Viking Age; 1000 AD.

Country: United Kingdom.

Loc.: Upper Esk Valley, Cumbria.

Travel: Pick-up at Ravenglass Railway Station. Easy connections from Manchester Airport.

Dur.: 2-week volunteer period; 6-week field school;June to July.

Age: Minimum 18.

Qualif.: No experience necessary. Participants must be able to walk a mile and lift 25 lbs.

Work: Excavation, survey, and remote sensing.

Lang.: English.

Accom.: Woolpack Inn. Field students will stay in purpose-built bunkhouse, basically a private youth hostel. Senior staff and volunteers may stay in the hotel portion of the Inn.

Cost: US$1,380 for 2-weeks; US$1,670 for 3 weeks; US$2,980 for 6 weeks. Room and board included. Personal expenses not included.

Applic.: Center for International Education at Michigan Technological University, www.mtu.edu/cie or call ++1 (906) 487 2160.

Notes: Contact Dr. Carl Blair

Società Friulana di Archeologia

c/o Civici Musei di Udine
Torre di Porta Villalta, Via Micesio 2, 33100 Udine Italy
Tel./Fax: ++39 (0432) 26560
E-mail: direzione@archeofriuli.it – sfaud@archeofriuli.it
www.archeofriuli.it

Desc.: Founded in 1989, during the excavation of Savorgnan Palace in Udine, the organisation carries out voluntary activities in cultural heritage, making excavations and restorations and promoting studies and publications in collaboration with Civici Musei of Udine and Soprintendenza del Friuli – Venezia Giulia. Thanks to meetings, courses for members, and lessons in the schools, it tries to promote the consciousness of the archaeological heritage of the region, also through exhibitions. Since 1991 it has published the annual review *Quaderni Friulani di Archeologia*.

Per.: Middle Ages and Protohistory; 10th–14th centuries AD.

Country: Italy.

Loc.: In the towns of Attimis, Nimus, Gradiscutta di Varmo, and Verzegnis in the Province of Udine in northeastern Italy.

Travel: All the sites are located near Udine and can be reached by bus from the railway station.

Dur.: 2 weeks.

Age: Minimum 18.

Qualif.: No experience necessary.

Work: Excavation, documentation, mapping, etc.

Lang.: Italian, English.

Accom.: In dormitory style structures.

Cost: EUR25–30 (approx. US$ 27–32). Board, lodging, and insurance included.

Applic.: By ordinary mail, fax, or e-mail.

Note: Participants must have steel-toed working boots, working gloves and clothes, water-bottle, safety helmet, etc.

South Cadbury Environs Project

Archaeology Department, Bristol University
The Laurels, Chapel Lane, North Cadbury, Yeovil BA22 7DE UK
Tel.: ++44 (1963) 220 435
E-mail: RTabor8387@aol.com
www.southcadbury.org.uk

Desc.: The project is set in the hinterland of Cadbury Castle at an Iron Age hillfort in Somerset. It places volunteers in a stunning landscape where they participate in geophysical survey, mini-excavation, and ploughzone sampling.

Per.: Neolithic, Bronze Age, Iron Age, Romano-British, early Medieval

Country: United Kingdom.

Loc.: Southeast Somerset

Travel: Meeting point at 1 Dairy Cottage, South Cadbury, at 9:30 on their first morning, unless otherwise arranged. Volunteers travelling by train or bus may be picked up from either Castle Cary railway station or Yeovil bus station (Glovers Walk).

Dur.: 2, 5-day weeks for international volunteers; April to November. 1 or more days per week for local volunteers; January to November.

Age: Minimum 18; local volunteers may be younger.

Qualif.: No experience necessary. Physical fitness is required.

Work: Survey, artefact collection, test pitting, and training.

Lang.: English.

Accom.: A list of available local accommodation is available on the website or upon application.

Cost: Accommodation and transport.

Applic.: On-line form. Contact Dr. Richard Tabor.

Notes: Participants in magnetic geophysical survey must be absolutely metal free, i.e., no inserted medical devices (metal pins, pacemakers, etc.), no piercings, and no clothing with metal zips, buttons, support wiring, hooks, etc.

South Quantock Archaeological Survey

King Alfred's College, Department of Archaeology
Winchester, Hampshire, SO22 4NR UK
Tel.: ++44 (1962) 841 515 (ext.2603)
Fax: ++44 (1962) 827 385
E-mail: p.marter@wkac.ac.uk
www.wkac.ac.uk/quantocks/

Desc.: The Southern Quantock Archaeological Survey aims to study crop mark sites identified from aerial photography in an area between Bishop's Lydeard and North Petherton in Somerset. The sites range in date from the later prehistoric to medieval periods. The Project provides training for undergraduates and MA students, working alongside volunteers and prospective students.

Per.: Late Prehistoric to Medieval.

Country: United Kingdom.

Loc.: Near Bishop's Lydeard, Taunton.

Travel: Meet at campsite (location provided with application pack). Collection from local rail station can be arranged.

Dur.: 1–4 weeks; June to July.

Age: Minimum 16.

Qualif.: No experience necessary.

Work: Excavation, finds processing, geophysical survey, topographic survey, test pitting, and environmental work.

Lang.: English.

Accom.: Camping. Volunteer must bring a tent and sleeping bag.

Cost: GB£10–12 (US$15-18) per day. Food and accommodation included.

Applic.: Request an application form from the above address (preferably be e-mail), providing full contact details (including name, address, and e-mail). Application forms will be sent out as soon as details of the season's costs are finalised. Applications must be returned by May 1. Places will be allocated on a first come first served basis.

Notes: Contact Phil Marter. Academic credit available with approval (a fee is payable). Consult the website for further details.

Stymphalos Project

University of British Columbia
Department of Classical, NE and Religious Studies
Vancouver, British Columbia V6T 1Z1 Canada
E-mail: hectorw@interchange.ubc.ca
www.arts.ubc.ca/cnrs/stymphal/

Desc.:	Since 1994, the Stymphalos Project has excavated 15 areas (houses, public buldings, sanctuary, fortifications, cemeteries, theatre, etc.) of a small mountain city of ancient Arcadia. Study and publication of the material is now underway and volunteers will be helping specialists in various areas like conservation, pottery, photography, drawing, etc.
Per.:	Classical Greek to early Roman.
Country:	Greece.
Loc.:	Arcadia.
Travel:	Details provided upon application.
Dur.:	3 weeks; July to August.
Age:	Minimum 18.
Qualif.:	No experience necessary.
Work:	Archiving, curation, photography, and illustration.
Lang.:	English.
Accom.:	Shared rooms with private facilities in modest village hotel. Meals in local taverna.
Cost:	CAD$300 (approx. US$200) per week. Airfare not included.
Applic.:	Contact Project Director Dr. Hector Williams.

SURTI – Society for Urban, Rural and Tribal Initiatives

Balliguda (Bandha Street)
Phulbani District (Kandhamal), Orissa India
Tel.: ++91 (68) 464 3447
Fax: ++91 (68) 464 3277 or (68) 464 3447
E-mail: surtiw@hotmail.com - youth@mail.unesco.or.kr
www.members.tripod.com/workcamps/travels/

Desc.:	SURTI organises workcamps and cultural programmes that involve tribal festivals of dance and song and visiting tribal villages and markets. Orissa has the third largest concentration of tribal people in India with different languages, religions, rituals, levels of acculturation, music, and dance.
Per.:	Modern.
Country:	India.
Loc.:	Different tribal villages in Orissa state.
Travel:	Participants are picked-up at the Bhubaneswar National airport or railway station with prior arrangement, and they must arrive in Bhubaneswar between 9:00 and 16:00, 1 day before the programme start date.
Dur.:	9–21 days; year round.
Age:	Minimum 17, maximum 50.
Qualif.:	No experience necessary.
Work:	Labour and cultural programmes with the village community.
Lang.:	English.
Accom.:	Hotels or guest houses at Bhubaneswar.
Cost:	US$100 per person for 9 days, US$150 for 15 days, US$180 for 21 days. US$600 for 10-day Holiday Camp (50% reduced student rate available). Bed, sheets, 2 meals, equipment, pick-up, and project transport included.
Applic.:	On-line form. Upon receipt, an information package is supplied. A confirmation letter from the participant must arrive 1 month before the date of arrival.
Notes:	Bring work clothes and shoes, a sleeping bag, toiletries, towels, and personal items.

Swaziland Cultural Development Project

WorkingAbroad
2nd Floor Office Suite, 59 Lansdowne Place
Hove BN3 1FL East Sussex UK
Tel.: ++44 (1273) 711 406 Fax: ++44 (1273) 711 406
E-mail: info@workingabroad.com
www.workingabroad.com/organis/swaziland1.htm

Desc.: Workcamp for the development of a cultural arts and crafts village using traditional building methods. Swaziland is a unique African Mountain Kingdom with several very interesting traditional ceremonies with dancing, drumming, and singing.

Per.: Contemporary.

Country: Swaziland.

Loc.: Village in Swaziland, Southern Africa.

Travel: Volunteers are met at the Johannesburg International airport.

Dur.: 8 weeks, with the possibility to extend; February to November.

Age: Minimum 18.

Qualif.: No specific skills are needed, although some previous experience in environmental education could be an asset, as well as any building, manual, technical, or arts and crafts skills.

Work: Building a Swazi arts and crafts cultural village using traditional building materials alongside local people; setting up an environmental education unit.

Lang.: English.

Accom.: Shared dormitories.

Cost: GB£550 (approx. US$820). Accommodation, self-catered food, training from local artisans, cultural tours, visits to game reserves, entrance fees to parks, internal transportation within Swaziland, airport pick-up and drop-off at Johannesburg International airport included. Airfare, travel/medical insurance, medical kit, and personal/private expenses not included.

Applic.: Contact the organisation for instructions.

Notes: Throughout each workcamp, volunteers have many field trip and individual exploration opportunities.

Tarbat Discovery Programme

University of York, Department of Archaeology
Kings Manor, York YO1 2EP UK
Tel.: ++44 (1904) 433 900
Fax: ++44 (1904) 433 902
E-mail: info@tarbat-discovery.co.uk
www.york.ac.uk/depts/arch/staff/sites/tarbat/

Desc.: The Tarbat Old Church, at Portmahomack, is located on the isolated peninsula on the Moray Firth north of Inverness. This location once played a major role in the Pictish and Viking sea-faring network. Research on the site on which the church stands has already recovered a number of Pictish stones from the foundations of the church, and excavations have revealed a major Pictish settlement comprising monastic buildings, artisan work areas, and agricultural buildings.

Per.: Pictish, Norse, and Medieval.

Country: United Kingdom.

Loc.: Portmahomack.

Travel: Details provided upon application.

Dur.: 2 weeks for volunteers; July to August. 3 weeks for field school in August.

Age: Minimum 18.

Qualif.: No experience necessary.

Work: Excavation, volunteering, and training.

Lang.: English.

Accom.: Confirmed prior to field season.

Cost: GB£540 (approx. US$800) for 3-week field school; GB£80 (US$120) for 2-week volunteer period.

Applic.: On-line form.

Teaching and Projects Abroad

Gerrard House, Rustington, West Sussex BN16 1AW UK
Tel.: ++44 (1903) 859 911
Fax: ++44 (1903) 785 779
E-mail: info@teaching-abroad.co.uk
www.teaching-abroad.co.uk

Desc.: Rediscover ancient cultures on the archaeology programme in Rumania and the Inca Projects programme in Peru. In Peru, volunteers work in the historic town and battlefield of Ollantaytambo. In Rumania, volunteers are working with the National Museum of History to investigate ancient Dacia and the medieval principality of Transylvania.

Per.: Inca in Peru and Iron Age in Rumania.

Country: Peru, Rumania.

Loc.: Ollantaytambo in the Andes; Dacia, Brasov county in the Carpathian mountains.

Travel: Details provided upon application.

Dur.: Typically 2–4 months. Duration is at the volunteers' choice.

Age: Minimum17, maximum 70.

Qualif.: No experience necessary.

Work: Physical work similar to dry stonewalling to reconstruct the Inca terraces and the canals of the Sacred Valley in Peru; excavation in Rumania with potential museum work.

Lang.: English, in Peru good spoken Spanish is necessary.

Accom.: Local host-families, hostels, or other types of accommodation.

Cost: GB£1,595 (approx. US$2,400) for Peru; GB£1,495 for Rumania, for programmes up to 3 months. A deposit of GB£195 (US$300) is required with the application. Food, accommodation, insurance, and staff support included. International travel not included.

Applic.: On-line form. Receipt of the application and deposit payment and a formal letter of acceptance will be sent within 15 working days. Apply at least 2 months in advance to allow time for visa and travel arrangements.

Tel Hazor Excavations Project

Institute of Archaeology, The Hebrew University of Jerusalem
Mount Scopus Jerusalem 91905 Israel
Tel.: ++972 (2) 588 2403/4
Fax: ++972 (2) 582 5548
E-mail: bentor@h2.hum.huji.ac.il
http://unixware.mscc.huji.ac.il/~hatsor/hazor.html

Desc.: Hazor was an ancient Canaanite and Israelite City located in the north of modern day Israel important in antiquity. It is the largest biblical-era site in Israel, covering some 200 acres. An important city in the region, Hazor is comprised of the upper city (the acropolis) and the lower city (the fortified enclosure) lying close to the north.

Per.: Early to late Bronze Age; 3rd millennium BC, 18th-century BC, 13th-century BC.

Country: Israel.

Loc.: Hazor is approximately 3 miles (5km) north of Rosh-Pinnah, northern Israel.

Travel: There is no direct bus from Ben-Gurion airport to Safed. Take a bus to Haifa central bus station, which has buses to Safed approximately every 20–40 minutes, then local bus to Gesher House (contact the organisation for a map to Gesher House).

Dur.: 3–6 weeks; June to August.

Age: Minimum 18.

Qualif.: No experience necessary.

Work: Excavation work at the site is 5:00–13:00, Monday through Friday, with additional work assignments in the afternoon and the evenings. Lectures during the week provide training in field archaeology and interpretation of finds.

Lang.: English, Hebrew.

Accom.: Gesher House on Mount Canaan in Safed, about 10 miles from Tel Hazor. 35 people per room. Due to space limitations, married couples will not be able to share the same room. Beds, mattresses, sheets, 1 pillow, and 1 blanket are provided per person.

Cost: US$750 per session (US$250 per week) or US$1,350 for the full 6-week term, payable at Hazor, in the volunteer's own country's currency. Bring a modest amount of money to cover personal expenses and additional travel before and after the dig.

Applic: On-line form air mailed to Dr. Amnon Ben-Tor including US$25 registration fee. (include a return address). All payments if made by check (personal, travellers' checks, bankers' checks) should be made in the applicant's national currency. (Note: remittance must be by check or money order payable to: The Israel Exploration Society, PO Box 7041, Jerusalem 91070 Israel; tel. 972-2-6257991; fax 972-2-6247772; e-mail: ies@vms.huji.ac.il; www.hum.huji.ac.il/ies/.)

Notes: Academic credit available with approval from home university. Participants receive a participation certificate.

See also:
Hebrew University of Jerusalem

Tell es-Safi/Gath Archaeological Project

The Institute of Archaeology, Martin (Szusz) Department of Land of Israel Studies
Bar Ilan University, Ramat-Gan, 52900 Israel
Fax: ++972 (3) 535 1233
E-mail: maeir@h2.hum.huji.ac.il
www.dig-gath.org

Desc.: This long-term investigation is aimed at studying the archaeology and history of Tell es-Safi, identified by most scholars as the Biblical city of "Gath of the Philistines" (the home of Goliath and Achish). It is among the largest tells (ancient ruin mounds) and most important archaeological sites in Israel. Continuous excavations are planned for at least the next decade..

Per.: Bronze and Iron Age, Chalcolithic period (5th millennium BC).

Country: Israel.

Loc.: On the border between the Philistia and the Judean foothills (Shephelah) in Central Israel, on the southern bank of the Elah valley in the Southern Levant, approximately halfway between Jerusalem and Ashkelon.

Travel: Details provided upon application.

Dur.: 2–4 weeks.

Age: Minimum 18.

Qualif.: No experience necessary.

Work: Excavation, post-excavation (e.g., pottery washing), lectures, field trips. Workdays are Sunday to Friday 6:00–13:00).

Lang.: English.

Accom.: Kibbutz Kfar Menahem, a short drive from the site. Air-conditioned rooms, a pool, and kosher food.

Cost: US$25 application fee plus US$300 per week, 2-week minimum, or US$1,150 for 4 weeks for volunteers; US$2,250 for 4 weeks for students. Food, accommodation, and travel from kibbutz to site and back, and for students the 6 credits from Bar Ilan University included. Medical and accident insurance, travel to and from Israel or airport to the kibbutz, and laundry not included. All participants must provide their own health and accident insurance.

Applic.: Deadline for registration and US$25 fee is May 1. Registration will be finalized once the on-line health, insurance, and conduct and behavior form is received followed by the receipt of a US$625 deposit (for minimum stay of 2 weeks), in cash (US funds only, no money transfers are accepted) or bank check, made out to "The Foundation for the Study of Eretz Israel". All remaining funds must be received by the first day of participation on the dig.

Notes: Academic credit available through Bar Ilan University.

See also:

Israel Foriegn Ministry

Temple of the Winged Lions Project

AEP—American Expeditions to Petra
15810 Chicory Drive
Fountain Hills, AZ 85268 USA.
E-mail: hammondp@aol.com
www.todacosa.com/petra/aep.htm

Desc.: The AEP is an independent archaeological expedition. Over 275 volunteer AEP members have worked on the site up to the present time. Interested persons (male or female), students (graduate or undergraduate), faculty, and other interested individuals are invited to apply.

Per.: As a result of recovered materials and external earthquake data, it was possible to date the temple from "the fourth day of 'Ab" (19 August), AD 28, to its destruction late in the evening of 19 May, AD 363, making it perhaps the most closely dated structure to have been excavated in the Middle East.

Country: Jordan.

Loc.: Petra.

Travel: Details provided upon application.

Dur.: 5–6 weeks; June to July.

Age.: Minimum 18.

Qualif.: No experience necessary.

Work: Participating expedition members will have a rotating schedule of restoration and conservation activities, laboratory work, excavation, and other archaeological assignments. The expedition has a 6-day work week, extending from Saturday to Thursday.

Lang.: English.

Accom.: Large private home in the Bedouin village of Umm Sihun, just outside of Petra. It is within walking distance of the site but transportation to and from the site is set up on a regular basis. The AEP also uses this house as its processing headquarters. This facility provides sleeping quarters, showers, dining facilities, work areas, and communal rooms to relax. Local cooks and housekeepers maintain the meals and general housekeeping. No other housing arrangements are permissible.

Cost: US$2,800. This covers on-site room and board (full season, less a 3-day break period), laundry, and group transportation (Amman-Petra-Amman). Airfare and transportation to the site not included.

Applic.: A detailed information packet may also be ordered. A non-refundable charge of US$25 is required for receipt of application packets to defray printing and shipping costs.The application deadline is March 1 and application approval by March 15. Participantion is limited to 30 persons.

Notes: Academic credit for participation must be made with the participant's home institution. No provision can be made for special diets, guests, or other unusual arrangements. Daily food menus are set and no individual variations are possible. Participating members of the expedition must be in good health and remain on for the full expedition season.

Terra Europaea, Inc.

334 Serrano Drive
San Francisco, California 94132 USA
Tel.: ++1 (209) 484 7256
Fax: ++1 (415) 338 1775
E-mail: ellis@terraeuropaea.org
www.terraeuropaea.org

Desc.: Terra Europaea is a non-profit group of archaeologists and educators dedicated to supporting heritage research and public education in eastern Europe. There are 2 projects: Scanteia late Neolithic Village, of the Cucuteni-Tripolye culture excavating prehistoric houses and uncovering impressive tricolour pottery; and Tropaeum Traiani Roman city, to conduct surveying and test excavations at rural settlements on buried aqueduct lines.

Per.: Late Neolithic to late Roman; 4350–4200 BC, 2nd–6th centuries AD.

Country: Romania.

Loc.: Scanteia is in Moldavia, northeast Romania; the Roman city is in Dobrudja, southeast Romania near the Black Sea coast.

Travel: Bucharest airport for pick-up; trains to Iasi (for Scanteia) or Constantza (for Tropaeum Traiani).

Dur.: 2 weeks per site; July 1–15 (Scanteia); July 16–31 (Tropaeum Traiani).

Age.: Minimum 20.

Qualif.: No experience necessary.

Work: Fieldwork, survey, methodology, photography.

Lang.: English.

Accom.: Hosted by families or boarded in schools or local winery. No running water: well water and sponge bath. Bring sleeping bag and mat. Hired cook prepares rural Romanian cuisine.

Cost: US$950 for 2-week project; US$1,550 for both projects in 4 weeks. Room, board, train transport, and pick-up included.

Applic.: Request forms by e-mail to be returned with US$50 deposit by March 15 and payment received by April 15.

Notes: Anti-tetanus and hepatitis vaccinations and insurance required.

Thistle Camps

National Trust for Scotland
Wemyss House, 28 Charlotte Square,Edinburgh, Scotland EH2 4ET UK
Tel.: ++44 (131) 243 9470
Fax: ++44 (131) 243 9593
E-mail: conservationvolunteers@nts.org.uk
www.thistlecamps.org.uk

Desc.: Thistle Camps are residential working holidays organised by The National Trust for Scotland to help in the conservation and management of countryside properties in its care. The camps vary from property to property in terms of duration, accommodation standard, work and cost.

Per.: Various.

Country: United Kingdom.

Loc.: Various.

Travel: Transportation provided from the pick-up point to the accommodation. Full details and timings will be sent 4 weeks before the start of the camp.

Dur.: 1–2 weeks, March to October.

Age: Minimum 16 (UK residents with written guardian consent), otherwise minimum 18.

Qualif.: Skills are welcome but not essential, as all camps are supervised by an experienced leader and property staff.

Work: Survey and excavation. Workday is 9:00–17:00, with lunch and tea breaks taken on site.

Lang.: English.

Accom.: Normally a Trust base camp or outdoor centre with heating, beds, and showers.

Cost: Varies depending on camp location, duration, and time of year. Reduced rates for students, unwaged, and retirees is given in brackets for each camp.

Applic.: Contact the National Trust for Scotland.

Notes: Bring raingear and warm clothing.

See also:
Ben Lawers Archaeological Field School

Tiwanaku Enclave

UREP — University Research Expeditions Program
University of California
One Shields Ave., Davis, California 95616 USA
Tel.: ++1 (530) 757 3529   Fax: ++1 (530) 757 3537
E-mail: urep@ucdavis.edu
www.urep.ucdavis.edu

Desc.: Arising on the shores of Lake Titicaca, the Tiwanakus are best known for their huge pyramids, expert metal and stone work, fine ceramics and textiles, and apparent use of hallucinogenic plants to expand their cultural influence. Researchers hope to learn how this archaic state expanded but then collapsed after only 600 years of existence. Although all periods of human occupation are present in the Puno region, this research will focus on the period of time in which the bay was incorporated into the Tiwanaku state, circa 700 AD.

Per.: Pre-Inca; 700 AD.

Country: Peru.

Loc.: Puno Bay, Juliaca, Peru.

Travel: Meeting point in Juliaca to be arranged.

Dur.: 2–4 weeks; August.

Age: Minimum 18; 16- and 17-year-olds can participate with project leader's approval.

Qualif.: Experience welcomed but not necessary.

Work: Site mapping, excavations and laboratory processing of artefacts, possibly survey work.High elevations can make physical tasks seem more strenuous.

Lang.: English, Spanish.

Accom.: Dormitory-style arrangements in house in Puno Bay. Limited water. Bring warm sleeping bag but mattresses are provided.

Cost: US$1,350 per session. Room and board included. Airfare not included.

Applic.: Post application with US$200 deposit.

Notes: Academic credit available with approval from home institutions.

See also:

UREP– University Research Expeditions Program

Trebula Mutuesca Archaeological Fieldwork

Mykenai di Emeri Farinetti & C. Snc, Servizi per l'Archeologia e la Cultura
Via A. Baldissera, 61 int.19, 00159 Rome Italy
Tel.: ++39 (06) 439 2136
Fax: ++39 (06) 439 2136
E-mail: mykenai@tiscalinet.it
www.mykenai.it

Desc.: This archaeological summer field school is organised jointly through the Archaeological Service of Latium (Soprintendenza Archeologica per il Lazio), the Municipality of Monteleone Sabino,and the Mykenai archaeological unit.

Per.: Early Roman.

Country: Italy.

Loc.: Monteleone Sabino, north of Rome.

Travel: Details provided upon application.

Dur.: Minimum 2 weeks; July to September.

Age: Minimum 18.

Qualif.: No experience necessary.

Work: Activities include 12 days of digging activities at the site of the Mid-Republican sanctuary of the ancient Trebula Mutuesca and afternoon lessons concerning the more recent methodologies of archaeological research.

Lang.: Italian.

Accom.: A school in the centre of the village

Cost: EUR185 (approx. US$200) per week. Room, board, and insurance included.

Applic.: On-line form at: www.mykenai.it/Download/Info+Quest%20-%20English.rtf. Complete first the questionnaire and return it via e-mail. The questionnaire is not an official application form. Once the questionnaire is received an application form is sent.

Ugrian Archaeological Project

The Ural State University
"Volot" Laboratory to Sergey Koksharov
51 Lenin avenue, Ekaterinburg 620083 Russia
Tel.: ++(7) 3432 or 55 70 05   Fax: ++ (7) 3432 or 55 74 01
E-mail: anshpitonkov@mail.ru
www.geocities.com/andr_shp/emder11.html

Desc.: The history and cultural heritage of the region of Lower Ob' (West Siberia) is almost unknown in the West. Meanwhile the area has hundreds of significant archaeological sites dated from 10,000 BC to 16th century AD. Emder fortress and associated necropolis is among the most attractive archaeological monument of West Siberia. The fortress is of Ugrian origin and represents a perfect object for studying material and spiritual culture of Finnish and Hungarian ancestry.

Per.: Iron Age; 7th–16th centuries AD.

Country: Russia.

Loc.: 185 miles (300km) northwest from Khanty-Mansiysk Autonomous District.

Travel: Specific details provided upon application.

Dur.: 2 weeks; July to August.

Age: Minimum 18.

Qualif.: No experience necessary.

Work: Excavation. Monday to Friday, Saturday half-day.

Lang.: English, Russian.

Accom.: Field camp setting. Lodging in tents with all meals will be prepared in the field.

Cost: US$250 per week. Airfare not included.

Applic.: Deadline May 31.

Notes: Academic credit available through the Ural State University. Bring personal trowel (optional), tent, sleeping bag, rain clothing, and all-weather boots. Participants should obtain necessary vaccinations, insurance, etc., prior to the trip.

See also:
Urals and Western Siberia Settlements and Burials

Underwater Archaeology International Field School

IAS – Istituto Attività Subacquee
Via Lombardi 12, 90144 Palermo Italy
Tel.. ++39 (335) 451533 or (348) 3311040
E-mail: marcello@mbox.infcom.it
www.infcom.it/subarcheo/ias.ing.html

Desc.: IAS (Institute for underwater activities) is one of the top institutions for underwater archaeology in Sicily and in Italy. IAS proposes, in cooperation with local cultural heritage authorities, courses of underwater archaeology to researchers, students or enthusiasts, within the framework of a EU project.

Per.: Classic, Roman, Medieval (Arab period).

Country: Italy.

Loc.: San Vito Lo Capo; western Sicily.

Travel: Plane, train, or boat to Palermo, then bus to San Vito Lo Capo.

Dur.: 20 days; May to September.

Age.: Minimum 18.

Qualif.: No previous experience required, but a strong interest in scientific methods to archaeological underwater excavations.

Work: Daily activities include: prospections; excavation with the air-lift; soundings; graphic surveys; photography; drawing; mapping. Lessons topics are: introduction to archaeology and underwater archaeology; ancient trade and naval construction; methods of archaeological research; analysis of archives and bibliographic sources; archaeological drawing and surveying. Activities are carried on in sites indicated by local authorities.

Lang.: English, Italian.

Accom.: In tourist apartments for 2–4 people.

Cost: Participation, room and board: EUR680 (approx. US$ 720) for one week, EUR980 for 2 weeks, EUR 1,300 for 3 weeks.

Applic.: Apply via e-mail, an application fee of EUR250 is required.

Notes: Dives are supervised by a specialist in hyperbaric medicine, who checks daily the health condition of the students. IAS awards also a Licence as "Archaeology Instructor" recognised by NASE (National Academy of Scuba Educator); see website.

UNESCO – United Nations Educational, Scientific and Cultural Organization

7, place de Fontenoy
75352 Paris 07 SP France
Tel.: ++33 1 45 68 10 00
Fax: ++33 1 45 67 16 90
www.unesco.org

Desc.: UNESCO was established in 1945. It has its headquarters in Paris, France and 73 field offices and units in different parts of the world. The goal of this international body is to mobilise governments and other international partners in favour of voluntary service to make available more programmes, projects, funding, and other support for young people. In this way young people around the world will be encouraged and aided in becoming volunteers and being responsible actors in their societies.

Per.: Various.
Country: Worldwide.
Loc.: Various.
Travel: Details provided upon application to project organisation.
Dur.: Typically minimum 2 weeks.
Age: 18–25.
Qualif.: No experience necessary.
Work: Diverse programmes available in a wide range of sectors including archaeology and culture.
Lang.: English or language of host country.
Accom.: Variable.
Cost: Inquire with project organisation.
Applic.: UNESCO does not recruit volunteers or organise volunteer programmes, workcamps, or exchange.

Urals and Western Siberia Settlements and Burials

Ural State University Archaeological Laboratory
51 Lenin Avenue, Ekaterinburg 620083 Russia
Tel.: ++(7) 34 32 or 55 70 05 Fax: ++(7) 34 32 or 55 74 01
E-mail: Svetlanasharapova@daes.ustu.ru – Ludmila.Koryakova@usu.ru
http://www2.usu.ru/arch_laboratory/eng/fldhom.htm

Desc.: Excavations of the Pavlinovo archaeological complex (fortress and kourgans/burial grounds) situated on an old river terrace consist of fortification features, a citadel feature, and a settlement area with numerous dwelling structure depressions.

Per.: Bronze and Early Iron Ages.

Country: Russia.

Loc.: Trans-Ural region, approximately 185 miles (300km) southeast of Ekaterinburg, on the left bank of the Iset River.

Travel: Fly to Ekaterinburg city direct or via Moscow. Participants are met at the airport. Train or bus to the field site.

Dur.: 1–4 weeks; July to August.

Age: Minimum 18.

Qualif.: Archaeological experience is desireable but not necessary. .

Work: Field survey, excavation, planning, profiling, artefact processing, and recording, lectures, and training.

Lang.: English.

Accom.: Tent camping in group setting (approximately 50 people). Meals are prepared in the field. 1–2 nights will be spent at the dormitory of the Ural State University in Ekaterinburg.

Cost: US$250 per week for the 3-credit option; US$200 per week for non-credit. Equipment, local travel, camp meals, and visa support included. Accommodation in Ekaterinburg upon arrival and departure from the project (about US$3–10) not included.

Applic.: Send statement of interest, personal, contact, and passport information, university status, address of the Russian Consulate in home city by mail, fax, or e-mail. Deadline May 31.

Notes: Bring trowel, personal items, tent, sleeping bag, raingear, all-weather boots, and personal insurance.

UREP – University Research Expeditions Program

University of California
One Shields Avenue, Davis, California 95616 USA
Tel.: ++1 (530) 757 3529
Fax: ++1 (530) 757 3537
E-mail: urep@ucdavis.edu
www.urep.ucdavis.edu

Desc.: The University of California organises research and volunteer projects where participants travel to locations worldwide and learn new skills, make new friends, and help contribute to a growing knowledge of the planet. UREP participants come from all walks of life: students, teachers, professionals, or active seniors, and no special experience is needed. Each participant is an active and full-fledged member of the research team and contributes an equal share to cover the project costs.

Per.: Various.

Country: Throughout Asia, Africa, Europe, and Latin and North America.

Loc.: Various.

Travel: Details to be confirmed with specific project.

Dur.: Typically 2 weeks; March to August

Age: Inquire with organisation for specific project.

Qualif.: No experience is necessary.

Work: Fieldwork, survey, excavation, etc.

Lang.: English.

Accom.: Group housing or camping.

Cost: US$800–2000. Costs vary with each project. Food and accommodation included. As a donation to the University of California, the costs may be tax-deductible.

Applic.: On-line form to be e-mailed or printed and posted to the above address. Include US$200 deposit.

See also:
Home and Hearth in the Bronze Age
Tiwanaku Enclave

USCAP – University of Sydney Central Asian Programme

Archaeology in Central Asia
Archaeology A14, University of Sydney NSW 2006 Australia
Tel.:++61 (2) 9351 2090 – Fax:++61 (2) 9351 7760
E-mail: alison.betts@archaeology.usyd.edu.au
www.arts.usyd.edu.au/departs/archaeology/CentralAsia
homepage.htm

Desc.: USCAP in collaboration with the Institute of History, Archaeology, and Ethnography (IHAE), Karakalpak Academy of Sciences takes a field team on archaeological excavations in Uzbekistan and a trip through the colourful Medieval Silk Road cities.

Per.: 4th century BC to 2nd century AD.

Country: Uzbekistan.

Loc.: The excavation headquarters are in ancient Chorasmia, the western province of modern Uzbekistan, set between the farmland and the desert, facing out on to a rolling dune-field covering the ruined city of Kazakl'i-yatkan.

Travel: All arrangements made by tour organisers (see Applic.).

Dur.: Approximately 3 weeks. September.

Age: Minimum 18.

Qualif.: No experience necessary.

Work: Excavation, drawing, planning, cleaning features, and recording finds.

Lang.: English.

Accom.: Excavation headquarters (USCAP 13 nights) in dormitory style accommodation, wirh electricity, hot showers, and outdoor 'squat' toilets. Cooking and cleaning provided. Hotel Uzbekistan among others during tours.

Cost: Approximately AUS$6,900 Sydney/Brisbane/Melbourne; GB£1,600/US$2,400 land only. Prices vary to consider international flights, departure taxes, meals in Uzbekistan, and guided tours and sight-seeing.

Applic.: For bookings and cost information, contact Odyssey Travel at www.odysseytravel.com.au, otherwise contact USCAP.

Valley of Peace Archaeological Project

Department of Sociology and Anthropology, New Mexico State University
Box 30001, Dept. 3BV, Las Cruces, New Mexico 88003-8001 USA
Tel.: ++1 (505) 646 1359   Fax: ++1 (505) 646 3725
E-mail: lislucer@nmsu.edu
www.ece.nmsu.edu/~lludeman/vopa/vopindex.htm

Desc.: The on-going research of this project is exploring how early Maya rulers replicated and expanded household rituals to acquire political power. The excavations focus on collecting ritual data, particularly information on termination, dedication, renewal, and ancestor veneration rituals.

Per.: Classic Maya; 250–850 AD

Country: Belize.

Loc.: Belmopan. Project site along the Belize River

Travel: Detail provided upon application.

Dur.: 4 weeks. June.

Age: Minimum 18.

Qualif.: No experience necessary.

Work: Survey and excavation. Monday to Friday; 6:30–14:30.

Lang.: English.

Accom.: Students will live in the capital of Belize, Belmopan in dorm-like conditions.

Cost: Approximately US$4,000–4,500. For out-of-state tuition, add an additional US$2,600. Tuition, transportation to and from Belize, room, and board included.

Applic.: Via e-mail only. Contact the project director Dr. Lisa Lucero.

Notes: Academic credit available with approval from home university. A list will be provided of necessary equipment, clothing, paperwork, and vaccinations.

VIMEX – Voluntarios Internacionales Mexico

Alfredo Elizondo No. 69
Col. Damina Carmona CP 15450 Mexico DF
Tel./Fax: ++ (525) 7 95 04 57
E-mail: vimex@laneta.apc.org
www.vimex.org.mx

Desc.: An 18th-century church at Quecholac, Puebla, was built by several religious orders like the Mercedarios and Agustinos among others. This church is an architectonic building of the Barocco. Local people want to reconstruct this church and several others that represent the evangelisation of the New Spain and the cultural heritage in general to turn them into national and international tourist attractions.

Per.: 17th–18th centuries.

Country: Mexico.

Loc.: Quecholac, Puebla, near Mexico city.

Travel: From the Mexico City airport, take a bus to Puebla. Arriving to Puebla CAPU bus station take another bus to Quecholac. The meeting point on the 1st day is at 16:00 in front of the Palacio Municipal (Municipal Palace) building.

Dur.: Inquire for available opportunities.

Age.: Minimum 18.

Qualif.: No experience necessary.

Work: Cleaning architecture, landscaping and beautifying restoration work, and painting. Monday to Friday, 30 hours per week.

Lang.: Spanish, English.

Accom.: Either in a local house, a hostel, or a hotel. Volunteers will cook their own meals and do housework

Cost: US$170 registration fee. Project costs vary.

Applic.: May be coordinated with CCIVS/ UNESCO , YAP, ALLIANCE, AVOS, or other workcamp organisation.

Notes: Bring light clothes, work clothes, sun protection, work gloves, and a cap or a hat. The weather is warm during the day but cold at nights.

Vindolanda Trust

Chesterholm Museum
Bardon Mill, Hexham Northumberland NE47 7JN UK
Tel.: ++44 (1434) 34 42 77
Fax: ++44 (1434) 34 40 60
E-mail: info@vindolanda.com
www.vindolanda.com

Desc.: The Vindolanda 'vicus', or Roman town outside the last fort at Vindolanda c. 212–300 AD, is among the best explored in Roman Britain and the Roman Empire as a whole, yet at least half of the area is believed to contain the 3rd-century town and late cemeteries yet to be explored. Trenches will be cut to explore the earlier military remains from the pre-Hadrianic era of the site, including the exploration of a deep fort ditch and locate features from the 2nd-century forts.

Per.: Roman; 100–300 AD.

Country: United Kingdom.

Loc.: Hexham Northumberland. About the centre of Hadrian's Wall near the village of Bardon Mill, 2 miles (3km) behind the Wall.

Travel: Must provide own travel. Some public transport but irregular. From the international airport in Newcastle-Upon-Tyne, take subway or taxi to the Once Brewed Youth Hostel or the Hayden Bridge Lodge in Vindolanda. Arrive on the Saturday and contact the organisation. Work will commence on Sunday.

Dur.: 5-day sessions; April to August.

Age: Minimum 16.

Qualif.: No experience necessary.

Work: Excavation of Roman fort and vicus. Sunday to Thursday.

Lang.: English.

Accom.: Information about local accommodation available on website. The Youth Hostel within walking distance from the project.

Cost: GB£50 for any session. Membership of the Friends of Vindolanda membership included.

Applic.: On-line form to email or send by post. See website for details.

Notes: Contact Andrew Birley, Assistant Director of Excavations.

Vive México

Morelia, Michoacán
Boulevard García de León 734-A
Fraccionamiento Chapultepec Oriente, CP 58280 Mexico
Tel./Fax: ++521 (443) 324 5170
E-mail: incoming@vivemexico.org
www.vivemexico.org

Desc.: Vive Mexico uses International Volunteer Service Projects to help in different projects for the culture, social, and ecological issues of Mexico and to promote intercultural exchanges and global understanding between the participants and the local communities involved in the projects. Vive Mexico works together with numerous members of the European Alliance of Voluntary Service Organisations, SCI, and YAP networks and others around the world.

Per.: Modern/contemporary.

Country: Mexico.

Loc.: Various locations.

Travel: From the international airport detailed travel instructions will be provided in the project Info Sheets.

Dur.: 3 weeks to 1 year.

Age: Minimum 18.

Qualif.: No experience necessary.

Work: Cultural, social, and ecological projects.

Lang.: English; Spanish is recommended and may be necessary.

Accom.: Schools, houses, tents, depending on project.

Cost: Varies with each project.

Applic.: Contact a partner organisation of Vive Mexico in home country. Vive Mexico can advise on which organisation may be appropriate. Further details provided upon application.

Notes: Bring sleeping bag and mat, comfortable working shoes, and swimwear. Vive Mexico works in alliance with GAIA, environmental NGO, México DF, Carlos B. Zetina 28, Depto 105, Colonia Condesa, tel. ++ (55) 2614 4767, workcamps@gaia.org.mx, www.gaia.org.mx.

VJF – Vereinigung Junger Freiwilliger eV

Hans-Otto Str. 7
10407 Berlin Germany
Tel.: ++49 (30) 4285 0603
Fax: ++49 (30) 4285 0604
E-mail: office@vjf.de
www.vjf.de

Desc.: Since 1990, the VJF has organised around 30–40 international annual workcamps in the European Union. It also organises workcamps in more than 50 countries worldwide, in cooperation with other organisations such as CCIVS and Allianceof European Voluntary Service Organisations (see listings).

Per.: Various.

Country: Germany and worldwide.

Loc.: Various.

Travel: Details provided with specific workcamp.

Dur.: 2–4 weeks, year round.

Age: Minimum 16 for German camps with parents' authorisation (VJF provides this form); mimumum 18 for international camps.

Qualif.: No experience necessary.

Work: Survey, archaeological research, mapping, excavations, reconstruction.

Lang.: English.

Accom.: Tents, lodges, or hostels, depending on location.

Cost: EUR15 (approx.US$16) membership fee. EUR60 for workcamps in Germany. EUR80 for members; EUR90 for students, unemployed, social workers; EUR110 for regular employees, for international camps.

Applic.: On-line form.

Volunteers For Peace International Workcamps

1034 Tiffany Road, Belmont, Vermont USA 05730
Tel.: ++1 (802) 259 2759
Fax: ++1 (802) 259 2922
E-mail: vfp@vfp.org
www.vfp.org

Desc.: This non-profit membership organisation has been coordinating international workcamps since 1982 and is a member of CCIVS at UNESCO and works in cooperation with SCI, Allianceof European Voluntary Service Organisations, and YAP (see listings).

Per.: Various.

Country: Various countries in Africa, Asia, Europe, the Americas, Middle East, and Oceania.

Loc.: Depending upon workcamp.

Travel: All transportation is arranged and paid for by the volunteer.

Dur.: 2–3 weeks per workcamp. Year round, typically June to September.

Age: Minimum 18. Teen camps for volunteers under 18.

Qualif.: No experience necessary.

Work: Excavation, field survey, restoration, etc., depending upon workcamp.

Lang.: English.

Accom.: Workcamps vary greatly in living conditions.

Cost: Registration fee of US$200 per workcamp (US$225 for volunteers under 18) plus mandatory membership of US$20. Food and accommodation included. Russian, African, Asian, and Latin American programmes may cost US$300–500.

Applic.: Register by fax, using a credit card for payment. There will be a penalty of US$100, payable in advance, for changing workcamp selections after registering.

Notes: Placement of nationals of countries other than the United States and Canada may be possible only if a partner organisation in the home country of the applicant does not exist.

Volunteers in Heritage Resources in the US Forest Service

USDA Forest Service-Modoc National Forest
800 West 12th Street, Alturas, California USA
Tel.: ++1 (530) 233 8731
Fax: ++1 (530) 233 8709
E-mail: ggates@fs.fed.us

Desc.: This program places American and International volunteers on National Forests across the US. The volunteers work primarily with archaeologists participating in archaeological surveys, some excavations, and lab work. Placements are usually for a minimum of four weeks and may last up to 12 weeks or more depending upon the volunteer and the individual forest.

Per.: Palaeo-Indian through Modern.

Country: United States.

Loc.: Nationwide.

Travel: Volunteers may be picked up at the nearest major airport/train or bus depot to the Forest.

Dur.: 4-12 weeks; May to October.

Age: Minimum 18.

Qualif.: No experience necessary.

Work: Excavation, survey, and laboratory work.

Lang.: English.

Accom.: Housing is provided free to the volunteer.

Cost: No costs apply. US$120 weekly is paid to the volunteer. Airfare not included.

Applic.: Open to all (J-1 Visa required for Internationals, for which the Agency will assist in obtaining).

Notes: Contact Project Director, Gerry Gates, Heritage Resource Program Manager, Modoc NF.

See also:

Passport in Time

Wadi ath-Thamad Project

Wilfrid Laurier University
Waterloo, Ontario N2L 3C5 Canada
Tel.: ++1 (519) 884 1970 X-6680
Fax: ++1 (519) 884 8853
E-mail: mdaviau@wlu.ca
www.wlu.ca/~wwwarch/jordan/

Desc.: This project involves several excavations – at a wayside shrine, a Neolithic village, and most importantly at the site of Khirbat al-Mudayna. This Iron Age site is a fortified town with features including a casemate wall, 6-chambered gate building with standing stones at the entrance, a temple, and a pillared building used for industrial purposes. Other buildings of interest in the area date to the early Roman period, with evidence of Nabataean culture.

Per.: Iron Age, Nabataean, early Roman, Neolithic.

Country: Jordan.

Loc.: The town of Madaba.

Travel: Details provided upon application.

Dur.: 6 weeks; June to August.

Age: Minimum 18.

Qualif.: No experience necessary.

Work: Excavation and survey.

Lang.: English.

Accom.: The Black Iris Hotel and Lulu's Pension.

Cost: CAD$2.200 plus CAD$50 application fee for Canadians; US$1,700 plus US$50 for non-Canadian team members per season. Lodging and 4 meals per day included. Airfare not included.

Applic.: Deadline March 5. Contact Dr. P. M. Michèle Daviau for further instructions.

Walls of Verona

Legambiente
Via Salaria 403, 00199 Rome Italy
Tel.: ++39 (06) 8626 8324/5/6
Fax: ++39 (06) 8626 8319
E-mail: legambiente.vol@tiscali.it
www.legambiente.com/canale8/campi/

Desc.: Verona is a very famous city in the northeast of Italy; it is a touristic place with a long history and culture, rich with historical monuments such as the famous Arena (the ancient Roman theatre). It is also a great example of fortified town with the walls and the surrounding area designated as a park. Unfortunately some parts of the area are still damaged and abandoned. The intent is to restore and revive of a large green space and restore a part of the park between 4 bastions of the 19th century and remains of walls of 16th century.

Per.: Early modern; 16th–19th centuries.

Country: Italy.

Loc.: Verona, northeast Italy.

Travel: Closest airport and railway station are in Verona. Staging area to be confirmed prior to project start date.

Dur.: 1 month.

Age: Minimum 18.

Qualif.: No experience necessary.

Work: Short-term volunteers work together with EVS (European Voluntary Service) volunteers in different activities: custody of the park, gardening, cleaning, guiding tourists through the park and participating on other Legambiente projects.

Lang.: Italian, French, or Spanish.

Accom.: In the old house of the guardian of the park "Raggio di Sole", very close to the centre of the town.

Cost: EUR130 (approx. US$ 140) plus membership fee.

Applic.: Inquire for further details.

See also:
Legambiente

Waterway Recovery Group

PO Box 114, Rickmansworth, Herts WD3 1ZY UK
Tel.: ++44 (1923) 71 11 14
Fax: ++44 (1923) 89 70 00
E-mail: enquiries@wrg.org.uk
www.wrg.org.uk

Desc.: Volunteers are needed to restore Britain's derelict canals with The National co-ordinating body for voluntary labour on the inland waterways of Great Britain.
Per.: 18th–19th centuries.
Country: United Kingdom.
Loc.: Various.
Travel: Details of the camp along with travel directions are sent a few weeks in advance. Pick-up at a nearby coach or train station is arranged.
Dur.: 1 day minimum, weekend or weeklong opportunities; year round.
Age: Minimum 17; maximum 70. Volunteer must be over 21 if English is a second language.
Qualif.: No experience necessary.
Work: Work may involve restoring industrial archaeology, demolishing old brickwork, driving a dump truck, clearing mud and vegetation, and helping at a National Waterways festival. Work may be either on weekends or weeklong canal camps.
Lang.: English.
Accom.: A village hall, sports centre, or similar style accommodation. Bring sleeping bag and mat.
Cost: GB£35 (approx.US$ 50) per week or GB£5 per day. Includes accommodation and food.
Applic.: Contact the Enquiries Officer at the above address.
Notes: Physically and mentally disabled volunteers may apply.

Western Belize Regional Cave Project
Belize Valley Archaeological Reconnaissance
Department of Anthropology, Indiana University
Student Buiding 130
701 East Kirkwood Avenue, Bloomingdale Indiana 47405-7100 USA
E-mail: BelizeMaya@aol.com
www.indiana.edu/~belize/

Desc.: This project is designed to introduce experienced participants to the fundamental approaches to the practice of speleoarchaeology and to provide training in a variety of archaeological techniques.

Per.: Prehistoric Maya.

Country: Belize.

Loc.: San Ignacio (called Cayo locally), western Belize.

Travel: Pick-up at Belize International airport.

Dur.: 2–4 weeks; June to August.

Age: Minimum 18.

Qualif.: Prior archaeological, spelunking, or caving experience is required. Previous experience in an archaeological field school is preferred. Owing to the strenuous and dangerous nature of cave reconnaissance excellent physical condition is imperative.

Work: Excavation, reconnaissance missions to locate and explore new caves, survey, laboratory analysis, illustration, identification, and documentation of cave art, cultural interpretation, lectures on Maya civilisation.

Lang.: English; Spanish is useful.

Accom.: Cahal Pech Village, a small hotel complex at San Ignacio. Small camps in the jungle with small thatched-roof huts ortents.

Cost: US$1,050 per 2-week session or US$1,750 per month. Lodging, meals, airport transportation, and daily project transport included. Travel, insurance, and personal items not included.

Applic.: Request application via e-mail and insturctions from Cameron Griffith; Co-Director. A brief resume is advised.

Notes: Academic credit available with home institution.

See also:

Belize Valley Archaeological Reconnaissance Project

Whitehall Farm

Northampton University
Simon's Cottage, Stowe Hill, Weedon, Northants NN7 4SF UK
Tel.: ++44 (1327) 342 581
E-mail: whitehallvilla@farmline.com
www.whitehallvilla.co.uk

Desc.: Volunteers are involved in the excavation of a Romano-British villa, bath-house, and associated landscape features. An unusual system of water management is also being investigated. The excavation is an important study for the wider area of Roman settlements.

Per.: Roman.

Country: United Kingdom.

Loc.: Near Junction 16 of M1, Northamptonshire.

Travel: Details provided upon application.

Dur.: 1 week; June to July.

Age: Minimum 18.

Qualif.: No experience necessary.

Work: Excavation, planning, surveying, finds processing, archiving, and training. Volunteers are expected to help with an Open Day public weekend.

Lang.: English.

Accom.: Campsite with full facilities available on site. Pubs and shops in walking distance.

Cost: GB£25 (approx.US$38) per week. Camping and training package included.

Applic.: On-line form. Contact Steve Young.

White House Bay Maritime Archaeological Project

Anglo-Danish Maritime Archaeological Team (ADMAT)
12 Penners Gardens, Langley Road, Surbiton, Surrey KT6 6JW UK
Tel.: ++44 (20) 83 99 12 84
Mobile ++44 (7951) 58 06 10
E-mail: maritime_archaeology@yahoo.co.uk – info@admat.org.uk
www.admat.org.uk

Desc.: This is a joint project of ADMAT with the Maritime Archaeological Department of the University of Bristol Field School in conjunction with the St. Christopher Heritage Society. This project is a unique introduction to maritime archaeology in the Caribbean. This is a 5-year project that aims to conduct maritime archaeology in the Caribbean and Latin America and survey historic wreck sites in and around St. Kitts, to assist governments to preserve and protect the underwater cultural heritage in the Caribbean, to assist volunteer students to take part in maritime archaeological field excavations and surveys, and to protect the European Underwater Maritime Cultural Heritage. They survey, record, and advise on how to protect, shipwrecks from the old European empires, which include 2 wreck sites and a careening site (the central section of the wreck stretches for over 30 metres). This is a major maritime archaeological project, and students, volunteers, and divers are given the opportunity to take part in the survey.

Per.: Early modern; 1600–1700s.

Country: St. Kitts, West Indies.

Loc.: St. Kitts, a Leeward Island in the eastern Caribbean near Nevis, St. Eustatius, Barbuda, and Antigua.

Travel: A project representative will meet participants at the St. Kitts airport.

Dur.: 2–4 weeks; April.

Age: Minimum 18.

Qualif.: No experience necessary. Training in the principles and practice of maritime archaeology.

Work: Maritime archaeology, survey, and excavation.

Lang.: English.

Accom.: Mule House in Brighton Plantations at White house Bay; 4 self-contained, self-catering apartments, which sleep up to 4 people comfortably (2 bedrooms, a lounge, kitchen, and dining area, plus separate bathroom with showers). The building is non-smoking. Maid service is provided once a week.

Cost: GB£600 (approx.US$900) per week (credits are extra). Fees include all administration, accommodation, food, tuition, and transport for the 2- or 4-week period. It is advisable to bring personal spending money. Airfare and travel, medical, and diving insurances not included.

Applic.: On-line form. Fees are payable in 3 stages, contact the organisation for details. Applications to participate in the field school are invited from students and members of the public.

Notes: Volunteers are required to provide their own personal diving equipment and must have either PADI Advanced Open Water or BSAC Sports Diver (or the equivalent under another agency) certification as a minimum and send copies of their diving qualifications with their booking. Original logbooks or certification cards and a medical statement must be presented to the ADMAT Diving Officer upon arrival. The University of Bristol accepts applications to credit this field school. A 2-week and a 4-week course are available at an additional charge payable to the University. Request confirmation of the acceptability of the course credits with home school.

Whittlewood Project

Centre for English Local History and the Medieval Settlement Research Group, Leicester University
Marcfitch House, 5 Salisbury Road, Leicester LE1 7QR UK
Tel.: ++44 (116) 252 5291
E-mail: RLCJ1@leicester.ac.uk
www.le.ac.uk/elh/whittlewood/index.htm

Desc.: The received wisdom that villages were formed at the time of the Anglo-Saxon invasions has been shown to be mistaken. It has been observed that villages were created during a complex of changes between the 9th–12th centuries. After a systematic assessment of Northamptonshire, Bedfordshire, Leicestershire (including Rutland), and Buckinghamshire, the Research Group has selected a group of 11 parishes in and around Whittlewood as the area with the best range of evidence.

Per.: Medieval.

Country: United Kingdom.

Loc.: The Buckinghamshire/Northamptonshire county boundary.

Travel: Details provided upon application.

Dur.: 1–2 weeks; July.

Age: Minimum 18.

Qualif.: No experience necessary.

Work: Documentary research, earthwork survey, fieldwalking, and geophysical survey.

Lang.: English.

Accom.: None provided.

Cost: None. Volunteers are responsible for their personal expenses, room, and board.

Applic.: Contact Dr. Richard Jones.

Workcamps For Young People in Brittany

Service Régional de l'Archéologie
Charles Foulon Avenue, 35700 Rennes France
Tel.: ++33 (2) 99 84 59 00 Fax: ++33 (2) 99 84 59 19
E-mail: contact.bretagne@culture.gouv.fr
www.culture.gouv.fr/bretagne
www.chantierbenevolebretagne.org

Desc.: Workcamps on archaeology and cultural heritage. General membership conditions vary from one site to another. For most excavation sites, good physical condition is required and motivation in order to take part in sustained physical work in the open air. The person in charge will provide more precise information on the site upon written request with a stamped addressed envelope for reply. Consult the websites for regularly updated lists of camps and the conditions and topic of each.

Per.: Various.

Country: France.

Loc.: Various.

Travel: Typical meeting point is at the site. Instructions provided upon application.

Dur.: 1 week to 1 month; June to October.

Age: Minimum 18, some camps open to younger volunteers.

Qualif.: No experience necessary.

Work: Restoration, reconstruction, and maintenance.

Lang.: English, French.

Accom.: Camping or rough accommodation. Bring sleeping gear.

Cost: Varies with each camp, but costs are typically a minimal contribution.

Applic.: Contact details provided with each camp on the website list of current camps.

Notes: Updated anti-tetanus vaccination is required; no restricting food diet. Security shoes are recommended on all the sites and sometimes necessary.

YAP – Youth Action for Peace

International Secretariat
3, Avenue du Parc Royal, 1020 Bruxelles Belgium
Tel.: ++32 (2) 478 9410
Fax: ++32 (2) 478 9432
E-mail: yapis@xs4all.be
www.yap.org

Desc.: YAP facilitates international workcamps in archaeological, environmental and conservation of parks, gardening, culture, and development projects.

Per.: Various.

Country: Throughout the Mediterranean, America, Asia, and Africa.

Loc.: Various.

Travel: Details provided upon application to specific project.

Dur.: 1–4 weeks, longer projects may be 3–12 months; year round.

Age: Minimum 18 (some projects for teenagers).

Qualif.: No experience necessary.

Work: Restoration, reconstruction, maintenance, public outreach, etc.

Lang.: English or language of host country.

Accom.: Varies from camping to hostelling, typically group settings.

Cost: Small registration fee and travel costs.

Applic.: Contact most convenient branch (consult website).

Yavneh-Yam Archaeological Project

Tel Aviv University Institute of Archaeology
Department of Classics, Ramat Aviv, 69978 Irael
Tel.: ++972 (3) 640 9938
Fax: ++972 (3) 640 6243
E-mail: fischer@post.tau.ac.il
www.tau.ac.il./~yavneyam/

Desc.: Yavneh-Yam has been occupied since early antiquity, as revealed both by historical sources and archaeological evidence. The site is mentioned for the first time as "muhazzi" in 15th–century BC Egyptian sources and later on as "the harbour of the people of Iamnia"(Yavneh-Yam). In Middle Age maps it is denominated "the harbour of the Jews".

Per.: Middle to Late Bronze Age, Iron Age, Persian, Hellenistic, Roman, Byzantine, and Early Islamic periods; 9th century BC to 7th century AD.

Country: Israel.

Loc.: Yavneh-Yam, the harbour of Jewish inland city Yavneh, is situated at an equivalent distance (about 20km) between Jaffa and Ashdod.

Travel: Details provided upon application.

Dur.: 2 weeks ; July to August.

Age: Minimum 16.

Qualif.: No experience necessary.

Work: Excavation, cleaning, surveying, finds processing, archiving.

Lang.: English.

Accom.: Youth village Ayanot (10-minute drive from the site) with 4 people per room with air conditioning, bathroom, and shower. Modern dining hall with a large variety of Israeli/Near Eastern cuisine.

Cost: US$650. Airfare not included.

Applic.: Contact Moshe Fischer.

YouthCamp – Voluntary Action for Youth

Athinas 13, Agia Varvara
Athens 123 51 Greece
Tel.: ++30 (210) 561 0728
Fax: ++30 (210) 562 1093
E-mail: info@youthcamp.gr – kpikramenos@hotmail.com
www.youthcamp.gr

Desc.: This independent, voluntary youth organisation that is striving to play a major role in the area of international voluntarism in Greece and Cyprus. Their aims are for the protection, conservation and development of natural and social environment; the promotion of voluntarism as an alternative way of democratic participation in all areas of social activity; the development of cultural relations among youth with different national backgrounds.

Per.: Various.

Country: Greece.

Loc.: Various locations.

Travel: Information Sheets define the time of arrival at a designated meeting place.

Dur.: 2–3 weeks; June to mid-September.

Age: 18–32.

Qualif.: No experience is necessary.

Work: Various duties. The workcamps are focusing on environmental, social, cultural, archaeological, and construction/renovation projects.

Lang.: English.

Accom.: Free accommodation at a local school or community centre. Living conditions provide all facilities to volunteers.

Cost: EUR100 (approx. US$108) per workcamp. Volunteers are provided with supplies for cooking. Some workcamps take the meals in a local tavern or restaurant. Travel costs not included.

Applic.: Contact the organisation.

Notes: An Information Sheet will be sent after application with all pertinent details.

APPENDICES

Analytical Table by geographic areas and periods

ORGANISATIONS AND PROJECTS	Europe – Prehistory	Europe – Classic /Iron Age	Europe – Roman	Europe – Early Medieval	Europe – Medieval	Europe – Renaissance/Post Medieval	Europe – Early Modern	Europe – Modern	Europe – Contemporary	Europe – Multiperiod	Middle East – Prehistory	Middle East – Greek-Roman	Middle East – Islamic/Medieval	Asia – Prehistory	Asia – Far East Civilisations	Asia – Modern /Contemporary	Africa – Prehistory / Palaeonthology	Africa – Modern/Contemporary	North America – Prehistory/Palaeonthol.	North America – Early Cultures	North America – Modern/Contemporary	Latin America – Prehistory	Latin America – Maya/Precolombian	Latin America – Pre-Inca/Inca	Latin America – Colonial/Modern	Caribbean	Oceania	Worldwide
Aang Serian Peace Village																		X										
Achill Island Field School						X	X																					
AIEP – Ass. for Ed., Cult and Work Int. Exchange Programs			X																									
Alchester Roman Fortress			X																									
Alexandria Archaeology Museum	X	X																										
Alliance of European Voluntary Service Organisations																												X
Alutiiq Museum and Achaeological Repository																			X		X							
Ancient Metal Production in Southern Jordan											X		X															
Ancient Nomads of Mongolia		X												X														
Anglo-American Project in Pompeii			X																									
ArchaeoExpeditions																												X
ArchaeoExpeditions—Belize																							X					
ArchaeoExpeditions—Canada																				X								
ArchaeoExpeditions—Spain	X																											
Archaeolink Prehistory Park	X	X																										
Archaeological and Architectural Field Work in Turkey												X																
Archaeological Excavations in Northern Spain	X									X																		
Arcaeology and Art							X																					
ArchaeoSpain		X	X	X																								
ArcheoClub d'Italia		X	X	X					X	X																		
Archeo-Venezia – Archaeological Field Work Camp						X																						
Arduwy Early Landscapes Project	X																											

Note: The organisations and projects are in alphabetical order by name or acronym. See the explanation of periods on pages 34-36.

ORGANISATIONS AND PROJECTS	Worldwide	Oceania	Caribbean	Latin America – Colonial/Modern	Latin America – Pre-Inca/Inca	Latin America – Maya/Precolombian	Latin America – Prehistory	North America – Modern/Contemporary	North America – Early Cultures	North America – Prehistory/Palaeonthol.	Africa – Modern/Contemporary	Africa – Prehistory / Palaeonthology	Asia – Modern /Contemporary	Asia – Far East East Civilisations	Asia – Prehistory	Middle East – Islamic/Medieval	Middle East – Greek-Roman	Middle East – Prehistory	Europe – Multiperiod	Europe – Contemporary	Europe – Modern	Europe – Early Modern	Europe – Renaissance/Post Medieval	Europe – Medieval	Europe – Early Medieval	Europe – Roman	Europe – Classic /Iron Age	Europe – Prehistory
ARKEOS																										X	X	
ASTOVOCT – Association Togolaise des Voluntaires Chretiens au Travail											X																	
Baga Gazaryn Chuluu Survey														X	X													
Baikal Archaeology Project															X													
Ba Ja Neolithic Project																		X										
Baldan Baraivan														X														
Bamburgh Research Project																			X		X	X	X	X	X	X		
Banstead																			X					X	X	X	X	X
Belize Valley Archaeology Reconnaissance Project						X																						
Ben Lawers Archaeological Field School																			X		X	X	X					
Billown Neolithic Landscape Project																												X
Black Mountain									X	X																		
Butser Ancient Farm																										X	X	
Cahuachi Consolidation – Proyecto Nasca					X																							
Canterbury Archaeological Trust Ltd.																			X		X	X	X	X	X	X	X	
Carnuntum																										X		
Castell Hanllys Training Excavation																										X	X	
Cathedral Camps	X																		X									
CCIVS – Coordinating Committee for International Volunteers Service																												
Center for the Study of Eurasian Nomads														X	X													
Chantiers Jeunesse								X											X									
Chinese Young Volunteers Association														X														

ORGANISATIONS AND PROJECTS	Worldwide	Oceania	Caribbean	Latin America – Colonial/Modern	Latin America – Pre-Inca/Inca	Latin America – Maya/Precolombian	Latin America – Prehistory	North America – Modern/Contemporary	North America – Early Cultures	North America – Prehistory/Palaeonthol.	Africa – Modern/Contemporary	Africa – Prehistory / Palaeonthology	Asia – Modern /Contemporary	Asia – Far East Civilisations	Asia – Prehistory	Middle East – Islamic/Medieval	Middle East – Greek-Roman	Middle East – Prehistory	Europe – Multiperiod	Europe – Contemporary	Europe – Modern	Europe – Early Modern	Europe – Renaissance/Post Medieval	Europe – Medieval	Europe – Early Medieval	Europe – Roman	Europe – Classic /Iron Age	Europe – Prehistory
Circumpolar Ethnographic Field School													X															
Club du Vieux Manoir																			X		X	X	X	X				
Colonial Landscape of St. Christopher			X																									
Combined Caesarea Expeditions																	X											
Compagnons Batisseurs																			X									
Concordia	X																											
Cornell Halai and East Lokris																											X	X
Cotravaux																			X									
Crow Canyon Archaeological Center									X																			
CVE – Caribbean Volunteer Expeditions			X																									
CVG – Conservation Volunteers Greece																			X									
CVS-BG – Cooperation for Voluntary Service Bulgaria																			X									
Cyprus Hills Archaeological Project										X																		
Czech American Archaeological Field School in Premyslovice Neolithic Village																			X									
Duensberg Project																										X	X	
Early Man in India															X													
Earthwatch Institute	X																											
Easter Island Cultures		X																										
Eco-Archaeological Park Pontecagnano Faiano																											X	X
Elderhostel	X																											
El Pilar Archaeological Reserve for Maya Flora and Fauna						X																						
Excavations at Capernaum																	X											

ORGANISATIONS AND PROJECTS

ORGANISATIONS AND PROJECTS	Europe – Prehistory	Europe – Classic /Iron Age	Europe – Roman	Europe – Early Medieval	Europe – Medieval	Europe – Renaissance/Post Medieval	Europe – Early Modern	Europe – Modern	Europe – Contemporary	Europe – Multiperiod	Middle East – Prehistory	Middle East – Greek-Roman	Middle East – Islamic/Medieval	Asia – Prehistory	Asia – Far East Civilisations	Asia – Modern /Contemporary	Africa – Prehistory / Palaeonthology	Africa – Modern/Contemporary	North America – Prehistory/Palaeonthol.	North America – Early Cultures	North America – Modern/Contemporary	Latin America – Prehistory	Latin America – Maya/Precolombian	Latin America – Pre-Inca/Inca	Latin America – Colonial/Modern	Caribbean	Oceania	Worldwide
Excavations at Kursi-Gergesa												X	X															
Falerii – Via Amerina		X	X																									
Farnese – Rofalco		X																										
Field School in East-Central Europe								X																				
FIYE – International Youth Exchange Foundation																												X
Footsteps of Man	X																											
Giurdignano Project – Megalithic Garden of Europe				X						X																		
Golden Hills Khazar Excavations				X	X					X																		
Gordon's Lodge Fieldschool	X	X	X	X	X	X																						
Gruppi Archeologici d'Italia																												
GSM – Genclik Servisleri Merkezi											X	X	X															
Hebrew University of Jerusalem											X	X	X															
Heidelberg College Experiential Archaeological Program																					X							
Heidelberg College Summer Undergraduate Field School																					X							
Helike Archaeological Excavations		X																										
Herstmonceux						X																						
Historical Archaeology in Bermuda																					X							
Hofstadir					X																							
Home and Hearth in the Bronze Age	X																											X
Horizon Cosmopolite																												X
Humayma Excavation Project												X																
Idalion Expedition											X	X																

ORGANISATIONS AND PROJECTS	Worldwide	Oceania	Caribbean	Latin America – Colonial/Modern	Latin America – Pre-Inca/Inca	Latin America – Maya/Precolombian	Latin America – Prehistory	North America – Modern/Contemporary	North America – Early Cultures	North America – Prehistory/Palaeonthol.	Africa – Modern/Contemporary	Africa – Prehistory / Palaeonthology	Asia – Modern/Contemporary	Asia – Far East Civilisations	Asia – Prehistory	Middle East – Islamic/Medieval	Middle East – Greek-Roman	Middle East – Prehistory	Europe – Multiperiod	Europe – Contemporary	Europe – Modern	Europe – Early Modern	Europe – Renaissance/Post Medieval	Europe – Medieval	Europe – Early Medieval	Europe – Roman	Europe – Classic /Iron Age	Europe – Prehistory
Iklaina Archaeological Project																											X	X
INEX Slovakia – Association for International Youth Exchange and Tourism																							X	X				
Ironbridge Gorge Museum Trust																					X							
Ischia di Castro																								X				
Israel Foreign Ministry																X	X	X										
JAC – Joint Assistance Center													X															
Jeunesse et Réconstruction																			X									
Judith River Dinosaur										X																		
Kalat Project																			X					X	X	X	X	X
Kendal Camp													X															
Kfar Ha Horesh Archaeology and Anthropology Field School																		X										
Koobi Fora Field School												X																
Körös Regional Archaeological Project																												X
KwaZulu Field Projects												X																
Lamanai Archaeological Project						X																						
Legambiente																			X									
Limpopo River Valley Archaeology Field School												X																
Lubbock Lake Landmark								X	X	X																		
Ma'ax Na Archaeology Project						X																						
Malta University																										X	X	X

246

ORGANISATIONS AND PROJECTS	Europe – Prehistory	Europe – Classic /Iron Age	Europe – Roman	Europe – Early Medieval	Europe – Medieval	Europe – Renaissance/Post Medieval	Europe – Early Modern	Europe – Modern	Europe – Contemporary	Europe – Multiperiod	Middle East – Prehistory	Middle East – Greek-Roman	Middle East – Islamic/Medieval	Asia – Prehistory	Asia – Far East Civilisations	Asia – Modern /Contemporary	Africa – Prehistory / Palaeonthology	Africa – Modern/Contemporary	North America – Prehistory/Palaeonthol.	North America – Early Cultures	North America – Modern/Contemporary	Latin America – Prehistory	Latin America – Maya/Precolombian	Latin America – Pre-Inca/Inca	Latin America – Colonial/Modern	Caribbean	Oceania	Worldwide
Mapping the Past																	X											
Maya Archaeology at Minanha																							X					
Maya Research Program																							X					
Midwest Archeological Center, National Park Service																			X	X	X							
Moab Archaeological Resource Survey Excavation																			X	X								
The National Trust										X																		
NICE – Never-ending International Work Camps Exchange														X	X	X												
Northern 'Sea Peoples' Excavation Project											X																	
North Pennines Heritage Trust					X																							
Notre Dame Archaeology Field School												X																
Ometepe Petroglyph Project																						X						
Paestum Project – Between Environment and History		X																										
Palaeoanthropology Field School in South Africa																	X											
Paleo-World Research Foundation Expeditons																			X									
Passport in Time																			X	X	X							
Pella Volunteer Scheme											X	X																
Piddington		X	X																									
Poulton Research Project	X		X		X					X																		
Pro International																												X

ORGANISATIONS AND PROJECTS

ORGANISATIONS AND PROJECTS	Europe – Prehistory	Europe – Classic /Iron Age	Europe – Roman	Europe – Early Medieval	Europe – Medieval	Europe – Renaissance/Post Medieval	Europe – Early Modern	Europe – Modern	Europe – Contemporary	Europe – Multiperiod	Middle East – Prehistory	Middle East – Greek-Roman	Middle East – Islamic/Medieval	Asia – Prehistory	Asia – Far East Civilisations	Asia – Modern /Contemporary	Africa – Prehistory / Palaeonthology	Africa – Modern/Contemporary	North America – Prehistory/Palaeonthol.	North America – Early Cultures	North America – Modern/Contemporary	Latin America – Prehistory	Latin America – Maya/Precolombian	Latin America – Pre-Inca/Inca	Latin America – Colonial/Modern	Caribbean	Oceania	Worldwide
Ramat Hanadiv Excavations												X																
Rempart																												X
Rochford Hundred Field Archaeology Group										X																		
Royal Tyrrell Museum Day Digs & Volunteer Preparation Program																			X									
Royal Tyrrell Museum Field Experience																			X									
Rural Ireland Lifeways Project																												
La Sabraneneque								X																				
San Giorgio Convent					X	X	X	X																				
Saveock Mill					X	X		X																				
SCI – Service Civil International									X	X																		X
SCI Spain – Servicio Civil Internacional										X																		
Sedgeford Archaeological and Historical Research Project			X	X																								
Semirechie and South Kazakhstan Archaeological Camp														X	X													
Sha'ar Hagolan – Archaeological Excavations and Neolithic Art Centre											X																	
Silchester Roman Town Life Project		X	X																									
Sino American Field School of Archeology (SAFSA)														X	X													
Slavia Project				X	X																							
SMELT Low Birker				X	X																							
Società Friulana di Archeologia	X																											
South Cadbury Environs Project	X	X	X	X																								

ORGANISATIONS AND PROJECTS	Europe – Prehistory	Europe – Classic/Iron Age	Europe – Roman	Europe – Early Medieval	Europe – Medieval	Europe – Renaissance/Post Medieval	Europe – Early Modern	Europe – Modern	Europe – Contemporary	Europe – Multiperiod	Middle East – Prehistory	Middle East – Greek-Roman	Middle East – Islamic/Medieval	Asia – Prehistory	Asia – Far East Civillisations	Asia – Modern /Contemporary	Africa – Prehistory / Palaeonthology	Africa – Modern/Contemporary	North America – Prehistory/Palaeonthol.	North America – Early Cultures	North America – Modern/Contemporary	Latin America – Prehistory	Latin America – Maya/Precolombian	Latin America – Pre-Inca/Inca	Latin America – Colonial/Modern	Caribbean	Oceania	Worldwide
South Quantock Archaeological Survey	X	X	X	X	X					X																		
Stymphalos Project		X	X	X																								
SURTI – Society for Urban, Rural and Tribal Initiatives																X												
Swaziland Cultural Development Project																		X										
Tarbat Discovery Programme		X		X	X																							
Teaching and Projects Abroad				X	X																			X				
Tel Hazor Excavations Project											X																	
Tell es-Safi/Gath Archaeological Project											X																	
Temple of the Winged Lions Project												X																
Terra Europea, Inc.	X		X							X																		
Thistle Camps		X																										
Tiwanaku Enclave																								X				
Trebula Mutuesca Archaeological Fieldwork		X																										
Ugrian Archaeological Project														X														
Underwater Archaeology International Field School		X	X		X																							
UNESCO – United Nations Educational, Scientific and Cultural Organization																												X
Urals and Western Siberia Settlements and Burials														X														
UREP – University Research Expeditions Program																												X
USCAP – University of Sidney Central Asian Programme															X													
Valley of Peace Archaeological Project																							X					
VIMEX – Voluntarious Internacionales Mexico																									X			

ORGANISATIONS AND PROJECTS

ORGANISATIONS AND PROJECTS	Europe – Prehistory	Europe – Classic /Iron Age	Europe – Roman	Europe – Early Medieval	Europe – Medieval	Europe – Renaissance/Post Medieval	Europe – Early Modern	Europe – Modern	Europe – Contemporary	Europe – Multiperiod	Middle East – Prehistory	Middle East – Greek-Roman	Middle East – Islamic/Medieval	Asia – Prehistory	Asia – Far East Civillisations	Asia – Modern /Contemporary	Africa – Prehistory / Palaeonthology	Africa – Modern/Contemporary	North America – Prehistory/Palaeonthol.	North America – Early Cultures	North America – Modern/Contemporary	Latin America – Prehistory	Latin America – Maya/Precolombian	Latin America – Pre-Inca/Inca	Latin America – Colonial/Modern	Caribbean	Oceania	Worldwide
Vindolanda Trust			X																									
Vive Mexico																									X			
VJF – Vereinigung Junger Freiwilliger eV										X																		X
Volunteers for Peace International Workcamps																				X	X							X
Volunteers in Heritage Resources in the US Forest Service																				X	X							
Wadi ath-Thamad Project											X	X																
Walls of Verona							X	X																				
Waterway Recovery Group							X	X																				
Western Belize Regional Cave Project																							X					
Whitehall Farm			X																									
White House Bay Maritime Archaeological Project																										X		
Whittlewood Project					X																							
Workcamps for Young People in Brittany										X																		
YAP – Youth Action for Peace																												
Yavneh-Yam Archaeological Project											X	X	X															X
Youthcamp – Voluntary Action for Youth	X											X	X															

ALPHABETICAL INDEX OF ORGANISATIONS AND PROJECTS

From the same publisher

Green Volunteers   The World Guide
to Voluntary Work in Nature Conservation

Over 200 projects worldwide for those who want to experience active conservation work as a volunteer. Projects are worldwide, year round, in a variety of habitats, from one week to one year or more. From dolphins to rhinos, from whales to primates, this guide is ideal for a meaningful vacation or for finding thesis or research opportunites.

Price £ 10.99   € 16.00 $ 14.95   Pages: 256

World Volunteers   The World Guide
to Humanitarian and Development Volunteering

Nearly 200 projects and organisations worldwide for people who want to work in international humanitarian projects but don't know how to begin. Opportunities are from 2 weeks to 2 years or longer. An ideal resource for a working holiday or a leave of absence. A guide for students, retirees, doctors or accountants, nurses or agronomists, surveyors and teachers, plumbers or builders, electricians or computer operators... For everyone who wants to get involved in helping those who suffer worldwide.

Price: £ 10.99   € 16.00 $ 14.95   Pages: 256

Archaeo-Volunteers   The World Guide
to Archaeological and Heritage Volunteering

Listing 200 projects and organisations in the 5 continents for those who want to spend a different working vacation helping Archaeologists. Placements are from 2 weeks to a few months. For enthusiastic amateurs, students and those wanting hands-on experience. Cultural and historical heritage maintenance and restoration and museum volunteering opportunities are also listed. The guide also tells how to find hundreds more excavations and workcamps on the Internet.

Price: £ 10.99   € 16.00 $ 14.95   Pages: 256